The Bible's Writings

The Bible's
Writings

An Introduction for Christians and Jews

David J. Zucker

WIPF & STOCK · Eugene, Oregon

THE BIBLE'S WRITINGS
An Introduction for Christians and Jews

Copyright © 2013 David J. Zucker. All rights reserved. Except for brief quotations in critical publications or reviews, no part of this book may be reproduced in any manner without prior written permission from the publisher. Write: Permissions, Wipf and Stock Publishers, 199 W. 8th Ave., Suite 3, Eugene, OR 97401.

Wipf & Stock
An Imprint of Wipf and Stock Publishers
199 W. 8th Ave., Suite 3
Eugene, OR 97401

www.wipfandstock.com

ISBN 13: 978-1-62032-738-8

Manufactured in the U.S.A.

*To my students throughout the years,
for their inquiring minds and enthusiastic responses*

Contents

Foreword by Victor H. Matthews | ix

1. Introduction to the Writings/*Ketuvim* | 1
2. Psalms | 13
3. Proverbs | 27
4. Job | 40
5. Song of Songs | 53
6. Ruth | 62
7. Lamentations | 72
8. Ecclesiastes | 86
9. Esther | 102
10. Daniel | 119
11. Ezra | 138
12. Nehemiah | 157
13. Chronicles (1 and 2) | 174

Glossary | 223
Bibliography | 227

Foreword

CHRISTIANS AND JEWS BOTH respect and are deeply attached to those Scriptures that we term respectively the Old Testament or the Hebrew Bible. In both religious traditions these sacred books are the source of rich learning as well as a body of literature that raises a number of questions and concerns. In the synagogue on a Sabbath morning as part of the regular service, the Torah Scroll is carried around and worshippers reach out to touch it, prior to its being set down on a lectern for a public reading. The congregation reveres the Torah and anticipates the weekly reading from the scroll, along with the teaching that will accompany it. A similar tradition is part of the regular ritual in Roman Catholic and Orthodox churches where there is a procession of the Gospel, prior to its being placed on the altar, and a set of readings are presented to the congregation. In countless Christian churches priests and pastors preach God's Word, sometimes basing their sermons on the books of the Old Testament/Hebrew Scriptures. More often the sermon is from the New Testament, but it is commonplace in numerous Christian religious denominations to read a selection from the Old Testament each week, and in some traditions to read from it on a daily basis.

In that sense the psalmist's words, spoken so many hundreds of years ago, ring true, "How very good and pleasant it is when kindred live together in unity" (Ps 133:1), and I might add, when they are willing to discuss openly a shared tradition. Does that mean that Christians and Jews read the same chapters when they read the Old Testament/Hebrew Scriptures or interpret them the same? The answer is both yes and no. Yes, when reading Isaiah in a Christian Bible these are pretty much the same words that one reads in Isaiah in a Jewish Bible. (You have to allow for slight differences in translation, and, occasionally, there are slight differences in the numbering of the verses of a given chapter.) However, Jews read these works within the context of the pre-Christian era and as part of their own history and tradition. For Christians, the Old Testament is often seen exclusively through the lens of the New Testament and the rise of the Christian movement. One of the chief values of Rabbi Zucker's volume is his attention to both of these styles of reading and his efforts to create a sense of value for both faith communities.

Other differences appear when you look at the table of contents of the Old Testament in a standard Christian Bible. You will notice that the arrangement of the books of the canon differs significantly from the order that one finds in the standard Jewish Bible, the *Tanakh: The Holy Scriptures* (Jewish Publication Society, 1985). Both versions of the Bible commence similarly: Genesis, Exodus, Leviticus, Numbers, and Deuteronomy. This is the first section in a Jewish Bible, what Jews call the Torah or the Pentateuch. In both editions, Joshua and Judges are the next books. Then, in the Christian version, the order changes: the next books are Ruth, Samuel, and Kings. Following these are Chronicles, Ezra, Nehemiah, and then Esther. This order follows a tradition that reaches back to the Greek translation of the Hebrew Bible, the Septuagint, about 2300 years ago or more. Jesus seems to know of this tradition, for he remarks, "These are the words which I spoke to you while I was still with you, that all things must be fulfilled which were written in the Law of Moses and the Prophets and the Psalms concerning Me" (Luke 24:44).

As Rabbi Zucker explains in this volume, a Jewish Bible follows a different canonical order for its scriptures. Jewish Bibles are traditionally divided into three sections: the *Torah* (meaning Teaching, Instruction, or Law), the Prophets (called in Hebrew *Neviim* and containing books of both history and prophecy), and the Writings (called in Hebrew *Ketuvim*, basically a collection including the Psalms and several wisdom books). These divisions are sometimes abbreviated into the acronym Tanak or Tanakh (*Torah, Neviim, Ketuvim*).

As one can see from the Table of Contents of this work the books of the third section are in the order: Psalms, Proverbs, Job, Song of Songs, Ruth, Lamentations, Ecclesiastes, Esther, Daniel, Ezra, Nehemiah, 1–2 Chronicles. That may seem a little unsettling at first for Christian readers, but the logic of this arrangement is made clear in this volume.

This book, *The Bible's WRITINGS: An Introduction for Christians and Jews*, is the final volume of a three-part series that began with *The Torah: An Introduction for Christians and Jews* (Paulist 2005), and then *The Bible's PROPHETS: An Introduction for Christians and Jews* (Wipf and Stock 2013). As in the previous works, the author devotes two segments to developing the historical context and major ideas of each book, taking the reader section by section and often chapter by chapter. Then the third part of each chapter is devoted to examples where the given work was utilized or quoted in the teachings of the New Testament writers. Next is a list of parallel teachings by the rabbis, showing how post-biblical Judaism understood those selfsame books. For many Christians these examples of rabbinic materials will provide unique and interesting—even surprising—insights into biblical interpretation from scholars who wished to place the ancient text into their own time and allow it to remain a living guide for their community. For Jews, the selections from the New Testament will show alterative ideas, namely how Christianity, through a different set of lenses, saw and reinterpreted Jewish Scripture. A short study section completes the fivefold approach to these sacred biblical writings and allows for further reflection as it discusses specific examples from the text.

I first met Rabbi Dr. Zucker many years ago when we served together on the same faculty in the Department of Religious Studies at Missouri State University. Rabbi Zucker is a scholar and a teacher whose love of the Bible is reflected in his many publications in journals, as well as books and chapters, often written with an interfaith Christian-Jewish audience in mind. Marv Wilson has described the author with these words: "Rabbi Zucker is one who cares deeply how Jews perceive Christians and how Christians perceive Jews" (from the Forework to *The Torah: An Introduction for Christians and Jews*). This volume, written for both Christians and Jews, will enhance a greater understanding between these two great faith traditions; it also will provide valuable lessons for all of us on how we may best learn from and about each other.

Victor H. Matthews
Dean of the College of Humanities and Public Affairs
Professor of Religious Studies
Missouri State University
Springfield, MO

1

Introduction to the Writings/*Ketuvim*

THIS VOLUME IS THE third and final work in a series that is an introduction to the Bible, written specifically for Christians and Jews. It offers a comprehensive, section-by-section and often a chapter-by-chapter overview to the world's most widely read book: the (Hebrew) Bible. This volume is unique in that a major feature offers examples of how the Christian Scriptures utilized the Hebrew Bible to further the ideas and ideals of Christianity; as well as offering examples where the ancient rabbis from a roughly parallel time period utilized the Hebrew Bible to further the ideas and ideals of Judaism.

The Bible is read by millions of people year by year. It is a sacred document, one that links Christians and Jews. Yet even the term "Bible" means one thing to Jews and something else to Christians. For Christians the Bible divides into two sections, the "Old Testament" followed by the "New Testament."

When Jews refer to a Bible, they mean a different—although in some ways very similar—set of books. For Jews the "Bible" is synonymous with the *TANAKH*, the threefold sacred scripture made up of the *Torah* (i.e., Teaching, Instruction, Law), the *Neviim* (Prophets), and finally the *Ketuvim* (Writings.) The books that make up those three sections are the same books that Christians would find in their version of the Old Testament. Yet, in many cases, the books in the Christian Scriptures are set out in a different order than that found in the Hebrew Bible (*TANAKH*). These differences between the order of the books are explained in a later section of this Introduction.

The third section of the Hebrew Bible, the Writings/*Ketuvim*, is composed of thirteen books, in this particular order: Psalms, Proverbs, Job, Song of Songs, Ruth, Lamentations, Ecclesiastes, Esther, Daniel, Ezra, Nehemiah, 1 and 2 Chronicles.

The Overall Structure of This Book

This volume, while it stands on its own, is also the final section of a three-part set. The previous works in the series are *The Torah: An Introduction for Christians and Jews* (Paulist, 2005) and *The Bible's PROPHETS: An Introduction for Christians and Jews* (Wipf and Stock, 2013). This volume is an introduction to the set of books in the Hebrew Bible that directly follow the Torah (i.e., the Pentateuch, the first five books of the Hebrew Bible) and the Prophets/*Neviim*.

Each chapter in this volume deals with one particular biblical book, and divides into five sections:

1, 2. An Introduction, and then various matters including geopolitical background, significant events, personalities, and concepts and divisions found in that particular book;

3. The particular book in the Christian Scriptures;

4. The book in rabbinic literature (see section below on "Rabbinic Literature");

5. Text study.

On occasion an asterisk (*) follows certain words. This indicates that the word appears in the glossary at the close of this work.

Translations used for this book (unless specifically otherwise noted) come from the New Revised Standard Version (NRSV*).[1] This is a modern translation with inclusive, gender-neutral language. Occasionally there are differences in the verse numbers in the Hebrew Bible* (*TANAKH*) and a Christian Bible. Verse numbers were added to the biblical text during the Middle Ages. No one knows with certainty why there are occasional discrepancies between the two versions. When there are variations in a particular verse quoted, the NRSV translation will be followed by the Hebrew* tradition, set apart in parentheses and marked with an "H." Real examples that will be found in this volume include Psalm 47:1–2, 8 (47:2–3, 9 H) and Song of Songs 7:2 (7:3 H).

I try to use gender-neutral language in terms for God. God cannot be described in terms of gender. God is neither a he nor a she. Yet the Hebrew language, like romance languages (French, Spanish, etc.), does not have a neutral case, only masculine and feminine nouns and pronouns. Unlike English and German, there is no "it." The default pronouns in the NRSV, as in this volume, when referring to God are "he," "him," and "his." While in

---

1. As published in *New Oxford Annotated Bible with the Apocryphal/Deuterocanonical Books* (1991), hereafter abbreviated *NOAB*.

the Bible God is most often described with masculine pronouns, feminine imagery is also used in the Bible. Isaiah explains that God says, "As a mother comforts her child, so I will comfort you" (Isa 66:13; cf. Isa 42:14; 49:15; 66:9). Since the word "Lord" has masculine overtones in most cases, unless quoting directly from a text this book uses the neutral term "God."

The last quarter of the twentieth century saw a flowering of woman-authored scholarship that continues to flourish in the twenty-first century. All people, women and men alike, are indebted to their contributions, many examples of which also have influenced and are included in this volume.

The Order of the Books of the Bible

As mentioned above, another term for the Jewish Bible is the *TANAKH**. *TANAKH* (sometimes *TANAK*) is an acronym; the letters T, N, and KH (or K) each refer to a word. These three words are *Torah** (Teaching), *Neviim** (Prophets), and *Ketuvim** (Writings). They refer to the three sections of the Jewish Bible. This is the order of the books of the Hebrew Bible* (Hebrew Scriptures*, Jewish Scriptures*, Jewish Bible*, *TANAKH*).

1. The Teaching/*Torah* contains Genesis, Exodus, Leviticus, Numbers, and Deuteronomy.

2. The Prophets/*Neviim* has two sections, the Former Prophets and the Latter Prophets. In order they are: (Former Prophets) Joshua, Judges, 1 and 2 Samuel, and 1 and 2 Kings; (Latter Prophets) Isaiah, Jeremiah, Ezekiel, Hosea, Joel, Amos, Obadiah, Jonah, Micah, Nahum, Habakkuk, Zephaniah, Haggai, Zechariah, and Malachi.

3. The Writings/*Ketuvim* consist of the Psalms, Proverbs, Job, Song of Songs, Ruth, Lamentations, Ecclesiastes, Esther, Daniel, Ezra, Nehemiah, and 1 and 2 Chronicles.

The Protestant Bible reflects the divisions of the Jewish Bible, but rearranges the order of the books in the second and third sections. Broadly speaking, the Torah (Pentateuch*) is followed by the "historical books," Joshua, Judges, Ruth, 1 and 2 Samuel, 1 and 2 Kings, 1 and 2 Chronicles, Ezra, Nehemiah, and Esther. Next come the "poetical books," or "Writings," made up of Job, Psalms, Proverbs, Ecclesiastes, and Song of Songs. This set concludes with the "prophetical books," Isaiah, Jeremiah, Lamentations, Ezekiel, Daniel, Hosea, Joel, Amos, Obadiah, Jonah, Micah, Nahum, Habakkuk, Zephaniah, Haggai, Zechariah, and Malachi.

The most striking difference is that in the Protestant Bible the Prophets (with the additions of Daniel and Lamentations) appear just prior to the Gospel* of Matthew.

The Roman Catholic Bible, in such versions as the Jerusalem Bible, New Jerusalem Bible, and New American Bible, follows a different order: Genesis, Exodus, Leviticus, Numbers, and Deuteronomy; then Joshua, Judges, Ruth, 1 and 2 Samuel, 1 and 2 Kings, 1 and 2 Chronicles, Ezra, Nehemiah, Tobit, Judith, Esther, 1 and 2 Maccabees, Job, Psalms, Proverbs, Ecclesiastes, Song of Songs, Wisdom of Solomon, Ecclesiasticus (Sirach), Isaiah, Jeremiah, Lamentations, Baruch, Ezekiel, Daniel, Hosea, Joel, Amos, Obadiah, Jonah, Micah, Nahum, Habakkuk, Zephaniah, Haggai, Zechariah, and Malachi. In the Catholic Bible, what is termed in the Protestant Bible as the Apocrypha appears as part of the Deuterocanonicals. The Roman Catholic Church shares this tradition with the Greek and Russian Orthodox Churches.

Terms of Reference

BCE and CE

"Before the Common Era" (BCE)* and "Common Era" (CE)* refer to *exactly the same periods* as "Before Christ" (BC) and "Anno Domini" ("In the year of our Lord," AD). Thus, 200 BCE is the same year as 200 BC, and 500 CE is the same year as 500 AD. The terms "Christ" (Messiah or Savior) or "In the year of our Lord" are certainly appropriate for Christians, but the more neutral and inclusive terms BCE and CE are rapidly becoming standard usage.

Do Christians and Jews Read the Same Book?

In the words of the Hebrew Bible (Jewish Scriptures, *TANAKH*) Christians and Jews share a common sacred literature. For Jews this Bible is the foundation for the ongoing and unbroken covenant with God. For Jews, it is not the "Old" Testament, having been succeeded by the "New" and improved Testament. It is *the* irreplaceable Testament.[2]

Jews appreciate that Christians understand the Christian Scriptures* (New Testament*) as God's new promise.[3] The authors of the Christian

---

2. Boadt, *Reading the Old Testament*, 4, 8–9; see also Brueggemann, *Introduction to the Old Testament*, 2–3. See also Signer, "Searching the Scriptures: Jews"; and Greenspahn, *Scripture in the Jewish and Christian Traditions*.

3. In the Christian Scriptures of Rom 9:2ff. and 11:1ff., Paul clearly states that God's covenant with the Jewish people is unbroken. Yet also look at Rom 9:14ff. and Heb 8:13; 9:15–20.

Scriptures write with a stated purpose: to convince people that the Messiah has come in the form of Jesus. "The gospels, like the other New Testament books . . . are the literary productions of a believing community . . . They are written with the aim of changing the reader or of building up the community's faith. In the Fourth Gospel, John says clearly, these things are 'written so that you may come to believe that Jesus is the Messiah, the Son of God, and that through believing you may have life in his name' (Jn 20:31)."[4]

Christians read the Hebrew Bible (which they call the Old Testament*) as the foundation stone of their own faith. "The first disciples and Christian writers . . . searched the Old Testament for passages that would throw light on the events of Jesus' life, death and resurrection. Matthew's Gospel is a case in point. It is filled with quotations from the Old Testament to explain each major step in Jesus' life . . . Even the church fathers . . . cited the Old Testament far more often than they did the Gospels."[5]

The first disciples and early Christian writers quote the Hebrew Bible as a source to teach new lessons and to explain God's purpose. Their writings parallel the teachings of the early rabbis, who often draw upon the Hebrew Bible to instruct and edify, and to understand God's purpose (see below the section "Rabbinic Literature").

Most Jews have never read the Christian Scriptures. Jews would be surprised to learn that the New Testament often quotes from or alludes to the Hebrew Scriptures. In like manner, most Christians are completely unfamiliar with the teachings found in rabbinic literature. They would be surprised to learn that the early rabbis often quote from the Hebrew Scriptures to support their Jewish teachings in a similar way as the writers of the New Testament support their Christian teachings in the Christian Scriptures.

This introduction to the third section of the Hebrew Bible is written primarily for Christians and Jews. It considers each of those books and explains how specific verses from the Hebrew Bible are quoted, paraphrased, or alluded to in the Christian Scriptures. This is followed by a major section that offers examples in which the early rabbis drew upon the same books of the Hebrew Bible to teach their lessons. Often these two perspectives see a very different message in the same verses.

A brief word about the New Testament. The New Testament begins with the Gospels. Then comes the book of Acts. This follows with a series of letters (the Epistles*) sent to various newly formed religious communities situated around the Mediterranean. For example, a letter (epistle) is sent to the nascent Christian church at Ephesus. This is the epistle Ephesians. Another letter is

---

4. *NOAB*, ix.
5. Boadt, *Reading the Old Testament*, 468.

sent to Corinth in Greece, hence Corinthians. Letters also go to individuals, such as Timothy and Philemon. The Christian Scriptures conclude with the book of Revelation.

For Christians, "Old" and "New" are more than merely synonyms for "former" and "latter." Broadly speaking, Christians understand the "Old Testament" to be God's original words to the Jews, and the "New Testament" to be the New Promise, an updated covenant or a revised contract. Old and New, therefore, take on a "value."

When Jews pick up a Christian Bible, they recognize that there are two parts. It is only the first section, however, that is sacred for Jews. The Christian Scriptures do not inform the Jewish religious experience.

Jews recognize that for Christians there is another scripture in addition to the Hebrew Bible. Jews understand that Christians regard this later scripture as holy and as a record of God's continuing relationship. For a Jewish understanding of the Christian Scriptures, see the recently published excellent volume, *The Jewish Annotated New Testament—New Revised Standard Version*. Edited by Amy-Jill Levine and Marc Zvi Brettler. New York: Oxford University Press, 2011. Jews nonetheless continue to believe that *for Jews* the original contract articulated in the Hebrew Scriptures is still binding. It continues to remain in place. For Jews the Hebrew Scriptures, as distinguished from the Christian Scriptures, continue to be the major source for understanding the ongoing covenant with God.

The Writings

What Are the Writings?

The Writings (*Ketuvim*), or as it is sometimes called, the *Hagiographa* (the Greek term for the Writings), is the last section of the Hebrew Bible to enter the canon. The Writings cover wisdom books, romance, drama, and history. Some of the books are written as poetry; others are prose accounts. The section begins with Psalms and Proverbs. Next comes Job. All three of these are termed "wisdom books."

- Psalms contain 150 songs and prayers, many of which praise God.
- Proverbs is a set of ethical maxims.
- Job is in essence a treatise on the question of undeserved suffering.

Next come the five books that form the "Scrolls," or in Hebrew, *megillas* (*megillot*), the most famous of which is Esther.

Song of Songs is love poetry. Ruth, set in the period of the judges, recounts how a Moabite woman entered the community of Israel. Lamentations includes dirges that recount the terrible days following the destruction of the first Jewish temple in 586 BCE. Ecclesiastes, like Proverbs, is a set of wise sayings, but it is written in the first person, and covers observations on living a full life. Esther, set in ancient Persia, recounts how a Jewish woman became a queen and saved the lives of her community.

Each one of these books is read on a separate Jewish holy day. During the Jewish liturgical year, on five holy days, in addition to the reading from the Torah and the Prophets (*Haftarah**), one of the five scrolls is read. Song of Songs is read on *Pesach*/Passover, in the early spring, the holy days that celebrate the Redemption from servitude in Egypt. The other four scrolls are Ruth (read at *Shavuot*/Weeks/Pentecost, in the late spring), Lamentations (read on *Tisha b'Av*, the ninth day of the Hebrew month of *Av*, in midsummer), Ecclesiastes (read on *Succot*/Booths/Tabernacles, in the early autumn), and Esther (read at *Purim*, generally in late winter).

The final five books generally could be called "historical" works. Daniel (like Esther) is set in ancient Persia, Ezra and Nehemiah reflect life in Jerusalem in the fifth century BCE, and the narrative of Chronicles covers much the same time period as the latter part of Samuel and all of Kings.

Women's Voices

Women's Voices Today

The last quarter or so of the twentieth century and the opening decade of the twenty-first has seen the blossoming of female scholars bringing their unique perspectives to the world of biblical scholarship. Some women would claim for themselves the term "feminist,"[6] others would not. Feminism is not a matter of gender identity, for there are both male and female feminists.

In any case, feminist thought, and certainly women writing offers a unique experience; it helps us to see more clearly the lives of women in the ancient world. We now recognize and have a better understanding of men and women's roles, as well as the degree and the effect to which patriarchy operated in the ancient world, and certainly today. Men as well as women have gained through the insights and scholarship of female writers.

---

6. Feminists, both female and male, reflect the theological spectrum. These include "evangelical women" who make "an important contribution to feminist hermeneutics, albeit from a more conservative position." Kroeger and Evans, *IVP Women's Bible Commentary*, xv.

In the introduction to their groundbreaking work, *Women's Bible Commentary* (2012), Carol A. Newsom, Sharon H. Ringe, and Jacqueline E. Lapsley, point out that with "increasing self-confidence and sophistication feminist study of the Bible has blossomed to become one of the most important new areas in contemporary biblical research." Women have raised new questions and "have posed . . . new ways of reading" that "have challenged the very way biblical studies are done." As these authors point out, feminist biblical studies take many different directions. "Some commentators have attempted to reach 'behind the text' to recover knowledge about the actual conditions of women's lives in the biblical period . . . Still others have tried to discover the extent to which even the biblical writings which pertain to women are shaped by the concerns and perspectives of men and yet how it can still be possible at times to discover the presence of women and their own points of view between the lines."[7]

Esther Fuchs has suggested that while a masculine approach to the Bible considers survival and security, a feminist view centers on "interpersonal politics, and [moves] from the public to the private"[8] sphere. Amy-Jill Levine explains that feminist analysis often "extends to questions of religion, class, race, ethnicity, and sexual preference, among others, and it often remarks on the interrelated or systematic nature of oppressive behaviors."[9]

Yet, we have to read carefully, for at times feminist analyses—as analyses from any theoretical viewpoint—can have their own particular perspectives. Levine observes, "Negative resonances that accompany the character in question are not infrequently ignored or excused. In some cases, the previously marginalized, the 'other,' becomes regarded as invariably right and good." Again, in Levine's words, one has to be aware of the "Power and Perniciousness of Interpretation."[10]

In the biblical era, men were positioned over women and were regarded as superior, stronger, and more spiritual. Yet, there also were privileges assigned among women: women who were free had a higher regard than women who were slaves. For example, in Genesis, as well as in the allegory found in the Christian Scriptures in Paul's Epistle to the Galatians, which is based on the figures of Sarah and Hagar (Gal 4:22—5:1), Sarah is "emblematic of what is desirable, promised, and legitimate and . . . [those texts] view Hagar as alien, atavistic, and rejected." Yet on the other hand, there are

---

7. Newsom, Ringe, and Lapsley, *Women's Bible Commentary* (2012), xxviii. These words are taken from the Introduction to the 1st ed. (1992).
8. Fuchs, "Feminist Hebrew Literary Criticism," 195.
9. Levine, "Settling at Beer-lahai-roi," 14.
10. Ibid., 18, 15.

contemporary feminist "readings that celebrate Hagar as representative of the oppressed: [as a woman who] struggles against elite privilege and social abuse,"[11] and epitomize Sarah as dominating and violent.

Levine points to Phyllis Trible's ground-breaking work, *Texts of Terror: Literary-Feminist Readings of Biblical Narratives* (1984), where, in the introduction to her chapter on Hagar, Trible features this epitaph for Hagar: "She was wounded for our transgressions; she was bruised for our iniquities." These words are a paraphrase from Isaiah's description of the Suffering Servant, and evoke images—certainly for Christians—of Jesus of Nazareth (cf. Isa 53:5; Matt 8:17; 1 Pet 2:22–24). Therefore they associate with Hagar images of someone who is completely innocent and fully exploited. Trible herself writes that, read "in light of contemporary issues and images, her [Hagar's] story depicts oppression in three familiar forms: nationality, class, and sex . . . As a symbol of the oppressed, Hagar becomes . . . the faithful maid exploited, the black woman used by the male and abused by the female of the ruling class, the surrogate mother, the resident alien without legal recourse, the other woman, the runaway youth."[12] Yet, at the same time, Levine points out that often such "positive reevaluation of one figure signals the denigration of another." She then goes on to ask, who are to be understood as Hagar's oppressors? "Hebrews? Israelites? Jews? The authors of the text? Men? Are they real people? . . . For some readers, the 'obvious' answer—anachronistically and overgeneralized—is 'the Jews.' For others, the answer is 'the text.'" The net effect is less to understand the biblical words in their context than to exchange one example of exploitation/victimhood for another. "Thus, while Hagar's various activities can be celebrated and her various persecutors condemned, it is unhelpful to view her solely as victim or unequivocally as 'good.'"[13]

In this volume, I refer to the scholarship of many women who bring their experiences as women, and/or their experiences as women who are reading and confronting these sacred words of the Bible. Their perspectives and perceptions provide valuable commentary adding new ways of seeing and understanding the ancient texts.

Women's Voices Then

Motherhood is probably the most important role women played in biblical times. This is congruent with patriarchal expectations of women. Given

11. Ibid., 15.
12. Trible, *Texts of Terror*, 27–28.
13. Levine, "Beer-lahai-roi," 19, 18.

ancient life spans, it was probable that for many women motherhood (including domestic functioning) and adulthood were practically coterminous. The Bible explains that Abraham had two or three wives, eight sons, and no daughters. Isaac had one wife and two sons. Ishmael had one wife, twelve sons, and one daughter. Jacob's twelve sons and one daughter were conceived through four wives. His brother Esau sired seven sons with three wives. The number of male versus female children seems remarkable and unlikely unless one accepts a divine plan. More likely, we can explain this phenomenon through a patriarchal bias, the conscious decision not to list all of the female children. How else can it be that 91 percent of all names mentioned in the Bible refer to men?[14]

Although conception and birth—actually bringing forth children/sons—is a prime virtue in motherhood, caring for, and more specifically caring for the interest of those children, is likewise important. This is reflected, among other places, in the early Samuel narrative, and then the Elijah-Elisha narratives in the books of Samuel and Kings.

Men and women are interdependent with each other. Women had roles in economic life as well as educational, managerial, and religious life. In ancient Israel daily "life centered on what can be called the 'family household,' which was the basic unit of society." Women may have had less power then men, but nonetheless they "figured prominently as authority figures in intrafamily matters . . . The Bible calls the household 'mother's household' rather than the usual 'father's household' in several passages concerned with marriageable daughters (Gen. 24:28; Ruth 1:8; Song 3:4; 8:2) . . . Such a role took women out of their own domestic contexts and gave them input into matters affecting land and property. It gave them direct influence over aspects of life that transcended their own immediate milieu."[15]

The statement to Eve in Genesis 3:16, "your desire shall be for your husband, and he shall rule over you," needs to be understood in terms of "sexuality in the context of a sanction for increasing the birthrate, not with general social dominance." As Carol L. Meyers points out, "there are no absolute statements in the Hebrew Bible of categorical male supremacy over women."[16]

In the Bible there are many examples of powerful women. That said, compared to the roles and depiction of men, these are only ever token examples. Deborah is a judge and also a prophet. Miriam, Huldah, Noadiah, and Isaiah's unnamed wife are all called prophets (Exod 15:20; 2 Kgs 22:14 / 2 Chr 34:22; Neh 6:14; Isa 8:3). Esther is a queen. The Bible mentions two

---

14. Meyers, "Every Day Life," 245.
15. Ibid., 246, 249.
16. Ibid., 250; cf. Adler, *Engendering Judaism*, 121–25.

"wise women" (2 Sam 14, 20), who advise, respectively, David and his chief general, Joab. Both these women use tact and negotiation to help solve family and political problems. Abigail saves her husband's life by her wise appeal to David, who later marries her (1 Sam 25).

Nonetheless, on the whole the near gender parity in the earlier biblical days eventually was supplanted by the monarchy and the demands of having a unified state, beginning in the beginning of the tenth century BCE, as urban life became more common. Over a period of years tribal and family units broke down and the household was no longer the dominant social unit. Centralized state-based units—military, civil, religious, and political classes with hierarchal structures—which were almost exclusively male, began to dominate. That said, the "ultimate displacement of females from the early parity they held with males in the premonarchic period and well into the monarchy in many rural quarters could not have come until the late preexilic period."[17]

On the whole, women have less political, social, cultural, ideational, and material power then men do in the overall patriarchy that characterizes the biblical world. Consequently, women in the Bible often have to resort to deception to achieve their goals. Deception is a very present theme in Genesis, but it appears also in other books, where it can characterize the negative behavior of certain women (Delilah in Judges, Jezebel in Kings, the woman of folly in Proverbs). In other moments it is praiseworthy, such as in the case of Esther. Some scholars believe it simply shows that deception is used by powerless characters and is not limited to women.[18] At times women use deception to further the divine plan.[19]

Women's Voices: A Cautionary Note

Although not limited to these books, some readers will want to approach the chapters on Ruth, Esther, and Lamentations with a sense of thoughtfulness and caution. This is especially true for Lamentations. As Kathleen O'Conner explains, "Women figure prominently in the book's description of war's atrocities and serve as symbols of the pain of the people." In Lamentations, the presentation of women mixes praise and censure, and it is largely the latter.

17. Meyers, *Discovering Eve*, 196; see also 189.
18. Jeansonne, *Women of Genesis*, 67.
19. "Rebekah's deception of the old and blind Isaac does not so much as hint at the wife's powerlessness versus her husband. It does not take into account that deception is Rebekah's only means of granting her preferred son a blessing. The fact is that Isaac, despite his dramatized impotence, is superior to Rebekah in power, yet it is Rebekah who is presented as a powerful woman who outsmarts an ailing old man." Fuchs, "Who Is Hiding the Truth?," 137.

Therefore, in spite of "the evocative beauty of Lamentations, there are reasons for women to be cautious when they approach it."[20] Likewise, the depictions and descriptions of Ruth and Esther merit an attentive approach to both the surface meaning of the narratives and their additional interpretations.

Rabbinic Literature

There is a vast corpus of writings known as "rabbinic literature." There is the Babylonian Talmud as well as the Jerusalem Talmud. Much of this is legal material. In addition, there are many collections of rabbinic homilies, collectively termed Midrash*. Whenever the Bible is not explicit or specific, the early interpreters of the post-biblical world (i.e., the rabbinic period), and their successors as well, sought to provide new insights as to what might be meant in a given context. Alongside the Bible, the rabbis developed a supplement, an additional way to understand what God desires of humans. The generic term for this exegesis or interpretation is *midrash* (plural, *midrashim**). The Hebrew for "sermon," *derasha*, is based on the word *midrash*. Through midrash, "a Scriptural passage yielded far more than could be discerned on the surface. The sacred words became an inexhaustible mine . . . of religious and ethical teaching."[21] As the *Babylonian Talmud* suggests, "One biblical statement may carry many meanings."[22] Tales and allegories, ethical reflections, epigrams and legends are all different ways in which midrash can be expressed.

Through their midrashim, the rabbis teach about the values of their time, such as the nature of God, opposition to idolatry, proper modesty, the importance of studying sacred texts, generosity, hard work, chastity, and loyalty. They also comment on differences between the Jewish community and other communities.

Midrash always develops out of the biblical text. Midrashic literature was first spoken, and later compiled by rabbis. The rabbis often disagree amongst themselves. To say that something is *a* rabbinic view, or even *the* rabbinic view, does not mean that all rabbis support that position or interpretation.[23]

20. O'Connor, "Lamentations," 278, 279.

21. A. Cohen, *Everyman's Talmud*, xviii; see also Signer, "Searching the Scriptures."

22. *Babylonian Talmud Sanhedrin* 34a. All references to the Babylonian Talmud that appear in this volume come from the Soncino edition; see the bibliography.

23. Not only are there differences of opinion among the rabbis, but there may be variations in some of the details of a given midrash in one midrash collection and another. Further, some midrash collections repeat a midrash that appeared earlier in that same volume. Although I quote a specific midrash, it does not necessarily mean—or not mean—that there are variations to be found.

2

Psalms

Introduction

THE PSALMS ARE A vast collection of diverse material, broadly termed "hymns." The book of Psalms is an anthology. Tradition ascribes the whole book of Psalms to the hand of King David (see below the section "Psalms in Rabbinic Literature"). This is based on David's fame as a musician (cf. 1 Sam 16:18ff.) David, however, could not have written all of Psalms. For example, in its superscription Psalm 30 refers to the "dedication of the temple," which was built by Solomon, David's son, long after David's death (see the Text Study at the close of this chapter, "Thanks for Healing"). Likewise, Psalm 137 unambiguously reflects a lament written during the Babylonian Exile, well over four hundred years following the time of King David. Scholarship suggests that the psalms were written and collected over a long period. Although some psalms are ascribed to David, there also are psalms that refer to Moses, Asaph, or Solomon. Others refer to groups of people such as the sons of Korah. Some have reference to musical instruments; others are without ascription.

There are psalms that have a group setting, and psalms that are spoken by individuals. The psalms reflect varied literary forms as well as different life situations. How they were used differs enormously, whether by individuals or in a liturgical setting.

Psalms is the first book in the third section of the Hebrew Bible, the Writings/*Ketuvim* (see the Introduction to this volume, specifically "The Order of the Books of the Bible"). It follows the prophecy of the book of

Malachi, the final book in the second section of the Hebrew Bible, the Prophets/*Neviim*. In the Christian Bible, Psalms follows Job.

"The importance of the Psalter for both Judaism and Christianity can hardly be exaggerated." From an early time, Jewish life on both an individual and a community level has been shaped by the Psalms. "In the prayer book, the midrashim, and the rituals of the synagogue" the influence of the psalms is pervasive. "Similarly for the Christian church, the New Testament is saturated with citations from the Psalter and such hymns as the 'Magnificat' [cf. Luke 1:46–55] reflect an unbroken continuity with the praises of Israel. The Psalter [. . . shapes] Christian liturgy in all the branches of Christendom both in the early, medieval, and Reformation periods. Even today many of the most enduring hymns of the church are based on Old Testament psalms."[1]

Since antiquity, the Psalms have been part of the liturgical life of the synagogue and the church. It is likely that they were part of the temple ritual in Jerusalem as well. The Talmud* suggests this in a number of places (*Babylonian Talmud Sukkah* 55a; *Babylonian Talmud Rosh Hashanah* 30b–31a).

The Psalms are revered for both public worship and private piety. "Probably no book of the Bible was known so well to medieval Christendom as the Psalms, and even today this book enjoys a unique place in the hearts of all readers of the Bible."[2]

In Hebrew, the book is termed *Sefer Tehillim* (Book of Praises). The term "Psalter" goes back to the Greek *psalterion*, which means a stringed instrument. A number of the psalms refer to musical accompaniment (cf. Pss 6 and 12; a *sheminith* may be an eight-stringed instrument.)

Many of the psalms begin with a *superscription*. This is a kind of dedicatory statement. It serves as an explanation through which the psalm is associated with a person or a group, or there is some information about how the psalm is to be recited.[3]

Traditionally there are five parts to the Psalter, corresponding to the five sections of the Torah. These divisions are: Psalms 1–41; 42–72; 73–89; 90–106; and 107–50.

---

1. Childs, *Introduction to the Old Testament*, 508; see also Sarna, *Songs of the Heart*, 23; Eaton, *Psalms*, 41–58.

2. Kugel, "Psalms," 833.

3. Schaefer, *Psalms*, 349–52.

In the Hebrew Bible, the superscription usually counts as a verse in its own right. Consequently, verse numbers often differ between the Hebrew Bible and the Christian Scriptures; for example, Psalm 48:1 [48:2 H]; 92:1 [92:2 H]. There are exceptions. Psalms 122 and 124 have a superscription, but the verses are the same in Hebrew Bibles and the Christian Scriptures.

Along with Proverbs and Job, Psalms is one of the longest books of poetry found in the Bible. "The chief characteristic of Hebrew poetry in the Bible is balance or symmetry, commonly called parallelism. Biblical poetry is also marked by the use of repetition, a fondness for alphabetical acrostics, and the employment of metaphor and simile."[4]

The Book of Psalms

Types of Psalms

There are various types of psalms, and several different ways to designate those divisions. The introduction to the Psalms in the *New Oxford Annotated Bible* (NRSV) offers these rubrics: hymns (with a subset of enthronement hymns and songs of Zion), laments, songs of trust, thanksgiving, sacred history, royal psalms, wisdom psalms, and liturgies.[5] Since these are broad definitions, some psalms fit into more than one designation.

Psalms do not fit a formal structure, such as that of a sonnet, which has fourteen lines, or a haiku, which has three lines of five, seven, and five syllables, respectively, and often celebrates nature.

Hymns (or Psalms of Praise)

In this category, a primary purpose is to praise God. Examples include, but are not limited to, Psalms 8 (see the Text Study at the end of this chapter, "God's Glory; Gifts to Humans"), 19, 33, 46–48.[6]

This type of psalm often begins with an invitation to worship, "Rejoice in the LORD, O you righteous, Praise befits the upright" (Ps 33:1). This is followed by the reasons for praise, "For the word of the LORD is upright, and all his work is done in faithfulness . . . By the word of the LORD the heavens were made, and all their host by the breath of his mouth" (Ps 33:4, 6). The psalm may conclude with a renewed summons to worship, "Our soul waits for the LORD; he is our help and shield . . . Let your steadfast love, O LORD, be upon us, even as we hope in you" (Ps 33:20, 22).

---

4. Limburg, "Book of Psalms," 5:528.

5. *NOAB*, 674. For an alternative list according to literary genre, see Boadt, *Reading the Old Testament*, 245. See also the analysis in *Women's Bible Commentary*, where the author offers ideas about types, as well as suggestions for "Listening for the Feminine in the Psalter." Declaissé-Walford, "Psalms," 224–26.

6. West offers many examples of each type of psalm. West, *Introduction to the Old Testament*, see notes 442ff.

Enthronement psalms celebrate God's sovereignty over the world. They are based on images of the coronation and rule of earthly rulers. Psalm 47 is an example (as are Pss 24, 93, 95–99): "Clap your hands, all you peoples; shout to God with loud songs of joy. For the LORD, the Most High, is awesome, a great king over all the earth . . . God is king over the nations; God sits on his holy throne" (Ps 47:1–2, 8 [47:2–3, 9 H]).

Examples of songs of Zion include Psalms 46, 48, 76, 84, 87, 122, and 132. Consider the lines, "Great is the LORD and greatly to be praised in the city of our God. His holy mountain, beautiful in elevation, is the joy of all the earth, Mount Zion, in the far north, the city of the great King" (Ps 48:1–2 [48:2–3 H]); likewise, "Pray for the peace of Jerusalem: 'May they prosper who love you. Peace be within your walls, and security within your towers'" (Ps 122:6–7).

Laments

Laments can be framed for an individual, or they can be communal laments. About a third of the psalms fit into the lament category. These psalms express "suffering . . . vulnerability and pain," doubts, desires, fear, and longing.[7] Individual psalm laments follow a familiar pattern. There is a kind of introduction, and then the problem is voiced. This is followed by a request for deliverance, an expression of assurance that God will respond, and finally a promise. Psalms that are either completely or in part individual laments include Psalms 3–7, 12, 17, 22–25. Psalm 22 is one of the best known of the individual lament psalms. "My God, my God, why have you forsaken me? Why are you so far from helping me, from the words of my groaning? O my God, I cry by day, but you do not answer; and by night, but find no rest" (Ps 22:1–2 [22:2–3 H]). In the Gospel of Mark, Jesus quotes from part of it while on the cross (Mark 15:34; cf. Matt 27:46).

Communal laments include Psalms 14, 44, 58, 60, 74, and 137. Psalm 137, unambiguously an exilic* communal lament psalm, expresses the sadness and depression of being exiled from Zion. "By the rivers of Babylon—there we sat down and there we wept when we remembered Zion . . . For there our captors asked us for songs, and our tormentors asked for mirth, saying, 'Sing us one of the songs of Zion!' How could we sing the LORD's song in a foreign land?" (Ps 137:1, 3–4).

---

7. Cottrill, "Articulate Body," 103.

Songs of Trust

Psalm 23 is an example of a song of trust. Others include Psalms 11, 16, 27, and 62. "The LORD is my shepherd, I shall not want . . . Surely goodness and mercy shall follow me all the days of my life" (Ps 23:1, 6). The writer of Psalm 62 expresses a similar confidence in God and God's care. "For God alone my soul waits in silence . . . He alone is my rock and my salvation, my fortress; I shall not be shaken . . . God is a refuge for us" (Ps 62:5-6, 8 [62:6-7, 9 H]).

Thanksgiving

Psalm 75 is a good example of a thanksgiving psalm. "We give thanks to you, O God; we give thanks; your name is near. People tell of your wondrous deeds" (Ps 75:1 [75:2 H]). In like manner, Psalm 92 offers thanks to God. "It is good to give thanks to the LORD, to sing praises to your name, O Most High; to declare your steadfast love in the morning, and your faithfulness by night" (Ps 92:1-2 [92:2-3 H]).

Sacred History

Psalms 105 and 106 address Israel's historical relationship with God. "He is the LORD our God . . . He is ever mindful of his covenant forever . . . the covenant that he made with Abraham, his sworn promise to Isaac, which he confirmed to Jacob . . . he had sent a man ahead of them, Joseph, who was sold as a slave . . . Then Israel came to Egypt . . . He sent his servant Moses, and Aaron whom he had chosen. They performed his signs among them, and miracles in the land" (Ps 105:7-10, 17, 23, 26-27). Psalm 106 speaks of the miracle at the Sea of Reeds* (Exod 14), where God rebuked the sea. The sea "became dry; he led them [Israel] through the deep as through a desert. So he saved them from the hand of the foe . . . The waters covered their adversaries; not one of them was left" (Ps 106:9-11).

Royal Psalms

In the royal genre are Psalms 2, 18, 20, 21, 45, 101, 110, and others (see the Text Study at the end of this chapter, "A Royal Psalm"). In Psalm 101, the ruler speaks to God, offering a pledge of righteousness. Attributed to David, this psalm may have been part of a coronation ceremony. "I will sing of loyalty and of justice; to you, O LORD, I will sing. I will study the way that is blameless ... I will walk with integrity of heart within my house; I will not set before my eyes anything that is base" (Ps 101:1-3).

Wisdom Psalms

Among the wisdom psalms are Psalms 1, 37, 49, 73, 78, and 91. Psalm 49, although recognized as one of the most difficult of the psalms to translate, does address the theme of the universality of death. It also speaks of the fleeting quality of life itself and the transient aspect of worldly wealth.[8] "Those who trust in their wealth and boast of the abundance of their riches ... no ransom avails for one's life, there is no price one can give to God for it ... the wise, they die; fool and dolt perish together ... when they die they will carry nothing away; their wealth will not go down after them" (Ps 49:6-7, 10, 17 [49:7-8, 11, 18 H]).

Liturgies

There are no statements in the Bible that indicate that the priesthood designated specific psalms for liturgical use in the Jerusalem temple. The Psalter itself does not associate any psalm with the Aaronide priesthood. However, as noted earlier in this chapter, statements in the Talmud indicate that psalms are recited at the temple.

The formal use of psalms in public worship began after the destruction of the second Jerusalem temple in 70 CE. "The penetration of the psalms into the liturgy represents a gradual process extending over the centuries ... in the talmudic period [c. 200 BCE—500 CE] the statutory prayers included no psalms whatsoever on Sabbaths and weekdays, and the only psalms recited were the *Hallel* [Pss 113-18] on the three Pilgrim Festivals [*Pesach*/Passover; *Shavuot*/Weeks/Pentecost; *Succot*/Booths/Tabernacles] and Hanukkah [Festival of Lights], and later ... on the New Moon."[9]

---

8. For an analysis of this psalm, see Zucker, "Riddle of Psalm 49."
9. Rabinowitz, "Psalms," 1323.

Acrostics, Superscriptions, and Selah

Acrostics

Two other features are evident when looking at the forms of the psalms. A number of the psalms are alphabetical acrostics. This means that the beginning letter of each verse follows the order of the Hebrew alphabet. In this group are Psalms 9, 10, 25, 34, 111, 112, 119, and 145 (see the Text Study at the close of this chapter, "An Acrostic Psalm"). Of these, Psalm 119 is the longest, for it features eight lines per Hebrew letter.

Superscriptions

Of the 150 psalms, all but 24 have some kind of superscription. The superscriptions come in various forms. They include the mention of a particular name, such as David (Pss 3–9, 11–32, 34–41, and so on), Asaph (50, 73–83), or the Korahites (42, 44–49, 84–85, 87–88). Other designations seem to have some kind of liturgical application. Regrettably, the titles for the psalms are for the most part unknown. Terms like *Mizmor* and *Shir* are used often, and probably have something to do with music, but their meaning is obscure.

As mentioned earlier in this chapter, in the Hebrew Bible the superscription often, but not always, counts as a verse in its own right.

Psalms without a superscription are termed "orphan psalms."

Selah

Then there is the word *Selah*. The term appears over seventy times in over three dozen psalms. It usually comes at the end of a verse, and occasionally in the middle, but never does it come at the beginning of a verse. Scholars and commentators throughout the ages have offered different explanations. There is no consensus as to what it means. Its etymology is obscure. It may be the addition of a later editor or scribe.

Psalms in the Christian Scriptures

In the final chapter of the Gospel of Luke, Jesus says, "These are my words that I spoke to you while I was still with you—that everything written about me in the law of Moses, the prophets and *the psalms* must be fulfilled" (Luke 24:44).

References to psalms permeate the Christian Scriptures. Jesus quotes psalms, suggesting that they refer to him. The Gospels and Epistles link psalm verses to Jesus' life.

A number of psalm verses are quoted repeatedly in the Christian Scriptures. For example, Psalm 110:1 appears in the Synoptic Gospels* (Matthew, Mark, and Luke) and several of the Epistles. Psalm 110 is attributed to David. It says, "The LORD says to my lord, 'Sit at my right hand until I make your enemies your footstool'" (v. 1). In Matthew 22:41ff. Jesus asks the Pharisees who they think is the Messiah. They reply, "The son of David." Jesus then asks them, "How is it then that David by the Spirit calls him Lord, saying 'The Lord said to my Lord, 'Sit at my right hand, until I put your enemies under your feet.'? If David thus calls him Lord, how can he be his son?" (Matt 22:44–45; cf. 26:64). Mark features a variation of this encounter, in which Jesus teaches at the temple (Mark 12:35–37; cf. 14:62; 16:19). Luke also features a parallel encounter, this time with some of the scribes (Luke 20:41ff.; cf. 22:69).

Acts 2 features the episode of the Holy Sprit pouring out on the apostles and their speaking in many tongues. Later in that chapter, Peter then refers to the opening lines of Psalm 110 (Acts 2:34–35). Jesus is described as being at the "right hand of God" in other places (Rom 8:34; Eph 1:20; Col 3:1, Heb 1:3, 13, et al.)

In Hebrews, the cryptic line in Psalm 110:4, "You are a priest *forever* according to the order of Melchizedek," is referenced several times (Heb 5:6, 10; 6:20; 7:1, 3, 17, 21; cf. John 12:34).

Psalm 2:7 states, "You are my son; today I have begotten you." Not surprisingly, the Gospel writers understood this as a reference to Jesus. Following Jesus' baptism by John at the Jordan River, as Jesus comes up from the water a voice from heaven calls out, "This is my Son, the Beloved, with whom I am well pleased" (Matt 3:17; Mark 1:11; cf. Luke 3:22; John 1:49). During the transfiguration narratives, variations of these words are repeated with the additional comment, "Listen to him" (Matt 17:5; Mark 9:7; Luke 9:35). In the Acts of the Apostles, Paul specifically mentions Psalm 2 and then quotes verse 7 (Acts 13:33). The author of Hebrews quotes the same line (Heb 1:5; 5:5).

Jesus cries out the plaint "My God, my God, why have you forsaken me?" while on the cross (Matt 27:46; Mark 15:34; Ps 22:1 [22:2 H]). A verse found later in that same psalm, "They divide my clothes among themselves, and for my clothing they cast lots" (Ps 22:18 [22:19 H]), is quoted directly in John's Gospel and referenced in the Synoptic Gospels (John 19:24; Matt 27:35; Mark 15:24; Luke 23:34).

"The stone that the builders rejected has become the chief cornerstone" (Ps 118:22) is featured in the Synoptics (Matt 21:42; Mark 12:10; Luke 20:17)[10] as well as in Acts and 1 Peter (Acts 4:11; 1 Pet 2:7; cf. 2:4, 6).

God's eternality, described so well in Psalm 102, "Long ago you laid the foundation of the earth . . . you endure . . . you are the same, and your years have no end," is echoed in the opening chapter of the Epistle to the Hebrews (Ps 102:25-27 [102:26-28 H]; Heb 1:10-12).

Psalms in Rabbinic Literature

There are references to psalms found in every midrash collection, and throughout rabbinic literature. Of particular note is the collection *Midrash on Psalms*.[11] The *Midrash on Psalms* was redacted about the tenth or eleventh century CE.

Why the book of Psalms is named for David. The Psalms are named for David because "his voice was sweet" (*Midrash Song of Songs Rabbah* 4.4.1[12]).

Moses gives the Torah; David gives the Psalms. "Moses gave the five books of the Torah to Israel, and corresponding to them, David gave the five books of the Psalms to Israel" (*Midrash on Psalms* 1.2 end).

A harp hung over David's bed—1. "A harp was suspended over David's bed. When midnight came, the north wind blew on it and it produced music of its own accord. David then arose and began to study Torah" (*Midrash Lamentations Rabbah* 2.22).

A harp hung over David's bed—2. A variation of this legend suggest that David studied Torah until midnight, and after midnight he composed songs and praises (*Babylonian Talmud Berakhot* 3b).

Earlier authorities. The rabbis suggest that the Psalter is based on the compositions of ten authorities: Adam, Melchizedek, Abraham, Moses, Heman, Jeduthun, Asaph, and three sons of Korah (*Babylonian Talmud Baba Batra* 14b-15a, *Midrash Ecclesiastes Rabbah* 7.19.4).

---

10. The biblical quotation used is from the Septuagint* translation. For a discussion of this, see Oesterley, *Psalms*, 94-95.

11. See the this title in the bibliography.

12. All references to *Midrash Rabbah* in this volume come from the Soncino edition; see the bibliography. Although David is credited with writing the Psalms, Jewish tradition acknowledges that he included the work of several others including Adam, Abraham, and Moses. See *Babylonian Talmud Baba Batra* 14b-15a and *Midrash Ecclesiastes Rabbah* 7.19.4, as well as the source for this note.

Eternal life. A person who recites Psalm 145 three times daily will inherit life eternal (*Babylonian Talmud Berakhot* 4b).

Different languages for activities. There are four languages: the Roman is best for battle; the Greek best for song; the Persian best for lamentations; and Hebrew is best for prayer, as alluded to in the verse "You hold them safe under your shelter from contentious tongues" (Ps 31:20 [31:21 H]) (*Midrash on Psalms* 31.7 end).

Different psalms praise God's works in the past, present, and future. Psalm 114:1 attests to God's actions in the past, "When Israel went out from Egypt." Psalm 115:1 attests to God's actions in the present, "Not to us, O LORD, not to us, but to your name give glory, for the sake of your steadfast love." Psalm 116:1 attests to God's actions in the time of the Messiah, "I love the LORD, because he has heard my voice and my supplications." Psalm 118:10 attests to God's actions in the times of Gog and Magog (the apocalyptic battle at the End of Days), "All nations surrounded me; in the name of the LORD I cut them off!" Psalm 118:28 attests to God's actions in the Time to Come, "You are my God, and I will give thanks to you; you are my God, I will extol you." Finally, Psalm 118:29 attests to God's actions in the World to Come, "O give thanks to the LORD, for he is good, for his steadfast love endures forever"[13] (*Midrash on Psalms* 26.6).

All of these are part of the *Hallel* (praise) psalms.

The Torah as a tree of life. Psalm 1:2–3 likens the person who studies (or recites) Torah day and night to a tree planted by water. Elsewhere (Prov 3:18), it explains that Wisdom is called a *tree of life*. The midrash explains, "Wisdom of Torah is called a tree of life because it is as precious as life itself to all living things" (*Midrash on Psalms* 1.19 beginning).

Text Study

Psalm 2; A Royal Psalm

Psalm 2 does not have a superscription, but from its context it appears to be a royal psalm, probably recited during the monarch's coronation.

---

[13]. For the rabbis, this psalm underscores clearly their belief that there are several separate, distinct, and discrete time periods, including the battle at the End of Days, the Time to Come, and the World to Come.

Verse 2. This verse speaks of "the LORD and his anointed." The Hebrew term translated as "anointed" is *mashiah̲*, from which the English word "messiah" derives.

In spite of the word "anointed," the psalm "is not Messianic. The expressions mentioned . . . refer to the earthly ruler, not to a Messianic king. It is only by reading-in later ideas that a Messianic interpretation is suggested. That *v.* 7 is quoted in Acts 13:33, Hebr. 1:5, 5:5 as in reference to Christ cannot [. . . find] support."[14]

Verses 4-9. These words are spoken by the ruler. The monarch explains that God holds those who would dare to rebel in great derision. The ruler is God's adopted child: "You are my son; today I have begotten you" (v. 7).

Verses 10-12. The rulers of the nations all about are urged to submit to God, lest they perish. Happy are those who take refuge in God.

Psalm 8; God's Glory; Gifts to Humans

The superscription ascribes this psalm to David. This could suggest that David is the author, or that it is "in the style" of a psalm written by David, or it could simply be an ascription meant to give this psalm a kind of cachet. The superscription also mentions that the psalm is "according to the Gittith." This may be some kind of musical style. Psalms 81 and 84 also mention the Gittith.

Verse 1 (2 H). God's name is majestic throughout the earth; God's glory is above the heavens.

Verse 2 (3 H) is very difficult to understand. It interrupts the flow of the psalm, and the meaning is not immediately clear. The NRSV offers a note that God's glory is "manifest in . . . the songs of children." The problem with this explanation is that infants do not sing, and just how the noises of infants would silence "the enemy and the avenger" is ignored.

Verses 3-6 (4-7 H). The psalmist considers the vastness of the heavens, the moon, and the stars. Compared to such marvels, humans are minute. Yet, despite this God raises humans to high honor. God grants them dominion over the earth, over all that God has formed. Humans are little less than divine (v. 5 [6 H]) and they are crowned with glory and honor.

Verses 7-8 (8-9 H). Sheep, oxen, beasts of the field, birds of the air, and fish of the sea are all are given over to the power of humans.

---

14. Oesterley, *Psalms*, 123; see also Goldingay, *Psalms*, 72–73.

"The phraseology in vv. 6-8 [7-9 H] reminds one of Gen. 1:26-28, in which 'dominion' over the rest of creation is clearly given to both male and female human beings. Two different words are used to express the idea of 'having dominion' in Gen 1:28 and in Psalm 8. Although human beings have often been tempted to misunderstand the nature of this assigned task, both words for 'having dominion' imply supervision for the good of the creation rather than exploitation of creation for the benefit of humankind."[15]

Verse 9 (10 H). Just as the psalm begins with praise of God's majesty throughout the world, so the same words close out this psalm. These verses are like bookends, bracketing the psalm.

Psalm 30; Thanks for Healing

The superscription ascribes this psalm to David, and adds that it is at the dedication of the temple (NRSV; House, with a note, the Temple, in NJPS/ TANAKH). As mentioned earlier in this chapter, it was King Solomon, David's son and successor, who built the temple in Jerusalem some years following David's death. As with Psalm 8, the reference here may mean that it was a psalm in the Davidic style, or perhaps a way to offer a cachet to the psalm.

This psalm divides about halfway through. The opening lines (vv. 1-5 [vv. 2-6 H]) thank God. The concluding verses (6-12 [7-13 H]) are more reflective.

Verses 1-3 (2-4 H). God is praised for bringing healing. The psalmist speaks of being drawn up, perhaps out of the depths of despair. "I cried to you for help, and you have healed me" (v. 2 [v. 3 H]). The psalmist makes specific reference to Sheol* and being in the pit. Sheol is a biblical term for the underground place where the dead go, whether they have been good or evil. They go to Sheol for a short period before they cease to exist. Sheol is a place of silence, where the dead neither remember nor praise God (Pss 6:5, 30:9 [30:10 H]; 49:15 [49:16 H]; 115:17.)

Verses 4-5 (5-6 H). "Sing praises to the LORD, O you his faithful ones" (v. 4 [v. 5 H]). These verses could have been said or sung by the psalmist, or this may be an invitation to the congregation to respond. The psalmist is hopeful. Difficulties are temporary; joy will follow.

---

15. Farmer, "Psalms," 142.

Verse 7 (8 H). "[Y]ou hid your face; I was dismayed." The assumption is that the person has done something reprehensible, and that God chooses not to respond. In the rabbinic literature this will be developed into the concept of *hester panim* ("hiding [the divine] face").

Verses 8–9 (9–10 H). In despair the psalmist tries to bargain with God. Do not let me reside in the pit, for how would I praise you there? This verse reflects the very human face of its author: he tries to convince God that it is in God's self-interest to offer salvation. In other words, if I were to die, who would praise you, God?

Verses 11–12 (12–13 H). The psalmist gives thanks with deeply evocative language. "You turned my mourning into dancing; you have taken off my sackcloth and clothed me with joy." Consequently, the psalmist promises to give eternal thanks.

Psalm 145; An Acrostic Psalm

The psalm is ascribed to David.

As noted earlier, a number of the psalms are constructed following the order of the Hebrew alphabet. This is not visually evident from the NRSV translation, although in some translations the alphabetic divisions are highlighted, for example in the NJPS/*TANAKH* and the Jerusalem Bible. Taking but the first five letters in the Hebrew alphabet, *alef, bet, gimel, dalet, hey*:

Verse 1 (*alef*): aromim-kha elohai . . . (I will extol you, my God . . .)

Verse 2 (*bet*): b'khol yom avar-kheka . . . (Every day I will bless you . . .)

Verse 3 (*gimel*): gadol Adonai . . . (Great is the LORD . . .)

Verse 4 (*dalet*): dor l'dor . . . (One generation shall laud your works to another . . .)

Verse 5 (*hey*): hadar k'vod . . . (On the glorious splendor . . .)

Psalm 145 is filled with praises and adoration of God. "A special feature is the earnestly expressed wish that" the knowledge of God be universally acclaimed. It "connotes God's rule from and to all time, in Heaven as on earth."[16] This psalm celebrates God's sovereignty, as do Psalms 98 and 99.

The term "praise" (*tehillah*) is found frequently in the Psalms. Psalm 145 is the only psalm to have that word, as part of its superscription.

---

16. Oesterley, *Psalms*, 572.

A number of the themes and phrases found in Psalm 145 are replicated from earlier psalms. For example, God's aspects of graciousness, mercy, being slow to anger, and abounding in steadfast love (vv. 8ff.) are found earlier in Psalms 86:5, 15; 100:5; 103:8. "All your works shall give thanks . . . your faithful shall bless you" (v. 10) echoes words in Psalms 103:22 and 134:1–2.

Psalm 145 is recited three times daily as part of the Jewish liturgy.

3

Proverbs

Introduction

PROVERBS SERVES AS A kind of instruction book. It teaches youth the way of morality. The advice is utilitarian. Proverbs stresses common sense virtues. These include self-discipline, proper manners, discreet speech, as well as the avoidance of laziness, improper companions, and ill behavior.

"It is not, of course, simply an anthology of wise sayings commonly heard in ancient Israel, though many of these are included in it . . . Rather, it is a source book of instructional materials for use in a school or in private study, for the cultivation of personal morality and practical wisdom."[1]

The overarching theme of Proverbs is fear of God (1:7; 9:10). Other major teachings include respect for parents and discipline in education; contrasting the behavior of the righteous with the wicked; the value of good friends and a loving wife; and civic virtues such as honesty, generosity, justice, and integrity. Other areas covered are self-discipline, particularly in sexual matters; knowledge of when to speak and when to remain silent; prudent planning for the future; proper manners before superiors; and the avoidance of foolish or careless behavior.[2]

Proverbs is the second book in the third section of the Hebrew Bible, the Writings/*Ketuvim* (see Introduction: "The Order of the Books of the Bible"). It follows Psalms and precedes Job. In the Christian Bible, while it follows Psalms, it precedes Ecclesiastes.

---

1. Scott, *Proverbs, Ecclesiastes*, 3; see also Fox, *Proverbs 1–9*, 3, 6–12.
2. Boadt, *Reading the Old Testament*, 418–19.

Another way to characterize Proverbs is as a collection or an anthology of ethical maxims. Short one-line sayings or principles make up most of the book. Everyday life provides metaphors for teaching wisdom. Generally, the wise saying is presented as poetic parallelism, using antithetical, synonymous, or synthetic characteristics, which is typical of biblical verse.

Antithetical: "A slack hand causes poverty; but the hand of the diligent makes rich" (10:4)

Synonymous: "The wise of heart is called perceptive, and pleasant speech increases persuasiveness" (16:21)

Synthetic: "Do not remove the ancient landmark that your ancestors set up" (22:28)

In a number of places, Wisdom is personified as a woman. Some biblical commentaries use the terms Lady Wisdom and her counterpart, Dame Folly;[3] the text itself, however, does not use these phrases. While commonly used, these descriptions are both quaint and antiquated. A more compelling and less strident pair of terms are Woman Wisdom and Woman Folly[4] (see the Text Study at the conclusion of this chapter, "Woman Wisdom versus Woman Folly").

In the Jewish Bible, the books of Proverbs, Job, and Ecclesiastes are commonly termed "wisdom literature."[5] Wisdom literature differs significantly from other parts of the Bible.

The book of Proverbs is attributed to Solomon, probably based on the comment that Solomon was the author of three thousand proverbs (1 Kgs 4:32 [5:12 H]).

---

3. For example, see *NOAB*, 812.

4. For Lady Wisdom and Dame Folly, see *NOAB* on Proverbs 9 and Fox, *Proverbs 1–9*, 300. For Woman Wisdom, Woman Folly, see Fontaine, "Proverbs," 148; and Murphy, *Proverbs*, 277–87. Alternatively, see comments about the two "women . . . wisdom . . . and the 'strange' woman or folly." Yoder, "Proverbs," 234–37.

Another commentator suggests that like "a prism, Proverbs catches the swirl of . . . ideas about and stories of women and distills them into the three strands of wise woman, foolish woman, and righteous woman." Hancock, "Wise Woman," 327.

5. In the Apocrypha (Deuterocanonicals), Sirach (Ecclesiasticus) and Wisdom of Solomon are also counted as wisdom literature.

The Book of Proverbs

Unlike many other parts of the Bible, the great themes of creation, redemption, and revelation are not part of this book. There are no clear references to Israel's history. Proverbs does not mention the exodus, the gift of the Ten Commandments, or the time spent in the desert. References to the capture of Canaan, the period of the judges, and the monarchy also do not appear here. Religious festivals and religious institutions, such as the priesthood, or specific mention of the temple in Jerusalem, are not part of the purview of Proverbs. The destruction of the temple, the Babylonian Exile, and the return likewise go unmentioned.

Proverbial sayings in the Bible are not limited to this one book.

> Besides traditional sayings preserved in narratives and prophetic literature, one finds similes and aphorisms in Psalms that closely resemble those in Proverbs. For example, Ps 37:16 expresses the judgment that the meager possessions of virtuous people are better than the abundance of many wicked persons. Similarly, [Ps] 37:21 states that a wicked individual borrows and cannot repay, but the righteous is generous and gives away... Ps 94:8–11 uses rhetorical questions in composing a didactic essay on divine sovereignty that hears, sees, and chastens. The motto in Prov 1:7a occurs in Ps 111:10a ("The fear of the Lord is the beginning of wisdom"); and the comparison of parental teaching with a lamp and light appears in Ps 119:105, here with reference to God's word.[6]

Proverbs is centered on living a prudent and moral life. There are references to God, but it is human willpower rather than God's redeeming action that is decisive.

The title for Proverbs in Hebrew is *Mishlei Shlomoh* (the proverbs of Solomon). A proverb is a *mashal* (*mishlei* [*mishlé*] = "proverbs of"). The Hebrew word *mashal* has additional usages. It can "designate a parable (Ps. 78:2), allegory (Ezek. 17:2), riddle (Prov. 1:6), taunt (Isa. 14:4), or oracle (Num. 23:18)."[7]

---

6. Crenshaw, "Book of Proverbs," 5:519.

7. West, *Introduction to the Old Testament*, 452 n. 50; see also Waltke, *Book of Proverbs*, 55–57.

Divisions in the Book of Proverbs

The book of Proverbs divides into several natural sections. Wisdom poems precede Proverbs of Solomon. A section containing Words of the Wise/Admonitions leads into Sayings of the Wise. A further set of proverbs is attributed to Solomon. Finally, the last two chapters contain the Words of Agur and then the Words of Lemuel's Mother, plus a description of the Worthy Woman/Capable Wife.

1:1—9:18	Praise of Wisdom
10:1—22:16	Proverbs of Solomon
22:17—24:22	Words of the Wise/Admonitions
24:23–34	Sayings of the Wise
25:1—29:27	Proverbs of Solomon (collected later)
30:1–33	Words of Agur
31:1–9	Words of Lemuel's Mother
31:10–31	A Worthy Woman/Capable Wife

Proverbs 1:1—9:18; Praise of Wisdom

The opening nine chapters feature long poems. This is in contrast to the short, pithy sayings found in much of the rest of Proverbs. The opening verses lay out the purpose of the book. "For learning about wisdom and instruction, for understanding words of insight, for gaining instruction in wise dealing, righteousness, justice and equity . . . to understand a proverb and a figure, the words of the wise and their riddles" (1:2, 3, 6). The goal is practical wisdom for living a good and prudent life. These opening verses then lead to the basic theme: "The fear of the LORD is the beginning of knowledge" (1:7).

> This section purports to give parental advice to children. The chief literary device is that of a father (the "I") speaking to a son (the "you"), for the most part warning against rival discourse and thus reinforcing an ideology, the ethos of the family. Readers assume the role of sons who must choose between those values that preserve society and alternative actions that undercut family stability. Various dangers threaten young men, but two stand out here: the encouragement from young companions to unite in an endeavor to get rich quickly through criminal activity and the seductive

invitation to sensual pleasure from illicit sources . . . Furthermore, the father confesses that he was once a child, in this way drawing adults into the discourse and uniting the generations. Occasionally, the father appeals to the authority of torah, a body of teaching that protects those who walk in its paths.

A mother's voice, although never audible, gives additional weight to the warnings against dangerous conduct. Because the principal threat to young men involves a specific kind of woman, the father's discourse receives an ally in feminine form.[8]

Proverbs 1:8 strikes a familiar note for this book. "Hear, my child, your father's instruction, and do not reject your mother's teaching." Of primary note is "instruction to the young." Similar language is often found (cf. 1:10, 15; 2:1; 3:1, 11, 21, etc.) Reference to parents is a recurring theme. It appears here and throughout Proverbs (6:20; 10:1; 15:20, etc.) Trust in God. Do not rely on your own insight. Learn to understand that God offers criticism and chastisements out of love. They are for your own good. "My child, do not despise the LORD's discipline or be weary of his reproof, for the LORD reproves the one he loves, as a father the son in whom he delights" (3:11–12).

In chapters 1, 8, and 9 the concept of Wisdom is personified. She offers her advice to youth. She does so openly and overtly. This is not esoteric knowledge. These are not insights for the elect, but for everyone. She raises her voice in public squares, at busy corners, and at the entrance of the city (1:20ff.; 8:2ff.; 9:3f.)

The most famous line of this section, indeed one of the most quoted lines from Proverbs, is "She is a tree of life to those who lay hold of her; those who hold her fast are called happy" (3:18). The subject of that particular line is Wisdom. Jewish tradition associates it with the Torah, and by extension Jewish learning as a whole. That verse and the verse that precedes it, "Her ways are ways of pleasantness, and all her paths are peace," as well as a verse from the next chapter, "For I give you good precepts: do not forsake my teaching" (3:17; 4:2), are incorporated into the synagogue liturgy. They are part of the prayers of the Torah service.

Wisdom is a prized possession. It brings insight, honor, length of days, and life itself (4:7, 8, 10, 13). By contrast, immoral people and evildoers are to be avoided at all costs. They eat the bread of wickedness and drink the wine of violence. The path of the righteous is like the light of dawn. The way of the wicked is deep darkness (4:17–19).

---

8. Crenshaw, "Book of Proverbs," 5:515; see also Davis, *Proverbs, Ecclesiastes*, 25–31.

Images are taken from the realm of nature. "Go to the ant, you lazybones; consider its ways, and be wise . . . it prepares its food in summer, and gathers its substance in harvest" (6:6, 8).

Proverbs 10:1—22:16; Proverbs of Solomon

Proverbs that are attributed to Solomon, or wisdom sayings, form this section. This may be the oldest section of the book. Wisdom and righteous living are linked; they contrast with fools and wickedness. Many of these discrete sayings are antithetical in style. This and that are good, but these and those are bad. For example, "The memory of the righteous is a blessing, but the name of the wicked will rot"; "The lips of the righteous know what is acceptable, but the mouth of the wicked what is perverse" (10:7, 32). Sometimes the verse begins with the desirable quality, sometimes with the negative. "Crooked minds are an abomination to the LORD, but those of blameless ways are his delight" (11:20). At other times, the second part of the verse adds an additional virtue. "Pleasant words are like a honeycomb, sweetness to the soul and health to the body" (16:24).

Proverbs 22:17—24:22; Words of the Wise/Admonitions

In the Greek version, this section starts with a kind of superscription: "The words of the wise." The first line then reads, "The words of the wise. Incline your ear and hear my words, and apply your mind to my teaching."

In the Masoretic Text* (MT*) (traditional Hebrew version), 22:17 reads, "Incline your ear and listen to the words of the sages; Pay attention to my wisdom" (NJPS/*TANAKH*).

Scholars suggest that there are many parallels in this section to the writings known as the Instruction (or the Maxims) of Amen-em-ope, an Egyptian sage (c. 1000 BCE). "The structure of the two is the same: a summons to hear 'thirty' . . . admonitions, a series of extended negative precepts. The first six and the ninth of these have topical and some verbal echoes of their Egyptian counterparts, but in a different order. The most striking verbal correspondence is the counsel against avarice in Proverbs 23:4–5: for wealth 'grows wings, like an eagle it flies away into the sky.' Amen-em-ope gives the same counsel but uses the simile 'geese' rather than an 'eagle.'"[9] The reference to "thirty sayings" is, "Have I not written for you thirty sayings of

---

9. Scott, "Book of Proverbs," 1272. See Matthews and Benjamin, *Old Testament Parallels*, 293–302.

admonition and knowledge?" (22:20). NJPS/*TANAKH* translates this as "a threefold lore," indicating in a note that the Hebrew is uncertain.

Proverbs 24:23–34; Sayings of the Wise

Proverbs 24:23–34, some eleven lines, serves as a short appendix to the third division in this collection of aphorisms. This section begins with the words, "These also are the sayings of the wise."

The latter five verses, 30–34, form a little parable in their own right. Similar to 6:6–11, they teach that a person who lacks initiative will end in poverty.

Proverbs 25:1—29:27; Proverbs of Solomon (Collected Later)

This is the second collection attributed to Solomon (see the section above, "Proverbs 10:1—22:16; Proverbs of Solomon"). Chapter 25 begins with an explanation that the following set of maxims are additional proverbs associated with Solomon. They were copied by officials of King Hezekiah of Judah. Although there is no indication in the text, there are internal similarities between the material found in the first three chapters (25–27), and likewise internal similarities between the following two chapters (28–29). "Throughout 25–27 precepts and similes predominate, rather than the declaratory sentences common in the first collection. The tone also is more secular and less moralizing; the name YHWH occurs only once, and then in a supplementary line. In 28–29, the resemblance to 10–22:16 is greater in both form and content. [The two sections, Proverbs 10:1—22:16 and 28:1—29:27,] have six proverbs in common, seven others are nearly identical, and four more have identical half lines. The virtues extolled and the vices held up to scorn are much the same."[10]

Proverbs 30:1–33; Words of Agur

This section subdivides into some words by the unknown figure Agur, and then a kind of response to him (vv. 1–9; 10–14). This is followed by a set of numerical proverbs, often using the formula, there are three or four things (Prov 30:15, 18, 21, 29). The prophet Amos used this three, then four image very powerfully in his rhetoric (Amos 1–2).

---

10. Scott, "Book of Proverbs," 1272.

Proverbs 31:1–9; Words of Lemuel's Mother

A mere nine verses are credited to the mother of someone named King Lemuel. There is a Lemuel mentioned in Genesis, but it is unlikely that this is the same figure. Her advice is to avoid wine and women. She also suggests people should judge righteously as well as defend the rights of the poor and the needy.

Proverbs 31:10–31; A Worthy Woman/Capable Wife

A worthy woman, or a capable wife, is the subject of these famous lines. It is an alphabetical acrostic. Alphabetical acrostics are found in the Psalms; they also feature in Lamentations. This set of proverbs is particularly interesting for the material it shares about domestic living arrangements, at least in well-to-do homes (see the Text Study at the conclusion of this chapter, "A Worthy Woman").

Proverbs in the Christian Scriptures

Although there are very few direct quotes from Proverbs in the Christian Scriptures, it is clear that the wisdom found in Proverbs influenced early Christian thought.

The Epistle to the Hebrews states, "My child, do not regard lightly the discipline of the Lord, or lose heart when you are punished by him; for the Lord disciplines those whom he loves, and chastises every child whom he accepts" (Heb 12:5–6). These verses are based on Proverbs 3:11–12, "My child, do not despise the LORD's discipline or be weary of his reproof, for the LORD reproves the one he loves, as a father the son in whom he delights." Likewise, Revelation 3:19 echoes Proverbs 3:12.

Paul's famous words addressing the gifts of the Spirit, that center on love, are found in 1 Corinthians. This includes the statement that love "bears all things, believes all things, hopes all things, endures all things." In this extended passage Paul reflects words that are part of Proverbs 10, "love covers all offenses" (1 Cor 13:7; Prov 10:12). An even closer reflection is found in 1 Peter, which states, "Above all, maintain constant love for one another, for love covers a multitude of sins" (1 Pet 4:8).

The Gospel of John's advice that "We know that God does not listen to sinners, but he does listen to one who worships him and obeys his will," sounds a great deal like the maxim, "The LORD is far from the wicked, but he hears the prayer of the righteous" (John 9:31; Prov 15:29).

Ephesians says in chapter 6, "And, fathers, do not provoke your children to anger, but bring them up in the discipline and instruction of the Lord." This may well be a restatement of "Discipline your children while there is hope; do not set your heart on their destruction" (Eph 6:4; Prov 19:18).

The notion that there are consequences for our actions is stated in Proverbs 24:12 where it asks rhetorically, "Does not he who keeps watch over your soul know it? And will he not repay all according to their deeds?" Matthew's Gospel expresses similar thoughts (Matt 16:27). Likewise, Romans states, "For he will repay according to each one's deeds" (Rom 2:6; cf. 2 Tim 4:14; Rev 2:23; 20:12–13; 22:12).

When the author of 1 Peter counsels, "Fear God. Honor the emperor," he recasts the advice, "My child, fear the LORD and the king, and do not disobey either of them" (1 Pet 2:17; Prov 24:21).

Paul's thoughts in Romans that "if your enemies are hungry, feed them; if they are thirsty, give them something to drink; for by doing this you will heap burning coals on their heads" is a slight rewording of Proverbs 25 (Rom 12:20; Prov 25:21–22).

The advice in Proverbs 27, "Do not boast about tomorrow, for you do not know what a day may bring," is the basis for similar advice in James (Prov 27:1; Jas 4:13–14).

Luke's description of some of the offenses of the Prodigal Son reflects the aphorism in Proverbs 29, "A child who loves wisdom makes a parent glad, but to keep company with prostitutes is to squander one's substance" (Luke 15:13; Prov 29:3).

In Matthew 23 Jesus states, "All who exalt themselves will be humbled, and all who humble themselves will be exalted." This is another way of explaining the instruction, "A person's pride will bring humiliation, but one who is lowly in spirit will obtain honor" (Matt 23:12; Prov 29:23).

Proverbs in Rabbinic Literature

Proverbs often is quoted in the standard collections of Midrash and in the Talmud. There also is a specific work devoted just to this biblical book, *The Midrash on Proverbs*.[11] *The Midrash on Proverbs* was redacted about the seventh century CE.

God used the Torah to create the world. "Wisdom" is considered as synonymous with the Torah. Proverbs 3:19–20 states, "The LORD by wisdom founded the earth; by understanding he established the heavens, by his

---

11. See this title in the bibliography.

knowledge the deeps broke open, and the clouds drop down the dew." God consults the Torah, which is preexistent with God, in creating the world (see the Text Study at the close of this chapter, "Wisdom Is a Woman") (*Midrash Exodus Rabbah* 47.4).

Words of Torah bring healing to the body. Words of Torah are healthful for all the limbs of the body. This is supported by the words, "For they are life to those who find them, and healing to all their flesh" (Prov 4:22) (*Midrash Leviticus Rabbah* 12.3).

God's presence is close to Israel's prophets; it is far from heathen prophets. Quoting "The LORD is far from the wicked, but he hears the prayer of the righteous" (Prov 15:29), it states that God appears to foreign prophets as one who comes from a distant land, or at night, for Israel's prophets God appears or calls directly (*Midrash Leviticus Rabbah* 1.13).

Chastisements of love. Human suffering should not be seen as something cruel or harsh. It is chastisement from a loving God. The term used is *yissurin shel 'ahavah* ("chastisements of love"). A classic description is found in the *Babylonian Talmud*. There it quotes the line, "For the LORD reproves the one he loves, as a father the son in whom he delights" (Prov 3:12) (*Babylonian Talmud Berakhot* 5a).[12]

Suffering now for a later reward. "Rabbi Eliezer said: Because God loves the righteous, he chastises them in this world, as it is said, *But he who loves him disciplines him early*" [13:24] . . . Because God loves Israel, he disciplines them . . . so that they will thereby achieve atonement for their sins in the coming future" (*Midrash on Proverbs*, ch. 13).

Humans are dependent on God; God is dependent on humans. The soul and the Torah are each compared to a lamp. The reference to a soul is "The human spirit is the lamp of the LORD" (20:27). The reference to the Torah is "For the commandment is a lamp and the teaching a light" (6:23). "God says to humans, 'My light is in your hand, this refers to the Torah'; and 'And your light is in my hand,' this refers to the soul. If you guard my light, I will guard your light, but if you extinguish my light, I will extinguish your light" (*Midrash Deuteronomy Rabbah* 4.4).

Evil is repaid with evil. In Roman times, citizens of the community of Bethar rejoice over the destruction of Jerusalem. In time, they are punished. This bears out the words, "Those who are glad at calamity will not go unpunished" (17:5) (*Midrash Lamentations Rabbah* 2.2.4).

---

12. See also Kraemer, *Responses to Suffering in Classical Rabbinic Literature*.

Be impartial in judgment. "Partiality in judging is not good" (24:23). With this, "Solomon made wisdom known to the sages, so that they would not respect persons in [rendering] judgment" (*Midrash on Proverbs*, ch. 24 beginning).

Solomon writes several biblical books. "Rabbi Jonathan said, first, [Solomon] writes the Song of Songs, then Proverbs, then Ecclesiastes. It is the way of the world. When a person is young, he composes songs; when he grows older he offers maxims; when he is old he speaks of the vanity of things" (*Midrash Song of Songs Rabbah* 1.1.10 end, and many other places).

Do not turn from Torah study. "Like a bird that strays from its nest is one who strays from home" (27:8). Someone who studies with the Sages, and then abandons this study is seriously condemned (*Midrash Ecclesiastes Rabbah* 1.15.2).

Text Study

Proverbs 8; Wisdom Is a Woman

Verses 1-5. Proverbs 8 personifies Wisdom in the form of a woman. As in Proverbs 1, she speaks in public, and invites simple ones to learn prudence as well as acquire intelligence. From her mouth utters truth and righteousness.

Verses 10-11. Wisdom's instruction is worth more than gold, silver, and jewels. Verses 18-19 reinforce this idea.

Verses 15-16. Rulers, kings, and nobles follow Wisdom's advice and rule justly.

Verse 22. This is quite a controversial verse. What does it mean when the text says, "the LORD created me at the beginning of his work"? How was Wisdom created? "The problem for monotheistic editors and translators both in antiquity and in modern times has been to avoid the notion that Woman Wisdom is either a sexually conceived child of God or a preexistent entity whom Yahweh acquires in order to begin creation."[13]

For the early rabbis, Wisdom is the same as Torah. God creates the Torah and then "consults" with it to create the world. Wisdom personified as a woman does not cause undue problems. In Hebrew, just as the word for wisdom is a feminine noun (*hokhma*), so is Torah a feminine noun.

Wisdom's preexistence is addressed in the opening lines of John's Gospel, "In the beginning was the Word [the *Logos*], and the Word was with God, and the Word was God. He was in the beginning with God" (John

---

13. Fontaine, "Proverbs," 148.

1:1–2). For John, Jesus is the Word. "And the Word became flesh and lived among us, and we have seen his glory, the glory as of a father's only son, full of grace and truth" (John 1:14).

Verses 22–31. Beginning with verse 22, Wisdom claims to be present with God *before* the beginning of the earth, as described in Genesis 1. "I was set up, at the first, before the beginning of the earth. When there were no depths . . . when there were no springs . . . Before the mountains had been shaped . . . when he had not yet made earth and fields . . . When he established the heavens I was there" (8:23–27).

Proverbs 9; Woman Wisdom versus Woman Folly

As noted earlier in this chapter, although the terms Lady Wisdom and Dame Folly are commonly used by way of descriptions, Woman Wisdom and Woman Folly are more compelling terms.

Verses 1–6 stand in contrast to the concluding six verses, 13–18. The opening verses are Woman Wisdom inviting the simple and immature to come to join in her carefully prepared feast that will lead to insight.

Verses 7–12 contain maxims about those who are scoffers and those who are wise.

Verses 13–18 are Woman Wisdom's counterpart, Woman Folly. Woman Folly is loud, ignorant, and knows nothing. She also invites the simple to join her in a feast, because "stolen water is sweet, and bread eaten in secret is pleasant." This latter way leads to death.

Proverbs 31:10–31; A Worthy Woman

A number of different terms are used to describe the woman praised and prized in this section: "capable wife" (NRSV, NEB*, NJPS/*TANAKH*); "worthy wife" (NAB*); "wife of noble character" (NIV*); "perfect wife" (Jerusalem Bible); and "good wife" (RSV*). The Hebrew word *'isha* can mean "wife" or "woman," depending on context.

Like some of the psalms and much of the book of Lamentations, these verses are set out in an alphabetical acrostic. Each verse follows the Hebrew alphabet in order.

The woman described here manages a well-to-do household. Mention is made of an expectation of gain. The woman deals with both wool and flax. She considers and purchases property. She arranges the planting of vineyards. She assigns tasks for her servant girls.

Work goes on at all hours. "Her lamp does not go out at night" (v. 18). The spinning of yarn, perhaps flax or wool (mention is made of a distaff, a rod on which the thread is wound, as well as a spindle) is a constant feature of her life. She makes coverings and linen garments, which are sold. She "supplies the merchant with sashes [or girdles]" (v. 24).

Her family praises her. She is prudent in the running of her household. She speaks wisely and utters wisdom.

"While there is evidence here of possibilities that only elite women could realize in their everyday lives (the purchase of land, for example, in v. 16), it is likely that this picture of rosy contentment and good fortune is held up as a goal to which all wives, regardless of their social status, ought to aspire . . . the success of this woman is viewed from the perspective of what she provides for her husband and children."[14]

---

14. Ibid., 152.

4

Job

Introduction

AT THE CENTER OF the book of Job is the unresolved (and probably irresolvable) question of undeserved suffering. "The book of Job is a rare and ingenious achievement. Its anonymous creator has fashioned a work [that is] unique . . . Though it partakes of the motifs and imagery of wisdom literature, it is infinitely more engaging and personal in its impact than anything written in the ancient Near East . . . As religion it is unrivaled in its proclamation of 'faith in spite of.' The obstacles to trust in God are presented ruthlessly and incisively, and the final triumph of faith is as rugged and convincing as the hero's most savage protests."[1]

Job, along with Proverbs and Ecclesiastes, is part of the wisdom literature of the Bible.

Job is the third book in the third section of the Hebrew Bible, the Writings/*Ketuvim* (see Introduction: "The Order of the Books of the Bible"). It follows Proverbs, and precedes Song of Songs. In the Christian Bible Job follows Esther and precedes Psalms.

With the exception of the prologue and epilogue, which appear in prose form, Job is written in poetic verse.

The biblical "narrative sets the action in (pre-)patriarchal times. Job's possessions, like those of the patriarchs, consist of cattle and servants;

---

1. Gottwald, *Light to the Nations*, 472–73.

not only his three friends but also his enemies (nomadic Sabeans and Chaldeans) come from the greater environment associated with Abraham's wanderings; . . . Job's life span exceeds that of the patriarchs; and his sacrifice of animals corresponds to the practice prior to official priests. The name Job recalls a folk hero associated in Ezek 14:14, 20 with Noah and Daniel . . . In accord with the universality typical of early wisdom, the hero seems to have been an Edomite, famous for the wisdom of its inhabitants."[2] Scholars are divided on the dating of Job, and ideas range from the seventh to second centuries BCE.[3]

There is only one female character in Job, his wife, and she is readily dismissed. Carol A. Newsom nonetheless points out that the book has quite some relevance for contemporary women. "What Job and his friends are debating turns out to include some important issues that feminist theology has been raising in recent years: the significance of personal experience as a source of religious insight, the importance and difficulty of solidarity among those who are oppressed, a critique of traditional models of God, and the relationship between human existence and the whole of creation."[4]

An Overview of Job

The opening chapter introduces Job, a completely righteous and blameless man. The scene suddenly shifts to the heavenly court. There is a figure termed Satan (the Hebrew word *Satan* means "'adversary' or 'accuser' . . . [it is] not the devil of New Testament thought"[5]). This figure suggests that the only reason that Job is God-fearing is because God blesses Job. Satan then challenges God with the statement, "But stretch out your hand now, and touch all that he has, and he will curse you to your face" (1:11; cf. 2:5). God agrees to the challenge, but cautions Satan to spare Job's life.

The core of the book of Job (chs. 3–37) is a set of discourses, written as poetry, between Job and his companions, Eliphaz, Bildad, Zophar, and Elihu. "The friends speak as the defenders of a rational and moralistic system and consequently view the problem from an external perspective. Job, however, knows 'the inner infinity of the suffering soul' and can only reject the answers of his orthodox counselors. His position is that not that he is without sin, but that he can find no wrong sufficiently great to justify

---

2. Crenshaw, "Book of Job," 3:858.

3. Clines, *Job 1–20*, lvii; see also Hartley, *Book of Job*, 17–20. Newsom (*Book of Job*, 16) suggests a date of the early Second Temple Period.

4. Newsom, "Job," 208.

5. *NOAB*, 625.

such thoroughgoing rejection at God's hands. Thus the friends' logic of just recompense provides no real defense of God's justice."[6]

The why of pain and suffering in general is not at the heart of this work. What is central is the question why there are instances where *the innocent* suffer without due cause.

Job's friends reflect the standard, popular view that suffering is a consequence of sin. This certainly is the broadly accepted view in the Bible. Job argues back that he is not aware that he has committed any acts that would result, or be deserving of, such unbearable punishment. He says, in effect, "I do not deserve this; this is unfair."

Throughout the book of Job many of the human characters present arguments and counterpoints. They seek to understand God's purpose.

At the conclusion of the book (chs. 38–41) God answers Job out of a whirlwind. God speaks of the overwhelming, awesome, and ultimately unknowable quality of divine power. Finally, in an epilogue (ch. 42) Job states his regret and acknowledges his presumption in voicing doubts about the ways of God. The book concludes with Job's health and wealth restored; in fact his fortune is doubled.

Interpreting Job's Suffering

Many have written about Job, and there are numerous interpretations about the book's essential meaning.[7] "Some see the final theophany and response

---

6. West, *Introduction to the Old Testament*, 459 (quoting Martin Buber, *The Prophetic Faith*, New York: Harper Torchbooks, 1960, 191).

7. "Because undeserved suffering posed an immense intellectual and religious problem for the sages, they sought arduously for a satisfactory answer. Their most common understanding, the *retributive*, is grounded in the order of the universe and the will of its creator. A second explanation, the *disciplinary*, derives from the context of the family, where well-intentioned parents punish their children as an act of love . . . A third approach to suffering, the *probative*, bears impressive witness to the disinterested nature of religion. God tests human hearts to ascertain whether or not religion is pure, and in doing so replaces human self-interest with the centrality of holiness. A fourth interpretation, the *eschatological*, contrasts present discomfort with future restoration, indicating that hope springs eternal in the human breast. A fifth suggestion, the *redemptive*, derives from the sacrificial system and the idea that the spilling of blood alone makes atonement. A sixth response, the *revelatory*, takes suffering as an occasion for divine disclosure of previously hidden truth, both human pride and the mystery of the living God. A seventh understanding of suffering, the *ineffable*, is a humble admission of ignorance before unspeakable mystery, one so profound that a self-revealing deity in the book of Job remains silent about the reason for Job's suffering and fails to affirm meaning behind such agony. An eighth explanation for suffering, the *incidental*, implies that an indifferent deity stands by and thereby encourages evil, which seems

as an affirmation that God's ways are a mystery. If humans cannot comprehend God's creation . . . why should they imagine that they can understand the precise mechanisms of God's justice? Others see Job's response as a claim that only faith may form a proper and adequate answer." Still a different approach is that when "Job triumphed, causing God to reveal himself, that revelation sought to communicate the essential difference between the natural order—which is ultimately inscrutable—and the moral order. The system of divine justice is *not* mechanistic, the author says. God is free from any moral order that we might seek to impose."[8]

That God speaks to Job is significant. The very fact of a divine response, that God feels compelled to argue against what Job says, or that God wants to offer Job an answer at all, is an important theological statement. It indicates that God and humanity share a relationship. God's addresses to Job may not be ultimately satisfying. "Neither speech can be said to offer a direct answer to Job's questions about the reasons for his own suffering and about the general lack of any discoverable relationship between men's characters and their fortunes . . . the implication is that one must serve God not only in spite of all adversity but without even the expectation of an explanation."[9] God's speech at the conclusion of the book of Job may not address Job's questions; nonetheless, God does reply. This is in marked contrast to Lamentations, which ultimately ends in silence.[10]

There is a further explanation. The book of Job shows that "God does not require that we blindly defend the divine system of justice. The pious individual may legitimately challenge and question, and God approves of doing so."[11]

Amazingly, the Bible makes no claim that Job is Jewish. Likewise, neither are Job's companions/friends identified as Jewish. In the Talmudic period, Rabbi Yoḥanan says, "There was no more righteous person among the nations of the world than Job" (["nations of the world" is a euphemism for non-Jews]. *Midrash Deuteronomy Rabbah* 2.5).

---

trivial to the High God who fashioned mortals to be subject to suffering as the human condition. All these understandings of suffering in one way or another find expression in the book of Job." Crenshaw, "Book of Job," 3:865–66.

8. Kraemer, *Responses to Suffering*, 32, 33. Kraemer refers to works by Nahum N. Glatzer and Stephen A. Geller; see Kraemer's endnotes 27, 30–35.

9. Ginsberg, "Book of Job," 119.

10. As it stands, the "book of Lamentations ends with absence. It ends with the absence of God and with the absence of survivors." Linafelt, *Surviving Lamentations*, 62.

11. Kraemer, *Responses to Suffering*, 33; see also Ehrlich, "Book of Job."

The Book of Job

Divisions in the Book of Job

Job 1–2	Prose prologue; God, Satan, Job and his companions
Job 3	Job's opening soliloquy
Job 4–27	Dialogue with companions/friends
Job 28–37	Monologues
Job 38:1—42:6	Dialogue with God
Job 42:7–17	Prose epilogue

Job 1–2; Prose Prologue; God, Satan, Job and His Companions

The first two chapters serve as a prose introduction to the core of the book, which is the dialogue concerning undeserved suffering. In these chapters, Satan places God in an untenable situation. If God refuses to accept Satan's challenge, it gives the impression that there is some basis to Satan's point that Job only reveres God because God rewards him. If God accepts the challenge, God appears heartless.

At the close of chapter 1, Job utters two famous statements, both contained in one verse: "Naked I came from my mother's womb, and naked shall I return there" and "the LORD gave, and the LORD has taken away; blessed be the name of the LORD" (1:21).

Chapter 2 presents Job with further reasons to doubt God. Most of his family are killed and his property stolen. He suffers from loathsome sores all over his body. Job's wife says to him, "Do you still persist in your integrity? Curse God, and die."[12] He replies to her that her response is foolish. "Shall we receive the good at the hand of God, and not receive the bad?" (2:9–10). The text explains that through all this Job does not sin with his lips.

Three companions/friends come to visit Job: Eliphaz, Bildad, and Zophar. To their credit, they do not rush in to offer their commiseration or advice. Rather they simply sit with him for a week in complete silence (2:13).

---

12. Pardes, *Countertraditions in the Bible*, 146–51. A more lighthearted approach to the book of Job is Van Wolde, *Mr and Mrs Job*.

Job 3; Job's Opening Soliloquy

The real drama of the book opens in chapter 3. Job's first words are to curse the day that he was born. He continues in this vein. Job comes close to saying that he wishes he were dead. "Truly the thing that I fear comes upon me, and what I dread befalls me. I am not at ease, nor am I quiet; I have no rest; but trouble comes" (3:25–26). That final phrase, "but trouble comes," is a wonderfully ironic statement, for in the very next chapter Eliphaz will begin the attempt to provide Job with answers for his sufferings.

Job 4–27; Dialogue with Companions/Friends

In chapters 4–5 Eliphaz begins to engage Job in conversation. He asks Job, "who that was innocent ever perished? Or where were the upright cut off?" (4:7). Eliphaz then takes the tack that by nature humans are sinful, and even angels are charged with error (4:17f.) He takes the argument further. He suggests that rebuke and chastisement are good for humans. God might punish, but will then redeem. "How happy is the one whom God reproves; therefore do not despise the discipline of the Almighty. For he wounds, but he binds up; he strikes, but his hands heal" (5:17–18). In this Eliphaz echoes advise offered in Proverbs (Prov 3:11–12).

Chapters 6–7 are Job's reply. He rejects Eliphaz's comments. Job denies he has done wrong (6:10, 24; 7:20).

Bildad in chapter 8 accuses Job of suggesting that God perverts justice (vv. 2–3). He insinuates that if people suffer, they must have erred.

Job replies in chapters 9–10. He claims his innocence and answers that God crushes him without cause (9:15, 17, 20f.) Job feels hounded by God. Job pleads that God should leave him alone (10:16, 20).

In chapter 11 Zophar labels Job as guilty (v. 6). Zophar tells Job that as a mortal he cannot understand God's ways (11:7f.) He implies Job is iniquitous and wicked.

Job replies in chapters 12–14. He proclaims his innocence. He agrees that with God are wisdom and strength (12:13). Job says that these companion/friends are speaking falsely of God (13:4, 7).

Eliphaz retorts that Job is "doing away with the fear of God." He hints that Job's suffering is due to his iniquity, for "The wicked writhe in pain all their days" (15:4, 20).

Job continues to protest his innocence, and accuses his companions of being "miserable comforters" (16:2). Bildad insists that Job is wicked (18:5ff.) but Job answers, "God has put me in the wrong." Job says further,

"Even when I cry out, 'Violence!' I am not answered; I call aloud, but there is no justice" (19:6–7) (see the Text Study section at the conclusion of this chapter, "Job Responds").

In chapter 22 Eliphaz again condemns Job. "Is not your wickedness great? There is no end to your iniquities." He tells Job to "Agree with God" and to accept God's instruction, for if Job returns to God, he will be restored (22:5, 21ff.)

In chapter 23 Job says he wants to present his case to God, but he cannot find God. Job complains, "If I go forward, he is not there; or backward, I cannot perceive him; on the left he hides, and I cannot behold him; I turn to the right, but I cannot see him" (23:8–9). These verses stand in marked contrast to the confident words of the psalmist who says, "Where can I go from your spirit? Or where can I flee from your presence? If I ascend to heaven, you are there; if I make my bed in Sheol, you are there . . . even the darkness is not dark to you" (Ps 139:7–12).

Bildad repeats some earlier arguments in chapter 25. Job replies that he will maintain his integrity, and he will hold on to his righteousness. Job says that his own heart does not reproach him (27:5–6).

Job 28–37; Monologues

Chapter 28 stands by itself. Job then speaks for three chapters, followed by a monologue by Elihu.

Chapter 28 is a "Hymn on the inaccessibility of wisdom . . . It is not addressed to anyone . . . The point is nevertheless clear: One can find precious stones that are deep in the earth [v. 1ff.], but no one can find wisdom (see also vv. 12, 20) because it is with God, who alone knows the *way* to wisdom (v. 23). In fact, his vision is perfect and hence he *sees everything* (v. 24)."[13] The chapter ends on a note reminiscent of Proverbs, "Truly, the fear of the Lord, that is wisdom; and to depart from evil is understanding" (Job 28:28; cf. Prov 1:7; 8:13).

In chapter 29 Job speaks of the many righteous acts he performed. In chapter 30 he bemoans that he is treated so badly; he speaks of his anger with God, and laments his condition. In chapter 31 at some length Job says, essentially, "If I have done wrong, then I would be deserving of punishment."

Chapters 32–37 are the discourses of a fourth companion/friend, Elihu. The Elihu section may be a later addition to the book of Job. It interrupts the flow of events. Towards the conclusion of chapter 31 Job says, "Here is my signature! let the Almighty answer me!" (v. 35). At the beginning of

---

13. *NOAB*, 654 n. 28.1–28.

chapter 38, God does reply to Job. This suggests that in an earlier version of the book there was no Elihu section. A further argument for the later addition of the Elihu section is that the epilogue to the book does not mention Elihu, although it does refer to Eliphaz, Bildad, and Zophar (42:9).

Elihu claims to be a young man, in contrast to Job (and perhaps to the other companions). He claims correctly that he is "full of words" (32:18). Initially in chapter 33, he does little more than summarize Job's complaints. He offers the obvious, "God is greater than any mortal" (v. 12).

Elihu is more interested in speaking than in listening to what Job might have to reply. Chapter 33 ends with the words, "If you have anything to say, answer me; speak, for I desire to justify you. If not, listen to me; be silent, and I will teach you wisdom" (vv. 32–33). Before Job has a chance to reply, Elihu continues directly, for chapter 34 begins, "Then Elihu continued and said: 'Hear my words, you wise men, and give ear to me, you who know'" (v. 1).

Elihu takes a very conventional approach: God will not do wrong. "Of a truth, God will not do wickedly, and the Almighty will not pervert justice" (34:12). He condemns Job, finding him without any support for his claims of innocence. "Job speaks without knowledge, his words are without insight . . . his answers are those of the wicked. For he adds rebellion to his sin" (34:35–37).

Elihu continues in a similar vein, asking Job to extol God, even if God is unknowable (36:24, 26). His speeches conclude with praises of God. Elihu implies that God is great, and therefore Job needs to submit. "The Almighty—we cannot find him; he is great in power and justice, and abundant righteousness he will not violate. Therefore mortals fear him." (37:23–24).

Job 38:1—42:6; Dialogue with God

The climax of the book of Job begins with chapter 38, where God suddenly speaks to Job in a whirlwind. God explains that Job will have a chance to respond. First God will raise some questions for him. God points out rhetorically that, as a mere human, Job lacks perspective. "Where were you when I laid the foundations of the earth? Tell me, if you have understanding. Who determined its measurements—surely you know!" (38:4f.) God continues, pointing out the differences between the divine and mere mortals. "Do you know the ordinances of the heavens? Can you establish their rule on earth? Can you lift up your voice to the clouds, so that a flood of waters may cover you? Can you send forth lightnings, so that they may go" (38:33–35). God's first soliloquy ends with the words, "Shall a faultfinder contend with the Almighty? Anyone who argues with God must respond" (40:2).

Job briefly responds with very few words. He does not really address the issues that God raises. "Job offers an elaborate statement—of silence. Is this evasive, or humility, or defiance? He does not say that he has sinned."[14]

God continues to address Job out of the whirlwind. God asks Job if he wants to defend himself at God's expense (40:8). God then asks Job if Job thinks he can do better at governing the world. In the final chapter, Job answers God and concedes that God is all-powerful, that God "can do all things." Job says that he had had heard of God, but now he understands better and consequently repents in dust and ashes (42:2; see v. 6).

Job 42:7–17; Prose Epilogue

In the epilogue, God restores to Job twice as much as he had before. He is restored to health, wealth, and happiness, and dies at an old age.

Job in the Christian Scriptures

The Epistle of James makes the only direct reference to Job found in the Christian Scriptures. "You have heard of the endurance of Job" (Jas 5:11; cf. "the patience of Job," [KJV]).

Paul does write of God's unsearchable ways. He asks, "For who has known the mind of the Lord? . . . Or who has given a gift to him, to receive a gift in return?" This echoes the line, "If you are righteous, what do you give to him; or what does he receive from your hand?" (Rom 11:34–35; Job 35:7).

In 2 Corinthians Paul offers the image of "a thorn was given me in the flesh, a messenger of Satan to torment me." This reflects God giving Satan large powers over Job (2 Cor 12:7; Job 2:6). The book of Revelation speaks of a time when "in those days people will seek death, but will not find it; they will long to die, but death will flee from them." In an early speech Job ponders why light is given to those bitter in soul, "who long for death, but it does not come" (Rev 9:6; Job 3:21). Another image in Revelation reflects words in Job. "These are the words of the holy one . . . who opens and no one will shut, who shuts and no one opens." At one point Job answers Zophar with the words that if God "tears down, no one can rebuild; if he shuts someone in, no one can open up" (Rev 3:7; Job 12:14).

In 1 Corinthians Paul slightly paraphrases Job, "He catches the wise in their craftiness" (1 Cor 3:19; cf. Job 5:13).

---

14. Ibid., 670 n. 40.3–5.

The author of 1 Peter writes of the "genuineness of your faith—being more precious than gold that, though perishable, is tested by fire—may be found to result in praise and glory and honor." This is similar to a speech spoken by Job. Job says that God "knows the way that I take; when he has tested me, I shall come out like gold" (1 Pet 1:7; Job 23:10). In Matthew Jesus explains, "For mortals it is impossible, but for God all things are possible." Among his final words, Job says to God, "I know you can do all things, and no purpose of yours can be thwarted" (Matt 19:26; cf. Mark 10:27; Job 42:2).

Timothy's statement that "we brought nothing into the world, so that we can take nothing out of it" (1 Tim 6:7) may well be based on Job's words, "Naked I came from my mother's womb, and naked shall I return there" (Job 1:21).

Job in Rabbinic Literature

Hope deferred makes the heart sick. "Hope deferred makes the heart sick" (Prov 13:12). This line from Proverbs is linked to a verse in Job, "What is my strength, that I should wait, and what is my end, that I should be patient? Is my strength the strength of stones, or is my flesh bronze?" (Job 6:11-12). The midrash then applies this teaching to the people of Israel in Egypt who wondered when God finally would redeem them (*Pesikta de-Rab Kahana, Piska* 5.3[15]).

God's love and justice are unfailing. Rabbi Judah bar Ilai quotes the line, "The LORD gave, and the LORD has taken away; blessed be the name of the LORD" (1:21), and then continues that if God gave, God gave in mercy; if God took, God took in mercy (*Midrash Leviticus Rabbah* 24.2).

The wicked choose not to repent. The line "The eyes of the wicked will fail" (11:20) is applied to wicked people who have a chance to repent and do not (*Pesikta de-Rab Kahana*, S. 3.2).

Comfort for Jerusalem: comparing Job, Lamentations, and Jeremiah. Just as Job was rewarded for his patience and his suffering, so will Israel be rewarded in a similar manner. A series of lines from Lamentations and Jeremiah are compared to lines in Job. These include:

> "They sat with him on the ground . . . and no one spoke a word to him" (Job 2:13).
> "The elders . . . sit on the ground in silence" (Lam 2:10).

---

15. See this title in the bibliography.

"The fire of God fell from heaven" (Job 1:16).
"From on high [God] sent fire" (Lam 1:13).

"I have sewed sackcloth upon my skin" (Job 16:15).
"The elders of daughter Zion . . . put on sackcloth" (Lam 2:10).

Job is told that "The Chaldeans . . . made a raid . . . and carried them off" (Job 1:17).

Jeremiah explains that "the city . . . has been given into the hands of the Chaldeans" (Jer 32:24).

The midrash ends with these words, "Now, taught Rabbi Joshua bar Nehemiah, if Job who was a sinner was eventually given a double recompense, so Jerusalem will eventually be given a double recompense of comfort." He quotes the line from Isaiah, "Comfort, O comfort my people" (Isa 40:1) (*Pesikta de-Rab Kahana, Piska* 16.6).

Peace above, peace below. Bar Kappara says, Great is peace. God makes peace in the heavens for the heavenly host among whom there is no jealousy, or hate, or contention, or wrangling, or quarrel, or strife, or envy. The source is "God . . . makes peace in his high heaven" (25:2). How much more is peace needed on earth (*Midrash Leviticus Rabbah* 9.9).

As you die, so are you resurrected. Quoting the verse in Job, "It is changed like clay under the seal, and it is dyed [note NRSV: and they stand forth] like a garment" (38:14), the rabbis suggest that if you die clothed, so are you resurrected clothed. They refer to passages in 1 Samuel where, when he is young, Samuel's mother makes a little robe for him (1 Sam 2:19). When the necromancer of Endor brings up the deceased spirit of Samuel, he is clothed, wrapped in a robe (1 Sam 28:14). Likewise, if you die blind or deaf, you are resurrected blind or deaf. "The Holy One said: . . . let them rise just as they went (to the grave) and afterwards I will heal them" (*Midrash Tanhuma, Genesis, Wayyigash* 11.9, Gen 46.28ff., part I[16]).

Job never existed. Rabbi Shimon ben Lakish says that Job never existed at all (*Midrash Genesis Rabbah* 57.4).

Job is a parable. Job never was and never existed, but is only a typical figure (*Babylonian Talmud Baba Batra* 15a).

When does Job live? Some say Job lives at the time of Moses, others that he is among those who return from the Babylonian Exile (*Babylonian Talmud Baba Batra* 15a).

---

16. See this title in the bibliography.

Job's wife. Job's wife is Dinah, Jacob's daughter (*Midrash Genesis Rabbah* 19.12, 57.4; *Babylonian Talmud Baba Batra* 15b).

The author of the book of Job. Moses writes the book of Job (*Babylonian Talmud Baba Batra* 14b).

Job serves God because of love. Job serves God because of love, as it is said, "Though he kill me, yet I will trust in him" (13:15)[17] (*Mishnah Sotah* 5.5).

Job serves God because of fear. Job serves God because of fear as it is said, the "man was blameless and upright, one who feared God and turned away from evil" (1:1) (*Mishnah Sotah* 5.5).

Job is a righteous Gentile. There is no more righteous man among the nations than Job (*Midrash Deuteronomy Rabbah* 2.4).

Text Study

Job 19; Job Responds

As noted earlier in this chapter, this soliloquy is one where Job retorts to his companions/friends that "God has put me in the wrong." Job says further, "Even when I cry out, 'Violence!' I am not answered; I call aloud, but there is no justice" (19:6–7).

Verses 1–3. Job does not sit passively and absorb the criticism he hears; rather he responds in righteous anger, suggesting that his comforters should be ashamed of what they are saying.

Verse 4. Job does not claim innocence, he claims injustice (see v. 7).

Verse 10. Job accuses God of breaking him down, of uprooting his hope like a tree.

Verses 13ff. Family is far away, relatives and friends have failed Job, guests in his house have forgotten him, servants ignore him, intimate friends abhor him, his bones cling to his skin, and he has barely escaped death.

Verses 25–26. The NRSV translates these verses, "For I know that my Redeemer lives, and that at the last he will stand upon the earth; and after my skin has been thus destroyed, then in my flesh I shall see God." The NJPS/TANAKH offers, "But I know that my Vindicator lives; In the end He will

---

17. Alternative translation, see *NOAB*, 639.

testify on earth—This, after my skin will have been peeled off. But I would behold God while still in my flesh."

The Hebrew term for "redeemer" or "vindicator" is *goel* (from the root *g-'a-l—gimmel-alef-lamed*). A *goel* ("redeemer/vindicator") is "a member of one's kinfolk who will avenge one's honor, or stand good for one's debts (compare Lev 25.25; Deut 25.5–10; Ruth 2.20)."[18] The notes go on to explain that there is some disagreement whether this redeemer/vindicator is a reference to "God, or a mediator (see 9.33–35), or a heavenly witness (see 16.19–21). In any case Job makes the magnificent affirmation that his justice will be recognized (therefore, ultimately by God). When will this be? The meaning of v. 26 is too uncertain a one on which to base a firm conclusion."[19]

Does this section in Job refer to the concept of physical resurrection of the dead? The answer is no. Resurrection is an idea that appears late in biblical thought, and "nowhere in the rest of the book does Job seriously consider the possibility [of physical resurrection] (see ch 14)."[20]

---

18. Ibid., 646 n. 19.25–27.

19 Ibid., 646 n. 19.25–27. See Wilson, *Job*, 207–10.

20. *NOAB*, 646 n. 19.25–27.

5

Song of Songs

Introduction

THE SONG OF SONGS is likewise termed the Song of Solomon, or the Canticle (of Canticles). In its present form, it reads as a secular love song between a man and a woman. The Hebrew title is *Shir ha-Shirim*. This translates as "The Song of Songs," but more idiomatically means "the best (or greatest) song." There are eight chapters in the book. It can be read as a unified whole, or as a set of some five to fifty individual love poems. "The Song ... [addresses] the emotion of desire. Desire remains the theme throughout the eight chapters ... the Song of Songs is not about sex per se, but about sexual yearning."[1] A man and a woman are the main speakers. The daughters of Jerusalem serve as a contrast or counterpoint for the woman's declarations (cf. 1:5; 5:8, 16). The woman has the majority of the verses. Her suitor sometimes is the ruler; sometimes he is a shepherd. The man and the woman each delights in, and describes the physical charms of, the other person. Throughout the Song of Songs, there are verses of yearning and self-description. There are statements of approval of and desire for the other. There are various settings for the lovemaking in the Song. These include "(a) the cultivated or habitable countryside; (b) the wild or remote natural landscape and its elements; (c) interior environments (houses, halls, rooms); (d) city streets."[2]

---

1. Walsh, *Exquisite Desire*, 29. See "How (Not) to Read the Song" in Hess, *Song of Songs*, 34–35; and Huwiler, *Biblical Women*, 98.

2. Falk, *Song of Songs*, 139. "The SoS appears to be a completely secular collection

The Song of Songs is the fourth book in the third section of the Hebrew Bible, the Writings/*Ketuvim* (see Introduction: "The Order of the Books of the Bible"). It follows Job and precedes Ruth. In the Christian Bible, the Song of Songs follows Ecclesiastes and precedes Isaiah.

The Book of Song of Songs

Authorship

King Solomon is the traditional author of Song of Songs. His name is mentioned several times in the text (1:1, 5; 3:7–11; 8:11–12). The Bible credits Solomon with multiple wives and his writing many songs (1 Kgs 11:3; 4:32 [5:12 H]). Solomon's authorship, however, is doubtful. It is more likely that these are secular love songs. At a point, they were edited into one book. In its present form it may well come from the Persian or Hellenistic period (c. 500–300 BCE). There are nearly fifty words that only appear in the Song. Many words show a similarity in style with Aramaic, the language that replaced Hebrew as the common language of Jews some time after the Babylonian Exile (586–538 BCE).

Interpretation

It is unclear if these verses are simply beautiful love poems or if there is a deeper meaning to the work. Suggested interpretations include that this book is an allegory, a cult myth based on a divine marriage between Israel and God (based on earlier Mesopotamian sources), a drama, an extended poem/song, or a series or anthology of poems/songs. "From a very early time, an allegorical interpretation provided theological meaning to an otherwise thoroughly erotic and secular poetry. The expressions of love were taken by Judaism as representing [God's] relation to Israel, and later by Christians as Christ's love for the church"[3] (see later in this chapter, "Song of Songs in the Christian Scriptures" and "Song of Songs in Rabbinic Literature").

---

of love lyrics, its allegorical interpretations notwithstanding . . . The primary subject of the SoS is . . . heterosexual love and its erotic manifestations." Brenner, "On Feminist Criticism of the Song of Songs," 28. There also are parallels with Egyptian love songs of an earlier era. See Matthews and Benjamin, *Old Testament Parallels*, 321–26.

3. West, *Introduction to the Old Testament*, 463. Garrett, *Song of Songs*, 59–76; see also Brenner, *Song of Songs*, 68–70. "Christians have through the centuries regarded the Song of Songs as one of the most religiously profound—and most difficult!—books of the Bible. Except for Genesis and the Psalms, the Song has generated more commentary than any book of the Bible. Medieval Christians especially were fascinated by it." Davis,

At its surface meaning, the Song of Songs is erotic poetry. Since this book does not mention the name of God, or include prophetic pronouncements or moral lessons, there were serious challenges by the rabbis to its being included in the biblical canon. The strong support for its inclusion by the great Sage Rabbi Akiva in the second century CE tipped the balance in its favor (*Mishnah Yadayim* 3.5).

The Song of Songs counteracts the idea that in the Bible "desire was constructed as male and as dangerous, something to be repressed or controlled—as we see in the laws governing sexual relations, the advice of Proverbs to young men, and the 'lessons' taught by the examples of heroes like Samson and David, led astray by their libidos."[4] The Song is unique in all of the Bible because "the woman is not cast in her traditional roles of wife, mother, sister, or in-law. Nor is she depicted as dealing with infertility, family dynamics, or the difficulties women face in a patriarchal power struggle. She is, in contrast, a young woman in love."[5]

Divisions in the Book of Song of Songs

As noted, there are differing interpretations on how to divide this book. Some suggest a unified whole. Others see it as a series of connected or separate love poems/songs. There are differences as to what constitutes a particular set, and there is no consensus among scholars as to these divisions.

Chapter 1

Verse 1. The Song opens with a title, ascribing it to Solomon.

Verses 2–7. The woman begins her song, mentioning in passing the "daughters of Jerusalem," which suggests that they might be there to hear her voice. She seeks to link up with her lover.

Verses 8–11. The man responds, comparing her to a mare among Pharaoh's chariots.

Proverbs, Ecclesiastes, and the Song of Songs, 231.

    4. Exum, "Song of Songs," 248.

    5. Rosenblatt, *After the Apple*, 243. Many praise the book, for it "advocates balance in female and male relationships, urging mutuality not domination, interdependence not enmity, sexual fulfillment not mere procreation, uninhibited love not bigoted emotions." Weems, "Song of Songs," 160.

Verses 12–14. The woman speaks, likening her lover to a cluster of henna blossoms.

Verses 15–17. It is unclear if this is the woman's voice, or the man's response to her.

Chapter 2

Verse 1. The woman self-describes as a rose of Sharon, a lily among the valleys.

Verse 2. The man responds, calling her a lily among brambles.

Verses 3–10a.[6] She praises her lover. She proclaims his fruit sweet to her taste. "Sustain me with raisins, refresh me with apples; for I am faint with love" she declares (v. 5). Again she addresses the daughters of Jerusalem (v. 7), asking them not to stir up or awaken love until it is ready. She sees her lover looking through a window. He speaks to her.

Verses 10b–15. In this section the man voices some of the most famous lines in the book. "Arise, my love, my fair one, and come away; for now the winter is past, the rain is over and gone. The flowers appear on the earth; the time of singing has come, and the voice of the turtledove is heard in our land" (vv. 10b–12).

Verses 16–17. The chapter closes as the woman speaks the equally famous words, "My beloved is mine, and I am his" (v. 16).

Chapter 3

Verses 1–5. Again the woman's voice opens up the chapter. She seeks her lover in the streets. At first, she cannot find him. When she does, she brings him to her mother's house. In verse 5, she addresses the daughters of Jerusalem. She asks them not to stir up or awaken love until it is ready.

Verses 6–11. Either the man is speaking, or perhaps a third party is describing a wedding procession. Specific mention is made of Solomon.

---

6. Hebrew sentences generally divide into two segments, divided by something like a comma. The first part is designated the a section (1a, 2a, 3a) and the second part the b section (1b, 2b, 3b).

Chapter 4

Verses 1–15. In a change of pace, the man's voice both begins and fills most of this chapter. He describes his lover as beautiful. Her eyes are like doves behind her veil. Her lips are a crimson thread. "Your two breasts are like two fawns, twins of a gazelle, that feed among the lilies" (4:5). She is flawless. He invites her to come with him. Her love is sweet, "how much better is your love than wine . . . honey and milk are under your tongue; the scent of your garments is like the scent of Lebanon" (4:10–11).

Verse 16. The woman responds. She calls upon the north and south winds to blow upon her garden, that its fragrance will be wafted abroad. She concludes with the words, "Let my beloved come to his garden, and eat his choicest fruits" (v. 16).

Chapter 5

Verse 1. Here the man responds to the closing verse of the previous chapter. He tells his lover that he is coming to his garden to drink wine and milk.

Verses 2–8. The woman awakes from a slumber. She looks for her lover. She says she had opened for him. Then suddenly he turned and was gone. She looks for him in the city. She cannot find him. She turns to the daughters of Jerusalem. She says, if you find him tell my lover that "I am faint with love" (5:8).

Verse 9. The daughters of Jerusalem respond to the woman's voice.

Verses 10–16. The woman describes her lover to the daughters of Jerusalem in powerfully evocative language. He is "radiant and ruddy . . . His head is the finest gold; his locks are wavy, black as a raven. His eyes are like doves . . . His arms are rounded gold . . . His legs are alabaster columns . . . His speech is most sweet." She concludes, "This is my beloved and this is my friend."

Chapter 6

Verse 1. Although not specifically labeled, the opening verse is likely spoken by the daughters of Jerusalem. They ask the woman where her lover has gone.

Verses 2–3. The woman responds. She repeats words spoken earlier, "I am my beloved's and my beloved is mine" (v. 3).

Verse 4-10. The man's voice returns. He calls her as beautiful as Tirzah, comely as Jerusalem. He praises his lover. He repeats some of his descriptions. He speaks of her teeth and her cheeks (6:6, 7; cf. 4:2, 3).

Verses 11-12. The woman speaks briefly. She suggests that she is being placed in a chariot.

Verse 13 (7:1 H). An unknown voice (perhaps the daughters of Jerusalem) asks the woman to return. She responds by asking why they look upon her.

Chapter 7

Verses 1-9 (2-10 H). The man admires and extols the physical beauty of his lover. He describes her feet, thighs, belly, breasts, and neck. He likens her breasts to a palm tree's clusters. He speaks of climbing the palm to lay hold of its branches. Her breath is the scent of apples. Her kisses are like the best wine (vv. 7-9 [8-10 H]).

Verses 10-13 (11-14 H). The woman responds. She speaks of her beloved's desire. She invites him to go to the fields where she will give him her love (v. 11, 12 [12, 13 H]) (see the Text Study section at the conclusion of this chapter, "Celebrating Love").

Chapter 8

Verses 1-4. The woman speaks. She wishes that she had known him even earlier in her life. Verse 4 returns to the earlier request to the daughters of Jerusalem. She asks them not to stir up or awaken love until it is ready.

Verse 5. It is unclear if the man or the woman is speaking.

Verses 6-7. The voice here is likewise unclear. It may be that each speaks these well-known words to the other. "Set me as a seal upon your heart, as a seal upon your arm; for love is strong as death, passion fierce as the grave. Its flashes are flashes of fire, a raging flame" (v. 6).

Verses 8-9. Since these verses are in the plural form, the daughters of Jerusalem are the likely speakers.

Verses 10-14. As the woman's voice began this book, so it closes it. She speaks of her own charms. Then she concludes with a call to her lover to join her.

Song of Songs in the Christian Scriptures

There are no verses from the Song of Songs quoted in the Christian Scriptures. Nonetheless, in the Middle Ages this book became the source for several writers, prominent among them the French ecclesiastic Bernard of Clairvaux. Bernard wrote many sermons wherein he suggested that the love expressed in the Song was but an allegory for the love of Christ for the soul and, in addition, the mystical union that came from this love. In the Middle Ages other Christian authors interpreted the Song of Songs as Christ's love for his Blessed Mother. The Song additionally provided sermonic material for Martin Luther, John Calvin, and the Puritan preachers, all who interpreted it allegorically, taking it far beyond the original book in the Hebrew Bible with its clear description of sexual love as a joyful and positive ideal.[7]

Song of Songs in Rabbinic Literature

Song of Songs is one of the five "scrolls." During the Jewish liturgical year, on five holy days, in addition to the reading from the Torah and the Prophets (*Haftarah*), one of the five scrolls are read. Song of Songs is read on *Pesach*/Passover, in the early spring, the holiday that celebrates the Redemption from servitude in Egypt.

The other four scrolls are Ruth (read at *Shavuot*/Weeks/Pentecost in the late spring), Lamentations (read on *Tisha b'Av*, the ninth day of the Hebrew month of *Av*, in the midsummer), Ecclesiastes (read on *Succot*/Booths/Tabernacles in the early autumn), and Esther (read at *Purim* generally in late winter). This is the same order in which these books appear in the Hebrew Bible.

Midrash Song of Songs Rabbah. The midrash collection *Midrash Rabbah* (the Great Midrash) devotes a whole book to the Song of Songs. *Midrash Song of Songs Rabbah* was redacted about the middle of the sixth century CE.

A uniquely sacred book. Rabbi Akiva, the great sage of the second century CE, states that Song of Songs is a uniquely sacred book (*Mishnah Yadayim* 3.5).

From synagogue to synagogue, schoolhouse to schoolhouse. "My beloved is like a gazelle" (2:9). Just as a gazelle leaps and skips from thicket to thicket and grove to grove, so does God leap from synagogue to synagogue, from schoolhouse to schoolhouse in order to bless Israel (*Pesikta de-Rab Kahana*, Piska 5.8).

---

7. Whiteley, "Song of Solomon," 348.

God observes Israel and speaks words of blessing. "My beloved is like . . . a young stag . . . he stands behind our wall, gazing in at the windows . . . My beloved speaks" (2:9–10). This means that God stands outside of the walls of prayer houses and study houses. God looks through the openings that are formed by the arms of the priests (when they raise their arms in blessing.) The priests then speak God's words to Israel (quoting Num 6:24), "The LORD bless you and keep you" (*Pesikta de Rab Kahana, Piska* 5.8).

Solomon writes the Song of Songs. Solomon writes the books of Proverbs, Ecclesiastes, and the Song of Songs (*Midrash Song of Songs Rabbah* 1.1.6).

How God's Revelation on Sinai reached Israel. "Let him kiss me with the kisses of his mouth!" (1:2). When God uttered the commandments on Mount Sinai, individual angels brought them to the Israelites, and person-by-person explained the rules and regulations. If the person agreed to follow the commands and to accept the divinity of God, the angel kissed that person on the mouth and taught him/her Torah (*Midrash Song of Songs Rabbah* 1.2.2).

Our children will be our sureties. "Draw me after you" (1:4). When God offers the commandments to Israel, God asks for sureties that they will really follow the divine teaching. The Israelites suggest their ancestors. God says that the ancestors committed faults. Then the Israelites offer the prophets as their sureties. God says this will not do. Finally, the Israelites pledge their children, and God agrees. The midrash then ties this to the verse in Psalms, "Out of the mouth of babes and infants you have founded a bulwark" (Ps 8:2 [8:3 H]), understanding bulwark as "strength," that is, Torah (*Midrash Song of Songs Rabbah* 1.4.1).

You are beautiful in what you do. "Ah, you are beautiful, my love; ah, you are beautiful" (1:15). This means that God regards Israel as beautiful in their performance of precepts and in deeds of kindness. This is both the performance of positive commands (i.e., do such and such) and negative commands (i.e., do not do such and such), in following daily prayers, and in affirming God's unity, the *Sh'ma** ("Hear, O Israel: The LORD is our God, the LORD alone," Deut 6:4) (*Midrash Song of Songs Rabbah* 1.15.1).

Moses and Aaron. "Your two breasts are like two fawns" (4:5). Just as the breasts are the beauty and the ornament of a woman, the glory and pride of a woman, so are Moses and Aaron the beauty and ornament, the glory and pride of Israel (*Midrash Song of Songs Rabbah* 4.5.1).

Text Study: Song of Songs 7; Celebrating Love

Verse 2 (3 H). The man describes the physical beauty of his lover in this and in several succeeding verses. As with much of biblical poetry, the second part of the verse is a conscious reflection or a restatement of the first section. Here he focuses on her navel or perhaps her hips. He suggests that they are as a bowl filled with wine; her belly is a heap of wheat encircled by lilies.

Verse 3 (4 H). Her two breasts are like fawns, twins of a gazelle. There is a sense of both the innocence and the excitement of young animals.

Verse 5 (6 H). Praising her magnificent head, he extols her flowing locks, suggesting that rulers are captivated by her tresses. As noted, many of the Hebrew words are of uncertain meaning.[8]

Verse 10 (11 H). The woman responds to her lover. In her words, "I am my beloved's and his desire is for me." She paraphrases words found earlier in the book where she says, "My beloved is mine, and I am his" (2:16; 6:3).

Verse 12 (13 H). She invites her lover to go out early to the vineyards, to see if the grape blossoms are in flower, if the pomegranates (a fruit with many seeds, hence a symbol of abundance) are in bloom. She promises there to offer him her love.

---

8. *NOAB*, 859.

6

Ruth

Introduction

THE BOOK OF RUTH reads like a historical romance. It tells the story of a young foreign woman's integration into Jewish life. The conclusion of the book reveals that Ruth will be the great-grandmother of King David. By extension, she is an ancestor of the Messiah, who will be a descendant of David. Ruth is central to the plot of the story. She appears in every chapter. Ruth, and her mother-in-law, Naomi, who likewise appears in each chapter, dominate the narrative. Women's voices fill this book. This is in contrast to the book of Esther, the only other book in either the Jewish or Christian Scriptures that bears the title of a woman. Although Esther is central to the plot of that book, she does not appear in each chapter, nor is her role so prominent in the narrative. These two books, however, share another quality. The women heroines are very resourceful. "Lacking direct power, [these] women use other means to achieve their goals—shrewdness, verve, wit, and just plain smarts. And because power for women traditionally comes from their identification and association with men, the shrewdness and smarts . . . [are] applied to winning or controlling a man."[1]

Ruth is the fifth book in the third section of the Hebrew Bible, the Writings/*Ketuvim* (see Introduction: "The Order of the Books of the Bible"). It follows the Song of Songs and precedes Lamentations. In the Christian Bible Ruth appears much earlier, following Judges and preceding Samuel. This is because in the Christian Bible the historical books precede the poetic, wisdom, and prophetic books.

---

1. Francine Klagsbrun, "Ruth and Naomi, Rachel and Leah," 268.

The Book of Ruth

History, Romance, or Polemic?

The book of Ruth can be read on several different levels. It might be a history, a romance, or a polemic. Many of the names in the book have symbolic value. Ruth also has inspired feminist interpretations of the book.

Is the narrative of Ruth part of the history of the house of David? The final verses list Ruth's descendants (4:17–22). This links her to the birth of David. Through Boaz, Ruth's husband, there likewise is a connection reaching backward to Perez, the son of Judah, one of Jacob's children (4:12, 18). In fact, the story of Ruth is the product of a later age, and this is a rewriting of history.

The genealogical connection to David is in addition to the romantic elements of the book. Ruth is an engagingly and endearingly told story. It depicts a young widow who leaves her native land to accompany her mother-in-law to a foreign country. In that land of ancient Judah, in time Ruth overcomes the local inhabitants' distrust of the "other." She establishes herself as a figure of great respect and honor. She marries well and establishes a royal dynasty. Ruth is a well-crafted story. "Within the structures of this tale, silences are as meaningful as the dialogues themselves . . . Chapter 1, containing the most provocative and memorable dialogues in the tale, ends with silence: the women's stunned, hushed reaction to the abundance that they encounter in Bethlehem, which contrasts starkly with their own destitution."[2]

Genealogical considerations and a romantic tale notwithstanding, one view is that the book may also well be a carefully written polemic. It suggests that "the author wished to show that a non-Israelite could become a faithful worshipper of the LORD. This would counter the books of Ezra and Nehemiah, both of which consider intermarriage wrong (see Ezra chs 9 and 10; Neh 10.30). Like the books of Jonah and Isaiah chs 40–55, Ruth affirms that the concern of the LORD extends beyond the people of Israel to people of every nation."[3]

A careful reading of Ruth suggests a very different and darker polemical purpose. "Ruth's Gentile background remains a stigma: her Moabite ancestry associates her with an aggressive form of seduction and with the taint of idolatry" (cf. Num 25:1ff.) Ruth is praised for her kindness. Yet,

---

2. Aschkenasy, "Language as Female Empowerment in Ruth," 119. See Lacocque's analysis of the book in terms of literary criticism in Lacocque, *Ruth*, 8–18.

3. *NOAB*, 332. Perhaps it raises "a religious argument" against the enforcement of endogamous marriages favored by Ezra-Nehemiah. Matthews, *Judges and Ruth*, 209. "The book of Ruth is unequivocally a story about God's redemptive love," explains Rowell, "Ruth," 146. See also Eskenazi and Frymer-Kensky, *Ruth*, xxxviii ff.

she consistently is termed "Ruth the Moabite." This highlights her foreign, non-Israelite origin. At the close of the book, "the Israelite woman Naomi, not the Moabite Ruth, becomes the acclaimed mother of Obed (4:17)." This action eclipses Ruth's role as mother. It obscures Obed's foreign stain. This interpretation suggests that a subliminal message of the book of Ruth is that "women's principal worth is in producing sons and that Gentile women, sexually manipulative and therefore dangerous, should not be fully incorporated into Israel. Perhaps Ruth's unconventional actions are acceptable in this book only because she is a Moabite."[4] Further, even though on one level this book celebrates Ruth's *ḥesed* (*chesed*, "lovingkindness"), at the same time, "Ruth's actions offer no means for improving the social system of Bethlehem. The book of Ruth offers no prescriptions for changing the circumstances in which women, either native or foreign, find themselves impoverished and unprotected. Women have a voice in the community, but that is all. Their fates are determined by men: their husbands and sons and the town elders."[5]

A still different explanation is that the author of Ruth consciously connects but also contrasts its narrative, and in particular its conclusion, to two early episodes in the Bible, specifically in the book of Genesis.[6] In both of these instances, that of Lot/Lot's daughters (Gen 19) and Judah/Tamar (Gen 38), women are ill treated; they are regarded as dispensable characters. Nonetheless, in its present form, the "tale of Ruth is purged of the many unseemly elements of the two previous" narratives.[7] "Such intertextual links are not mere niceties,"[8] but a deliberate decision to link together the three stories. In each of those cases the father (father-in-law) regards his daughters (daughter-in-law) as expendable. These are tales of crass and immoral behavior in their own right, and additionally each leads to incest. The book of Ruth suggests a response: that men in authority should protect the vulnerable and look after their welfare. In the book of Ruth, Boaz rescues

---

4. Levine, "Ruth," 78–79.

5. Ibid. 78. Ruth as reflecting the plights of foreign workers is discussed in Brenner, "Ruth as Foreign Worker."

6. "Ruth evokes Genesis in a number of ways. First, the book explicitly mentions some of the ancestors in Genesis by name: Rachel, Leah, Judah, Tamar, and Perez . . . there are some parallels and allusions . . . Ruth's Moabite origin brings to mind the story of Lot's daughters and the birth of Moab (Gen. 19:30–37)." Eskenazi and Frymer-Kensky, *Ruth*, xxi.

7. Aschkenasy, "Language as Female Empowerment in Ruth," 121.

8. Eskenazi and Frymer-Kensky, *Ruth*, xxii. The authors refer to Fisch's exploration of this issue: Fisch, "Ruth and the Structure of Covenant History." Nielsen has written, "Ruth belongs within an intertextuality of women's stories that deal with infertility and the triumph over it. The most obvious examples of women who do their utmost to get a son [include] . . . Lot's daughters . . . and Tamar." Nielsen, *Ruth*, 13.

Ruth from widowhood and provides her with an heir; he also redeems the history of their two families, his own and that of Ruth. Through this device the book's message rewrites ancient wrongs.[9] As Ilana Pardes observes, "the Book of Ruth violates a whole array of conventions, the primary one being the gender of its protagonists."[10]

Divisions in the Book of Ruth

Chapter 1

The narrative sets the book of Ruth in the period when the judges ruled (c. 1200–1000 BCE). In response to a famine, a family leaves their home in Bethlehem in Judah and settles in Moab. The principals are Elimelech, his wife Naomi, and their two sons, Mahlon and Chilion. Elimelech dies in Moab. His two sons marry Moabite women, Orpah and Ruth. After a decade in Moab, the two sons die childless. This leaves a household made up of three widows.

Naomi hears that the famine in Judah has ended. She desires to resettle in her ancestral home. Orpah and Ruth accompany her on her return. Along the way, Naomi actively dissuades and discourages her daughters-in-law from continuing on this journey to Judah. She suggests that they go back each to her mother's house. Naomi does not say so directly, but she infers that these women are more likely to remarry within their own cultural surroundings. After an initial protest that Naomi rejects, Orpah leaves. Ruth remains adamant that she will accompany Naomi on her journey. Ruth then speaks the most famous words in the book:

> "Do not press me to leave you or to turn back from following you!
> Where you go, I will go; where you lodge I will lodge;
> your people shall be my people, and your God my God.
> Where you die, I will die—there will I be buried.
> May the LORD do thus and so to me, and more as well, if even
> death parts me from you!" (1:16–17)

The chapter concludes with the women arriving in Bethlehem at the time of the late spring/early summer harvest. In response to the welcome by the townspeople, Naomi claims she has come back empty (!) and that God has dealt harshly with her. Naomi neither acknowledges Ruth's presence with her, nor does she introduce her daughter-in-law.

---

9. Zucker, "Throwaway Women."
10. Pardes, *Countertraditions in the Bible*, 99.

Chapter 2

This chapter commences with what seems to be an unimportant, or perhaps irrelevant, piece of information. Naomi has a relative on her late husband's side, Boaz. Boaz is wealthy and a prominent figure in the community.

The narrative then explains that Ruth volunteers to go out to work. Since it is harvest time, she plans to be a gleaner. She wants to support the two of them. Naomi encourages her to do so. *By chance* (!), Ruth starts to glean in a field belonging to Boaz. Then Boaz *coincidentally* arrives from Bethlehem. He sees Ruth working. He enquires about her from one of his employees. The man identifies her as Ruth the Moabite, the woman who had come with Naomi. The servant explains further that Ruth has been working diligently all day.

Boaz approaches Ruth. He encourages her to glean in his field. Boaz explains that he has instructed his employees not to bother her. She asks him why he would show such kindness to her, especially since she is a foreigner. He replies that he has heard good reports about her. He knows that she left her native land and has been a support for Naomi.

At mealtime, Boaz invites Ruth to sit beside the other reapers. He encourages her to partake of the food, which she does. Boaz further instructs his employees to favor her. At day's end she returns to Naomi bringing about an ephah of barley (about two-thirds of a bushel). Naomi congratulates Ruth on her industriousness. Ruth tells Naomi that she has met Boaz. Naomi encourages Ruth to remain working there throughout the summer. Ruth continues until the end of the barley and wheat harvests.

Chapter 3

Naomi suggests to Ruth that the time has come to move matters along. The goal is to secure a stable future for Ruth. Naomi tells Ruth that this very evening Boaz will be at the threshing floor, winnowing barley. Naomi proposes that Ruth should quietly go there. She is to wait until Boaz has bedded down for night. Ruth should then uncover his feet and lie down. Boaz will tell her what to do. Ruth agrees to the plan.

That evening Boaz suddenly awakes. He finds Ruth, who asks him to "spread [his] cloak" (v. 9) over her, for he is her closest kin (see the Text Study at the end of this chapter, "Spreading One's Cloak"). Boaz praises her for her action. He explains that there is a closer next-of-kin. He promises Ruth that he will settle the matter in the morning. Before sunrise, Boaz sends Ruth back to Naomi, carrying six measures of barley.

Chapter 4

The closing chapter features Boaz at the city gate. This is where people transact community business. He times his presence there just when the man who is the closer relative to Naomi/Ruth than Boaz comes by. Boaz convenes a quorum of elders. He explains that Naomi wishes to sell a parcel of land that had belonged to her husband Elimelech. The nearer next-of-kin expresses his interest in acquiring the land. Boaz then adds an additional fact: along with the land will come Ruth, and by implication, the obligation of Levirate marriage (see the Text Study section at the end of the chapter, "Levirate Marriage"). Hearing this, the nearer next-of-kin decides to bypass the offer of land. He invites Boaz to acquire it in his own right. Boaz readily agrees. Boaz and Ruth marry. They have a son, Obed. Naomi takes pride in her new grandchild. The chapter concludes with the genealogies linking Ruth to David, and Boaz backwards to Perez and forwards to David.

Symbolic Names in Ruth

A person's name is their fame. Often in biblical texts names carry symbolic meaning. Alternatively, the Bible often puns on a person's name and some related event. For example, Abram takes on the new name Abraham, meaning the "ancestor of a multitude" (Gen 17:5). The name Isaac relates to the word for *laughter* (Gen 21:6). The name Jacob has links with the words for *heel* (Gen 25:26) and *supplants* (27:36).

Many names in Ruth have symbolic value. At times the play on the name is a positive connection, and at times it is negative. A number of these puns/interpretations of names are found in *Midrash Ruth Rabbah* 2.5. The narrative begins in the land of Judah, in Bethlehem. Bethlehem literally means "house of bread," or euphemistically "breadbasket," as in the United States and Canada where the Midwestern states and provinces are referred to as the breadbasket because of the abundance of grain grown there. The difficulty is that there is no bread in Bethlehem because of the famine.

Elimelech, Naomi's husband's name, can be translated euphemistically as "I am a king" (*eli* = to me; *melekh* = king). By extension, this can mean "I am a powerful person." In fact, Elimelech is not royalty, nor is he powerful. He flees his native land and then he dies. He leaves his wife impoverished.

Mahlon and Chilion have linguistic affinities to the words for *illness* and *devastation*. In short order, both sons die.

Naomi is based on the word for *pleasantness*. At the close of the book, she will know pleasantness when her grandson is born. Yet, initially Naomi only knows hardship. When she returns to Bethlehem, she tells those who greet her, "Call me no longer Naomi [pleasant], call me Mara [bitter] for the Almighty has dealt *bitterly* with me" (1:20).

Boaz can be read as the phrase "in him is strength." Boaz is a strong and positive figure in the book.

The name Ruth probably is related to the word for *kindness* or *friendship* (*re-ut*), from the root *r-'-h* (*resh-ayin-hey*). More to the point, her name is familiar to English-speaking people. Someone who lacks compassion is *ruthless*, and so by extension the name Ruth means *compassionate* or *caring*.

Ruth: Women Reading/Women Writing

One of the blessings that have come out the feminist movement is a rich body of literature written by women, about women in the Bible. At various points in this volume, material has been quoted from insights found in *Women's Bible Commentary*, edited by Carol A. Newsom, Sharon H. Ringe, and Jacqueline E. Lapsley (2012.) Other important books by women are *Reading Ruth: Contemporary Women Reclaim a Sacred Story*, edited by Judith A. Kates and Gail Twersky Reimer (1994); *Ruth*, by Kirsten Nielsen (1997), and the Jewish Publication Society's Commentary on Ruth by Tamara Cohn Eskenazi and Tikva Frymer-Kensky (2011).[11] Kates and Reimer note that often "women recognize ways in which a traditional text speaks to their experience as women, but when they turn to commentary, they find little that speaks to either their experiences as women or their experiences as women reading/confronting a biblical text."[12] To address this concern, they bring together a variety of Jewish women's voices. Among them are biblical scholars; scholars of Jewish studies; women with expertise in women's studies, literary studies, philosophy, psychology, and sociology; as well as psychiatrists, rabbis, mothers, daughters, friends, and lovers. In several cases, these descriptions overlap in the same person. Contributions to this particular work include a verse-by-verse commentary, a lesbian interpretation of the book, and many other essays that challenge a more traditional understanding of Ruth.

---

11. Lee, "Ruth"; see also the books by Kates and Reimer, Nielsen, and Eskenazi and Frymer-Kensky, where notes in these volumes suggest still other works authored by women about Ruth and other biblical books.

12. Kates and Reimer, *Reading Ruth*, xviii.

Ruth in the Christian Scriptures

The closing verses of Ruth list the Judah-to-David genealogies (4:12, 17–22). These names are part of the Gospel of Matthew's genealogical chart (Matt 1:3–6). Luke 3:31–33 offers similar material.

Ruth in Rabbinic Literature

Ruth is one of the five "scrolls." During the Jewish liturgical year, on five holy days, in addition to the reading from the Torah and the Prophets (*Haftarah*), one of the five scrolls are read. Ruth is read at *Shavuot*/Weeks/Pentecost, the holy days that celebrate the late spring harvest.

The other four scrolls are Song of Songs (read at *Pesach*/Passover in the early spring), Lamentations (read at *Tisha b'Av*, the ninth day of the Hebrew month of *Av*, in the midsummer), Ecclesiastes (read at *Succot*/Booths/Tabernacles, in the early autumn), and Esther (read at *Purim* generally in late winter).

Midrash Ruth Rabbah. The midrash collection *Midrash Rabbah* (the Great Midrash) devotes a whole book to Ruth. *Midrash Ruth Rabbah* was redacted about the sixth century CE.

Judging judges. Ruth is set in the time when the "judges ruled" (i.e., judged) (1:1). A place that has a judicious judiciary fares well. Likewise, if the judiciary is corrupt, trouble ensures. "Woe to the generation which judges its judges" (*Midrash Ruth Rabbah* 1.1).

Naomi instructed Ruth in Judaism. The words "So the two of them *went on*" (1:19) in Hebrew is *taylakhnah*. The root of the word for "go" (went) is the same as the root of the word *Halakhah**, normative Jewish law. Thus, "So the two of *them went on*" is interpreted to mean that Naomi instructed Ruth in normative Jewish law (*taylakhnah*/*halakhah*) (*Midrash Ruth Rabbah* 2.12 end).

Boaz studied Torah. The text explains that, following his meal at the threshing floor, Boaz was "in a contented mood" (3:7). The Hebrew literally means "his heart was good." Why was his heart good? He recited the blessings after meals. He also studied Torah (*Midrash Ruth Rabbah* 5.15).

Spousal preferences. Boaz was considerably older than Ruth. One sage suggests that generally a person prefers a poor young spouse to a wealthy old one (*Midrash Ruth Rabbah* 6.2).

Six pious descendants. Boaz gave Ruth six measures of barley (3:15, 17). This corresponds to the six righteous descendants of Ruth and Boaz, each of whom had six outstanding virtues. The six are David, Hezekiah, Josiah, Hananiah-Mishael-Azariah, Daniel, and the Messiah. The midrash then lists six virtues for each person (*Midrash Ruth Rabbah* 7.2).

God's involvement. How was it that the next-of-kin who was the closer relative to Naomi/Ruth just *happened to be walking by* the city gate when Boaz was seeking to encounter him? Boaz played his part in this drama. Ruth and Naomi did as well. God then said, "I too must play mine!" God *arranged* for the man to be walking by. Had the next-of-kin been at the far ends of the earth, God would have caused him to fly and bring him there (*Midrash Ruth Rabbah* 7.7).

David honors his great-grandmother, Ruth. Based on a line in Psalms, there is a tradition that King David rose in the middle of the night to praise God ("At midnight I rise to praise you," Ps 119:62). "David said: It is my duty to arise at midnight and to praise you for the wonders that you have done with my ancestor (Ruth) at midnight, as it is stated [in Ruth 3:8–9]: NOW IT CAME TO PASS AT MIDNIGHT THAT THE MAN WAS STARTLED. SO HE TURNED ASIDE, <AND HERE WAS A WOMAN LYING AT HIS FEET>. THEN HE SAID: WHO ARE YOU? AND SHE SAID: I AM YOUR HANDMAID RUTH" (*Midrash Tanhuma, Numbers and Deuteronomy, Beha'alotekha* 3.19, Num 10:1ff., part 6[13]).

Text Study

Ruth 3:8ff. Spreading One's Cloak

At Naomi's direction, Ruth goes to the threshing floor. Unbeknown to Boaz, Ruth watches as he winnows some barley. Then, having eaten a meal, he lies down to sleep. She quietly enters the building. She uncovers his feet, and lies down. When he awakens, he is surprised to see someone. In the darkness, he does not recognize her. When asked who is there, Ruth identifies herself. She says to Boaz, "I am Ruth, your servant; spread your cloak over your servant, for you are next-of-kin" (3:9).

"To *spread* one's *cloak over* a woman means to take her for one's wife. There is a slight overtone of sexual intimacy in the passage, since *feet* (vv. 4, 8) in Hebrew can be a euphemism for 'genitals.' That the relationship between Ruth and Boaz is honorable according to the standards of their

---
13. See this title in the bibliography.

time, however, is shown by subsequent events."[14] Kirsten Nielsen, however, provocatively suggests that Ruth uncovered her own genitals.[15]

The issue of "next-of-kin" refers to Levirate marriage.

Ruth 4:1–10; Levirate Marriage

Levirate marriage (the term is based on the Latin word *levir*, meaning "brother-in-law") is a concept that seeks to protect and promote property lines within a family. The biblical source is Deuteronomy 25:5–6, with supplemental information provided in verses 7–10.

When a woman was widowed without offspring, the man's brother (or near next-of-kin) was obligated to marry the woman in order to impregnate her. The resulting children were then counted as part of the descendants of the original husband.

If the woman did not marry her brother-in-law, then according to biblical law, when she married a *stranger*, she would take the family inheritance with her to this new relationship.

Not every next-of-kin wanted, or was able, to take on the obligations and responsibilities of a new wife. When the next-of-kin chose not to marry the widow, he could perform the ceremony known as *halitza*. Through *halitza* the widow was released from the Levirate tie. She could marry someone else (see Deut 25:7–10). Part of this ceremony involved the public removal of the sandal belonging to the next-of-kin.

What is described in Ruth 4:7ff. does not comport in all phases to the description in Deuteronomy. Indeed, current scholarship now challenges the notion that "Ruth's marriage to Boaz represents a levirate marriage."[16]

In any case, the ceremony in Ruth clearly is based on older traditions.

---

14. *NOAB*, 335.

15. Nielsen, *Ruth*, 69–70. There are many "sexual overtones that permeate [this third] . . . chapter (repetitive use of the verbs 'to lie down, ' 'to enter,' 'to know') . . . [which] underscore Ruth's sexual vulnerability." Further, there is a sense of "secrecy, ambiguity, and danger. Identities are kept hidden; the narrative speaks only of 'the man' and 'the woman' . . . the night becomes a moment of uncovering on multiple levels." Despite these facts, Lee leaves the impression that sexual intercourse did not take place. Lee, "Ruth," 147.

16. Eskenazi and Frymer-Kensky, *Ruth*, xxxv; see discussion of this point in xxxv–xxxviii. See Bronner, "Regime of Modesty," 78.

7

Lamentations

Introduction

LAMENTATIONS CONTAINS FIVE SHORT chapters. They are mournful songs, dirges, or poems expressing great sadness. Women speak some lines; men speak others. There are both dialogues and monologues. A "lament conveys the full range of the language of suffering."[1] The English term "lamentations" is the translation of the Greek word meaning "dirges." A dirge is a slow, sad song or poem, or perhaps a music composition expressing mourning or grief. This describes the content of Lamentations. The Hebrew word for the noun "lament" or "lamentation" is *qinah*. Curiously, it does not appear even once in the whole book of Lamentations.[2]

The name that the Hebrew Bible uses for the title of this book is *Eikha* (literally "how"), which is the first word in the first verse. "How lonely sits the city that once was full of people! How like a widow she has become, she that was great among the nations! She that was a princess among the provinces has become a vassal" (1:1). The "city that once was full of people" is Jerusalem, and the speakers are lamenting its destruction by the Babylonians. Only the first and second chapters refer specifically to Jerusalem by name (1:7, 8, 17; 2:10).

---

1. Westermann, *Lamentations*, 92.
2. The Hebrew word *qinah*, "lament" or "lamentation," appears in this form only a dozen times in the whole Bible. Ezekiel uses it eight times, Amos once, and Jeremiah three times. Amos and Ezekiel briefly use slight variations of *qinah*, and it also appears once in Samuel (2 Sam 1:17) and once in Chronicles (2 Chr 35:25).

Several of the chapters (1, 2, 4, 5) are in the form of a communal lament or funeral dirge. Chapter 3 consists of the words of an individual speaking of the grief borne at this difficult time. Although there is no direct relationship between the chapters, nor is there "any progression of thought . . . it is striking how many of the same themes appear in all five chapters. All deal with the misery of the siege and the sorrow of the survivors."[3]

Lamentations is the sixth book in the third section of the Hebrew Bible, the Writings/*Ketuvim* (see Introduction: "The Order of the Books of the Bible"). It follows Ruth and precedes Ecclesiastes. In the Christian Bible the book of Lamentations follows directly upon the prophecy of Jeremiah, prior to the book of Ezekiel. Some Bibles list the book's title as "The Lamentations of Jeremiah."

Acrostics

Of Lamentations' five chapters, the first four are alphabetical acrostics in Hebrew. The opening words of successive verses follow the order of the Hebrew alphabet. The final chapter also reflects the Hebrew alphabet in that it has twenty-two lines (the number of letters in the Hebrew alphabet).

Geo-Political Background

Lamentations addresses the near unbearable burden of grief experienced by the survivors of Jerusalem, following the city's destruction by the Babylonian army in 586 BCE.

> The "land had suffered the full horrors of invasion from the Babylonian armies, and was defenseless against the border raids from Edomite tribes. Their capital city, Jerusalem had been captured, looted and destroyed; the king and the royal household, the nobles and the priests, everyone in fact who was capable of exercising influence . . . had been taken into exile or had fled for safety to Egypt . . . for those left in Judah as for those taken into exile there was no political future." It is nearly impossible to gauge the emotional devastation, depression, and utter dejection the survivors feel. The Jerusalem Temple's destruction means the "total collapse of their religious faith and hope. For the city was the place that Yahweh had chosen (Dt. 12:5, etc.). Moreover since the great reformation of King Josiah, Jerusalem and the Temple were the unique centres of the religion of

---

3. Childs, *Introduction to the Old Testament*, 594.

Yahweh's people (2 Kg. 23), where alone the sacred rites might be performed. The conclusion was inescapable; either Yahweh had been defeated by the deities of the invading armies, or he had abandoned his ancient people."[4]

The survivors react differently. Some people, without doubt, turn to the deities of the invading armies. Some seek solace or guidance from the ancient deities of the land. Others see in this catastrophe the realization of the prophecy of leaders such as Jeremiah.

God specifically told Jeremiah to "raise a lamentation on the bare heights, for the LORD has rejected and forsaken the generation that provoked his wrath" (Jer 7:29). This allows for different answers and different approaches. Divine judgment leads to self-evaluation, confession, and self-criticism. The tragedy of the temple's demolition, the destruction of Jerusalem, and the subsequent suffering, are all proof that God is reproving Israel for her faithlessness.

This does not happen immediately. Lamentations reflects more the painful description of life facing the survivors. Yet, there are indications in these chapters that some people begin to see purposeful divine judgment and the possibility of hope even within the midst of their pain.

The Book of Lamentations

The Theology of Lamentations

In the Bible, a common explanation for suffering is divine retribution. That element appears in Lamentations. God makes Zion "suffer for the multitude of her transgressions" (1:5). In Leviticus 26 and Deuteronomy 28, Israel is told what will happen if she turns from God's commands. Jeremiah is clear that if Judah persists in her immoral ways, she will be punished.

Lamentations proclaims that God is the one who brings devastation to the land. "The Lord has become like an enemy; he has destroyed Israel . . . he has destroyed his tabernacle; the LORD has abolished in Zion festival and sabbath" (2:5, 6). This was expected. God warned what would happen. "The LORD has done what he purposed, he has carried out his threat; as he ordained long ago, he has demolished without pity" (2:17).

Flowing out of this theology is the idea that Israel did wrong. It needs to admit these transgressions. This is expressed directly. "Woe to us, for we have sinned!" (5:16; cf. 3:42). Introspection is required. This too appears in the book. "Let us test and examine our ways, and return to the LORD" (3:40).

---

4. Herbert, "Lamentations," 563; see also Dobbs-Allsopp, *Lamentations*, 1–3.

Yet, "Lamentations is strikingly uncommunicative concerning the nature of Israel's sins. One searches the book almost in vain for the mention of a specific sin. Idolatry is not mentioned. Nowhere do we hear of the sins for which classical prophecy threatened destruction: social injustice, oppression of the weaker classes, bribery, and so on. Only 4:13 appears to specify a sin: 'It was for the sins of her prophets, the iniquities of her priests, who had shed in her midst the blood of the innocent.'"[5]

The traditional belief that God will take back the people finds expression in Lamentations. Praising God, the author of chapter 3 proclaims, "The steadfast love of the LORD never ceases, his mercies never come to an end . . . The LORD is good to those who wait for him . . . For the Lord will not reject forever. Although he causes grief, he will have compassion" (3:22, 25, 31, 32).

For all that, there also are examples where the author(s) of these laments vent(s) anger at God and challenge(s) divine decisions. The punishment is inappropriately disproportionate. Do women need to resort to cannibalism? Should priest and prophet be killed within God's own sanctuary? (2:20).

The close of the book poses the questions, "Why have you forgotten us completely, Why have you forsaken us these many days?" (5:20). There is no reply.

There are indications in the book that a section of the survivors see some kind of purposeful divine judgment in their plight (3:37–42). Some even express the possibility of hope even within their pain (3:22–24). As it stands, however,

> the book of Lamentations ends with absence. It ends with the absence of God and with the absence of survivors. Zion receives no response to her petitions on behalf of her children, the suffering man of chapter 3 has only the ghosts of salvation oracles past on which to rely, and the communal voice of chapter 4, waiting 'in vain for deliverance,' ends in chapter 5 as a community that is forgotten and forsaken, rejected and raged against . . .
>
> The poetry of Lamentations, for all its bleak recognition of rampant destruction, nevertheless maintains a drive—even a demand—for survival . . . Second Isaiah (chapters 40–55 in the biblical book of Isaiah) strives to match this drive for survival so prominent in Lamentations.[6]

---

5. Tigay, "Lamentations," 1369.
6. Linafelt, *Surviving Lamentations*, 62, 63.

Divisions in the Book of Lamentations

Chapter 1

The opening lines portray Jerusalem as a maiden. "From daughter Zion has departed all her majesty" (v. 6). She is like a widow. She weeps bitterly. Tears are on her cheeks. The poem divides nearly perfectly into two sections. Verses 1–11a serve as statements about Zion. She is described in the third person. "She weeps bitterly in the night... her downfall was appalling, with none to comfort her" (vv. 2, 9). The specific identification with Jerusalem appears in verses 7 and 8.

Verses 11b–22 gives voice to Jerusalem herself. She opens her discourse with the words of an appeal to God. "Look, O LORD, and see how worthless I have become. Is it nothing to you, all you who pass by? Look and see if there is any sorrow like my sorrow... For these things I weep; my eyes flow with tears" (vv. 11–12, 16). Verse 17 briefly departs from the first person narrative and speaks about Jerusalem, but then verses 18–22 return to Jerusalem's voice.

Chapter 2

This chapter continues in a similar pattern. The first ten verses speak in the third person. They describe what is happening to Jerusalem. The term "daughter Zion" appears several times. The first verse establishes God's humiliation of the city. Verses 2–5 mention physical and political aspects. These are the dwellings of Jacob: flaming fire and destroyed palaces and strongholds. The kingdom and its rulers are dishonored. Verses 6–7 turn to the temple and its ritual. God "has broken down his booth... [and] destroyed his tabernacle." Neither festival nor Sabbath is celebrated. God "has scorned his altar [and] disowned his sanctuary." Verses 8–10 address physical objects: ramparts, walls, gates, and bars. There is no viable leadership. The king and princes are exiled. The prophets do not receive visions. The elders are silent.

Beginning with verse 11 and continuing to the end of the chapter, the text is in the first person. He or she addresses Jerusalem and commiserates with her losses. "What can I say for you... O daughter Jerusalem... For vast as the sea is your ruin; who can heal you?" (v. 13). False prophets are blamed for their deceptive visions and for not criticizing iniquity. Jerusalem is personified. She is asked to cry out to God. The final verses are a plea to God, bewailing the fate of the city. "Look, O LORD, and consider! To whom have you done this? Should women eat their offspring, the children they have borne? . . . The young and the old are lying on the ground in the streets; my young women and my young men have fallen by the sword; in the day of your anger you have killed them, slaughtering without mercy. You invited my enemies from all around . . . on the day of the anger of the LORD no one escaped or survived; those whom I bore and reared my enemy has destroyed" (vv. 20–22).

Chapter 3

The third chapter is the longest in the book. It is the "ideological core." The author "reflects on the meaning of suffering. The opening description of his suffering (3:1–18) concludes with his observation: 'I thought my strength and hope had perished before the Lord' (3:18). However, he takes hope in the realization that God's kindness and mercy have not ended . . . but are renewed every morning (3:21–23). Furthermore, God is good to those who trust Him and seek Him; it is good to accept one's suffering and wait in silence for God's deliverance."[7]

Personal distress and pain fill the first eighteen verses. The writer unambiguously claims that God is the source of the pain experienced. The suffering is deeply felt. "I am one who has seen affliction . . . against me alone he turns his hand . . . he has made my flesh and my skin waste away . . . He has walled me about so that I cannot escape . . . He shot into my vitals the arrows of his quiver . . . my soul is bereft of peace; I have forgotten what happiness is" (vv. 1, 3, 4, 7, 13, 17).

Nonetheless, for all this pain and suffering, still the writer has hope. "The steadfast love of the LORD never ceases . . . The LORD is good to those who wait for him . . . the Lord will not reject forever" (vv. 22, 25, 31).

Chapter 3 declares that God has brought these calamities. They are chastisements for wrongdoing. "Is it not from the mouth of the Most High that good and bad come? Why should any who draw breath complain about the punishment of their sins?" (vv. 38–39). These disasters and misfortunes are proper punishments. The speaker claims wrongdoing. "Let us test and examine our ways, and return to the LORD . . . We have transgressed and rebelled" (vv. 40, 42).

The closing verses turn inward. They describe the painful and pitiful conditions faced in Jerusalem. The writer explains that he has called upon God. God answered, "Do not fear!" (v. 57). He is confident that God has heard. Eventually God will bring vengeance on those who have brought

---

7. Tigay, "Lamentations," 1372.

such misery. The final three verses are an invitation to pay back in kind the devastation wrought by Israel's enemies. "Pay them back for their deeds... Give them anguish of heart... Pursue them in anger and destroy them" the writer asks of God (vv. 64–66; cf. 4:21–22).

While the first four chapters are written as an alphabetic acrostic, chapter 3 is a triple acrostic. Each consecutive letter of the alphabet starts three verses in a row.

Chapter 4

The first half of this chapter contains some of the most painful descriptions of the devastation faced by the inhabitants of Jerusalem.

A number of disconnected themes run through the latter half of this chapter (see the Text Study section at the conclusion of this chapter, "The Plaint of the Survivors"). These themes include laying blame on the iniquities of prophets and priests, the cruelty of the unnamed enemies who pursued Jerusalem's citizens after the city's fall, and finally a promise of vengeance that shall befall Edom for its attacks on the hopeless and helpless refugees.

Chapter 5

This final chapter returns to a communal lament. Although not mentioned by name, the first verse is a plea to God to remember Jerusalem. The next seventeen verses describe the terrible conditions faced by the survivors. The final verses turn and offer a plea to God.

This chapter might be written months, or perhaps even some years, after the fall of the city. There is a sense that some time has passed since Jerusalem's destruction. There are contradictory statements. On one hand, the past generation is blamed for these terrible circumstances. "Our ancestors sinned; they are no more, and we bear their iniquities." Yet, there is an admission of sin. "The crown has fallen from our head; woe to us, for we have sinned!" (vv. 7, 16).

The closing verses are a plea for mercy. They ask God to restore Israel to its earlier glory. Technically, the final verses end with the words "... renew our days as of old—unless you have utterly rejected us, and are angry with us beyond measure" (vv. 21–22). In Jewish translations of the Bible, however, there is a tradition of ending books on a more positive note. Consequently, verse 21 is repeated after verse 22, thereby ending with the words, "Take us back, O LORD, to Yourself, and let us come back; renew our days as of old!" (NJPS/*TANAKH*).

Who Wrote Lamentations?

There is a tradition that Jeremiah is the author of Lamentations. Jeremiah prophesied in the years leading up to the destruction of the temple in Jerusalem in 586 BCE, and for some years after. He saw firsthand the devastation that the Babylonian army brings. He had warned that this would take place.

As noted earlier, the Hebrew word for the noun "lament" or "lamentation," *qinah*, does not appear in the book of Lamentations. Jeremiah specifically does use the word lament/lamentation/*qinah* in chapters 7 and 9 of the book that bears his name. For example, "Cut off your hair and throw it away; raise a *lamentation* [*qinah*] on the bare heights, for the LORD has rejected and forsaken the generation that provoked his wrath" (Jer 7:29). In chapter 9 Jeremiah says, "Take up weeping and wailing for the mountains, and a *lamentation* [*qinah*] for the pastures of the wilderness, because they are laid waste so that no one passes through" (Jer 9:10 [9:9 H]). Likewise, "Hear, O women, the word of the LORD, and let your ears receive the word of his mouth; teach to your daughters a dirge, and each to her neighbor a *lament* [*qinah*]" (Jer 9:20 [9:19 H]).

The book of Chronicles explains that Jeremiah writes a lament [*qinah*] for King Josiah. That had happened twenty years before the destruction of the temple, for Josiah died in 609 BCE (2 Chr 35:25).

There are many reasons to think that Jeremiah did not write the book of Lamentations. Jeremiah's concerns are not reflected in Lamentations. He speaks of social justice and moral change. He urges the people to have greater and deeper faith. Trust in God! That is the way to achieve salvation. "Thus says the LORD: Do not let the wise boast in their wisdom, do not let the mighty boast in their might, do not let the wealthy boast in their wealth; but let those who boast boast in this, that they understand and know me" (Jer 9:23–24 [9:22–23 H]).

Jeremiah holds out hope for a new covenant between Israel and God. "I will make a new covenant with the house of Israel . . . I will put my law within them, and I will write it on their hearts" (Jer 31:31, 33).

Jeremiah explains that, more than the cult, God wants the people's trust and obedience. Jeremiah predicts defeat, but, after defeat, a future of hope.

None of these ideas or concepts are found in Lamentations.

The book of Lamentations features alphabetical acrostics in four of its five chapters. The final chapter has twenty-two verses, the same number as the Hebrew alphabet. There are no alphabetic acrostics in all fifty-two chapters of Jeremiah. Chapter 5 of Lamentations is written from the viewpoint of people who continue to live in Jerusalem, years after the temple's destruction. Jeremiah leaves Jerusalem a few weeks after that sad event (Jer 43–44).

"Although there is no evidence outside the book itself that permits us to date its composition, . . . a date after 586 and well before 538, when Cyrus permitted the Jews to return from exile, is most likely."[8]

Women in Lamentations

Nancy C. Lee points out that the woman's voice in Lamentations "goes beyond women's traditional mourning of dirge-singing to lead a dialogical debate about God's justice in the context of" the destruction of the community. This "is a striking challenge to the tradition's then-current theologies and acceptable gender roles."[9]

"Women figure prominently in the book's description of war's atrocities and serve as symbols of the pain of the people." That said, the images of women are a mixture of praise and condemnation, but mostly condemnation. Therefore, in spite of "the evocative beauty of Lamentations, there are reasons for women to be cautious when they approach it."[10]

In its opening lines, Lamentations describes Jerusalem "like a widow." She had been a "princess among the provinces." She was "great among the nations." Now she sits lonely, a vassal state (1:1). Spurned by her former allies, who have turned on her, lonely Jerusalem grieves her position. "She weeps bitterly in the night, with tears on her cheeks . . . she has no one to comfort her; all her friends have dealt treacherously with her, they have become her enemies" (1:2).

Recurrent phrases in the book refer to "daughter Zion" (1:6; 2:1, 4; 4:22 etc.) A variant term is "daughter Jerusalem" (2:13, 15). In this role she appears both as a victim of the horrors of war, and as an eloquent spokesperson for the people. She "expresses her sorrow with language of intense feeling (1:16, 20; 2:11). Ultimately she discards the role of victim (Lam. 1) to become God's adversary, challenging divine mistreatment of herself and her people (2:20–22)."[11]

---

8. Hillers, "Book of Lamentations," 4:138; see also Longman, *Jeremiah, Lamentations*, 327–30. The "authorship of the book . . . [ascribed] to Jeremiah [is] due to an erroneous interpretation of 2 Chronicles 35:25 . . . the laments described in Chronicles were for the death of Josiah [in 609 BCE], not for the destruction of Jerusalem [in 586 BCE]." Flesher, "Lamentations," 392.

9. Lee, *Lyrics of Lament*, 160.

10. O'Connor, "Lamentations," 278, 279. I am grateful to my friend and colleague Rabbi Dr. Bonita E. Taylor for reading this section on "Women in Lamentations" and making valuable comments.

11. O'Connor, "Lamentations," 280.

The image of Jerusalem as a woman is double-edged. On the positive side, it honors women in a very prominent role. Elsewhere Jerusalem is termed God's faithful city (Zech 8:3ff.). Jerusalem is praised as God's earthly footstool. This proximity to God is offered as high praise. It conveys great honor (1 Chr 28:2; cf. Lam 2:1). God rejoices in Jerusalem (Isa 65:18ff.)

Women are portrayed as speaking forthrightly and challenging God's justice. Daughter Zion, or as O'Connor describes her, Daughter of Zion, "is God's beloved daughter." She "articulates her own pain and ultimately demands that God redress what seems to be divine injustice . . .

"In chap. 2 she abandons self-recrimination altogether and shouts in outrage at God for killing the young women and men of the city, for 'slaughtering them without mercy' (2:21) . . .

"The daughter of Zion's voice evokes the pain of women who have lost their children, who know sexual abuse, who are victims of war and famine."[12]

Yet, on the negative side, Jerusalem becomes a symbol for the government and people of Judah, and their rebellion against God. She is a wanton woman with "lovers" who have now abandoned her. God "has made her suffer for the multitude of her transgressions" (1:2, 5).

In very graphic language, chapter 1 describes Jerusalem as a menstruating woman. Her "uncleanness was in her skirts" (1:9). The word used here for uncleanness

> refers to ritual impurity, which could have several origins. Among the possibilities specific to women are uncleanness from menstruation (Lev. 15:19–30) or from adultery (Num. 5:19). Daughter of Zion's uncleanness comes from adultery . . . Menstrual uncleanness, nonetheless, is an aspect of daughter of Zion's shame in chap. 1. Among her enemies she has become a "filthy thing" (*niddah,* 1:17). The Hebrew word used here has the general meaning of "impurity" but often refers specifically to menstruation. In 1:8 a similar word, translated "mockery" (*nidah*), may create a pun on *niddah* . . .
>
> The daughter of Zion's shame involves her body in still another way. "All who honored her despise her, for they have seen her nakedness" (1:8). In ancient Israel the exposure of the body caused profound disgrace, and stripping may have been part of the punishment of prostitutes or newly taken slaves . . . the occasion for the daughter of Zion's nakedness is not specified, but her degradation and bodily humiliation are clear.[13]

12. Ibid., 282.
13. Ibid., 280. O'Connor goes on to suggest that Lam 1:12–27 portrays Jerusalem

The horrors of war are well depicted in Lamentations. Young men and elders are exiled, abused, or killed. This likewise is the fate of women young and old. The book explains, "my young women and my young men have fallen by the sword." Further, "my young women and young men have gone into captivity" (2:21; 1:18). "Women are raped in Zion, virgins in the towns of Judah" (5:11).

Most horrible is the famine that overtakes Jerusalem. "'Infants and babes faint in the streets of the city' (2:11). Mothers listen to their babies cry for food and watch them die on their breasts (2:12). 'Children beg for food, but no one gives them anything' (4:3–4) . . .

"Hunger leads to horror" when Lamentations reports that these devastating conditions have led to cannibalism. The "'hands of compassionate women have boiled their own children; they became their food' (4:10). To describe the terrible consequences of divine punishment, daughter of Zion hurls an accusation at God, 'Should women eat their offspring, the children they have borne?' (2:20) . . .

"If women did participate in cannibalism, it was probably not to feed themselves but feed other starving children."[14]

Taken as a whole, however, the dominant images of women in Lamentations are as victims of war, or as being punished for their immoral and reckless behavior.

Lamentations in the Christian Scriptures

There are no direct quotes from Lamentations in the Christian Scriptures. There are, however, some phrases or allusions that suggest the writers sought to connect with this biblical book. When Jesus is on the cross, some people come by and deride him, or shake their heads in derision. This action is similar to the lines in Lamentations. "All who pass along the way . . . hiss and wag their heads at daughter Jerusalem" (Lam 2:15, cf. Matt 27:39; Mark 15:29).

The words in chapter 3, "You have made us filth and rubbish among the peoples," find a similar reflection in the Epistle to the Corinthians, "We have become like the rubbish of the world, the dregs of all things, to this very day" (Lam 3:45; 1 Cor 4:13).

In John's Gospel Jesus says, "I am the light of the world. Whoever follows me will never walk in darkness but will have the light of life" (John 8:12). This

---

as an abused woman, and "Most disturbing of all, chapter 1 indirectly justifies abuse of women by portraying God as the abuser" (281).

14. Ibid., 281–82.

contrasts with the opening lines of chapter 3, where the writer proclaims, "he has driven and brought me into darkness without any light" (Lam 3:2).

Lamentations in Rabbinic Literature

The collection *Midrash Rabbah* (the Great Midrash) devotes a whole book to Lamentations. It was redacted at about the end of the fifth century CE.[15] *Midrash Lamentations Rabbah* discourses on the destruction of the temple in Jerusalem, the sufferings of the survivors, as well as the pain of exile. There are references to the Bar Kokhba (Bar Koziba) revolt against the Romans in 135 CE. In *Midrash Rabbah* the predominance of quotations featuring the book of Lamentations appear in the collection *Midrash Lamentations Rabbah*. Many other midrash collections, however, also quote from Lamentations.

Lamentations is one of the five "scrolls." During the Jewish liturgical year, on five holy days, in addition to the reading from the Torah and the Prophets (*Haftarah*), one of the five scrolls are read. Lamentations is read in midsummer on *Tisha b'Av*, the ninth (day of the Hebrew month) of Av. *Tisha b'Av* commemorates the destruction of the temple by the Babylonians in 586 BCE, but also the second temple's destruction by the Romans in 70 CE.

The other four scrolls are Song of Songs (read at *Pesach*/Passover in the early spring), Ruth (read at *Shavuot*/Weeks/Pentecost in the late spring), Ecclesiastes (read at *Succot*/Booths/Tabernacles in the early autumn), and Esther (read at *Purim* generally in late winter).

Narratives of suffering. Using the categories of martyrdom, privation, needless slaughter, and cannibalism, there are multiple entries for the line, "For these things I weep" (1:16) (*Midrash Lamentations Rabbah* 1.16.45).

A mother and her seven sons martyred. This martyrdom of Miriam, daughter of Tanhum, and her sons (in *Midrash Lamentations Rabbah*) is based on the accounts found in the Apocrypha's 2 Maccabees (where she is named Hannah) and the Pseudepigrapha's 4 Maccabees. The connecting line to Lamentations is "For these things I weep" (Lam 1:16) (*Midrash Lamentations Rabbah* 1.16.50).

An argument in favor of resurrection. "The steadfast love of the LORD never ceases . . . they are new every morning; great is your faithfulness" (3:22–23) is the prooftext for a belief in physical resurrection. "Rabbi Alexandri says,

---

15. Herr, "Lamentations Rabbah," 1378.

Because you renew us [in life] every morning, we know that great is your faithfulness for the resurrection of the dead" (*Midrash Lamentations Rabbah* 3.23.8).

Throwing stones away. Ecclesiastes' observation that there is a time to "throw away stones" (Eccl 3:5) finds support in the line, "The sacred stones lie scattered at the head of every street" (Lam 4:1) (*Midrash Ecclesiastes Rabbah* 3.8.2).

New insights in the Torah. When people take the time to study, they will learn new insights in the Torah. "They are new every morning; great is your faithfulness" (Lam 3:23) (*Tanna Debe Eliyyahu, Eliyyahu Rabbah,* ch. 18, p. 94 [210][16]).

Double comfort. Why in Isaiah 40:1 does it repeat the word comfort ("Comfort, O comfort my people")? This is to counterbalance the words in Lamentations where weeping is doubled, "She weeps bitterly [lit. "weeping, she weeps]" (Lam 1:2) (*Pesikta Rabbati, Piska* 30.3[17]).

Although Lamentations speaks in pain, Isaiah promises healing. A series of quotations from Lamentations contrast with a series of quotations from Isaiah that foretell a wondrous future. For example, "From daughter Zion has departed all her majesty" (Lam 1:6) is contrasted with "Who is this that comes . . . so splendidly robed?" (Isa 63:1). Likewise, "Jerusalem sinned grievously" (Lam 1:8) is contrasted with "I have swept away your transgressions like a cloud, and your sins like mist" (Isa 44:22) (*Pesikta Rabbati, Piska* 29/30 B.4).

Remembering the destruction of the temple. It is incumbent upon us to remember the destruction of the temple. "My soul continually thinks of it and is bowed down within me" (3:20) (*Pesikta Rabbati, Piska* 29.1).

Text Study: Lamentations 4; The Plaint of the Survivors

Verses 3–4. Animals feed their young, but conditions are so ghastly, so horrific, and privation is so rampant, that children beg for food, and infants perish in terrible thirst.

---

16. See this title in the bibliography.
17. See this title in the bibliography.

Verses 7-9. Before Jerusalem's capture and destruction, people live in luxury. They are healthy and vibrant. Now they are gaunt, filthy, and their bones protrude for lack of nourishment.

Verse 10. Mothers resort to cannibalism to provide for their surviving children (see 2 Kgs 25:3).

Verses 11-12. God gave full vent to divine anger, and the nations all about were amazed.

Verse 13. The sins of priests and prophets who shed the blood of the righteous are named as the cause for Jerusalem's destruction. No further details are offered.

Verses 14-16. Survivors are defiled with blood. They become fugitives and wanderers. God shows no regard for them. Neither priests nor elders are honored.

Verses 18-20. Those who escaped, the fugitives who sought refuge, were pursued by the enemy. It is likely that this refers to the neighboring Edomites, not to the Babylonian armies. The Edomites took advantage of Judah's destruction. The next verses call for revenge.

Verses 21-22. As the citizens of Jerusalem are termed Zion's daughter, so here Edom's daughter becomes a phrase for that country. As they wrought destruction, so in time will they be destroyed. They shall drink from the cup of suffering and pain. They will be stripped of their power (see Obad 8-14).

8

Ecclesiastes

Introduction

LIKE PROVERBS, ECCLESIASTES PRESENTS practical advice. Like the book of Job it offers reflections on the problems of life and religion. Ecclesiastes stands apart from many of the books of the Bible because its concerns are neither Israel's history nor its covenantal relationship with God.

Ecclesiastes is unique in that, with the exception of the epilogue, it is all written in the first person.

Ecclesiastes sometimes is referred to by its Hebrew name, *Qoheleth* (*Koheleth*).

Ecclesiastes, along with Proverbs and Job, is part of what is commonly termed "wisdom literature." As mentioned earlier in this volume in the chapter on Proverbs, this wisdom literature constitutes material that is very different from other parts of the Bible.[1] Wisdom literature provides advice on how someone might achieve a successful life. It also offers thoughts as to the problems of life, and what is the meaning of existence.

Ecclesiastes is the seventh book in the third section of the Hebrew Bible, the Writings/*Ketuvim* (see Introduction: "The Order of the Books of the Bible"). It follows Lamentations and precedes Esther. In the Christian Bible Ecclesiastes follows Proverbs and precedes Song of Songs.

---

1. In the Apocrypha (Deuterocanonicals), Sirach (Ecclesiasticus) and the Wisdom of Solomon are counted as wisdom literature. Certain psalms, or parts of psalms, are also designated as part of wisdom literature, though there is no general consensus which psalms would be included. See the chapter on Psalms in this volume. Fox (*Ecclesiastes*, xi) suggests Psalms 1, 19 (vv. 8–15), 34, 37, 111–12, and 119.

The Title; Contents

The opening verses speak of the "Teacher" or the "Preacher."

"The words of the Teacher . . . Vanity of vanities, says the Teacher, vanity of vanities! All is vanity" (1:1–2). Compare NJPS/*TANAKH*: "The words of Koheleth [Qoheleth] . . . Utter futility!—said Koheleth—Utter futility! All is futile!"

As noted, the Hebrew name of this book is *Qoheleth* (*Koheleth*). The root of this word, *q-h-l* (*quf-hey-lamed*), "has to do with an assembly or congregation (an 'ecclesia,' hence the Greek and Latin form, Ecclesiastes). The name, then, would seem to mean 'leader of an assembly.' The term 'Preacher' goes back through Luther (*Prediger*) to Jerome (*concionator*), but the author is not a preacher, nor is this a series of sermons."[2]

The book often is described as pessimistic in its nature. Certainly, the author suggests that life is predetermined; God controls it. "God . . . has appointed a time for every matter, and for every work" (3:17). Nothing changes, no matter what humans do. "What has been is what will be, and what has been done is what will be done; there is nothing new under the sun" (1:9). Not only is there nothing new, but this is compounded by the fact that we do not remember what has been, nor will those who follow us remember our deeds. Even if people seek knowledge, it is futile, a folly, a "chasing after wind. For in much wisdom is much vexation, and those who increase knowledge increase sorrow" (1:17–18, cf. 2:12–15).

Whether one is wise or foolish, death is our common lot. Even though people can have some sense of the past and the future, still they cannot know what God wants. People simply cannot and "do not know the work of God, who makes everything" (11:5; cf. 3:11; 8:17).

God has set "a time for every matter under heaven." Whatever God has done "endures forever; nothing can be added to it, nor anything taken from it; God has done this, so that all should stand in awe before him" (3:1, 14).

Ecclesiastes explains, "the fate of humans and the fate of animals is the same; as one dies, so dies the other . . . humans have no advantage over the animals." Since death is our common destiny, and no one "knows whether the human spirit goes upward and the spirit of animals goes downward to the earth," the best we can do is to get on with life and enjoy what we do (3:19, 21).

In many ways the advice offered in Ecclesiastes is repetitive. In addition, the author can be inconsistent; he sometimes contradicts his own advice.[3]

---

2. *NOAB*, 841.
3. Gordis, *Koheleth*, 69.

At its close, the book advises people to be God-fearing and obedient to the divine will. Ecclesiastes enjoins people to hold God in awe, and to "keep his commands, this submissive, subservient obedience to God without expectation of reward being the 'whole of man' (*Eccl.* 12.13), the entire purpose of his existence."[4]

In terms of the structure of Ecclesiastes, "[l]eaving aside the superscription in 1:1, there remain a thematic refrain (1:2) and a poem (1:3–11) at the beginning, and a poem (11:7—12:7) plus a thematic refrain (12:8) at the end. Together with the superscription, the two epilogues (12:9–11, 12–14) enclose the book in a kind of envelope. The first poem demonstrates the aptness of the thematic statement in the realm of nature, and the final poem shows the accuracy of the theme on the human scene. Nature's ceaseless repetition illustrates the utter futility of things, as does the eventual disintegration of the human body."[5]

Authorship

At various points in Ecclesiastes, the author claims to be both the son of King David and a ruler in his own right (1:1, 12). Although the name of Solomon (David's son and successor) does not appear in the book, traditionally he is credited with writing Ecclesiastes (*Midrash Song of Songs Rabbah* 1.1.10). There also is a tradition that Hezekiah copied out or perhaps transcribed Ecclesiastes. This statement in *Babylonian Talmud Baba Batra* 15a is based on a line in Proverbs that "These are the *other* proverbs of Solomon that the officials of King Hezekiah of Judah copied" (Prov 25:1).

The books of Kings and Chronicles describe King Solomon as wise and wealthy (1 Kgs 3:12; 4:22ff., 29ff.; 1 Chr 29:3; 2 Chr 1:12, etc.).

Despite the claim for Solomonic authorship, there are many arguments that challenge the concept of Solomon writing this book. If the author intended to ascribe Ecclesiastes to Solomon, why did he not do so directly? Why use the obscure term Qoheleth/Teacher? "Far from pretending to be the work of a king, the book reflects the standpoint of a commoner at many points. Such are the lament on the oppression of the weak ([Eccl] 4:1f.), the sardonic comment on corruption in government (5:7 [English, 5:8]), the sense of fear of royal authority (8:2–5; 10:20), the resigned remarks of unworthy leadership (10:5ff.), and the complete absence of any national motif in the book."[6]

---

4. Schwartz, "Ecclesiastes," 213.
5. Crenshaw, "Book of Ecclesiastes," 2:273.
6. Gordis, *Koheleth*, 40–41.

Dating Ecclesiastes

The language of the book also argues against Solomon's authorship. "Ecclesiastes is clearly postexilic [c. 500 BCE or later]. Numerous words and linguistic uses are more characteristic of rabbinic Hebrew than of the classical (pre-exilic*) biblical language . . . There is also evidence for the influence of Greek thought, with which Jews came into contact in the Hellenistic age, in the third or early second centuries B.C.E . . . a third-century B.C.E. dating is the most likely."[7]

The Book of Ecclesiastes

Ecclesiastes is filled with observations about life, and the pointlessness of finding lasting meaning in what one achieves. All is futility; all is vanity. Much of what the author writes is characterized as pessimistic, cynical, unorthodox thought, and written with a sense of grievance.

Divisions in the Book of Ecclesiastes

Unlike the book of Proverbs, the book of Ecclesiastes is not a series of unrelated pithy statements. There is some kind of direction to the book, but there is no consensus as to what is its overarching structure, or whether there is one. One generally accepted view suggests these divisions:

Ecclesiastes 1:1	Superscription
Ecclesiastes 1:2–11	Initial poem
Ecclesiastes 1:12—6:9	An investigation of life
Ecclesiastes 6:10—11:6	The author's conclusions
6:10-12	Introduction
7:1—8:17	Humans cannot find out what is good for them to do
9:1—11:6	Humans do not know what will come after them
Ecclesiastes 11:7—12:8	Concluding poem
Ecclesiastes 12:9-14	Epilogue[8]

---

7. Fox, *Ecclesiastes*, xiv.
8. Ibid., xvi. Lohfink (*Qoheleth*, 8) suggests a chiastic structure to Ecclesiastes.

Ecclesiastes 1:1; Superscription

As noted earlier in this chapter, the opening verse refers to "The words of the Teacher [Preacher], the son of David, king in Jerusalem."

Ecclesiastes 1:2–11; Initial Poem

Verses 2–3. Vanity of vanities, all is vanity, all is futile. All is "utterly senseless"; all is "utterly absurd."[9] The author then asks rhetorically, what do people gain from their work? Nothing really has value, let alone lasting value. The specific phrase "under the sun" is a euphemism for human life. A similar phrase the author uses is "under heaven" (1:13; 2:3; 3:1) (see the Text Study at the conclusion of this chapter, "Familiar Passages").

Verses 4–9 serve as an answer to the question, what do people gain from their work? Generations come and go; the earth remains. The sun rises and sets. Wind blows aimlessly. Streams run into the sea, but the sea is never full. People are never satisfied with what they see or hear. Ultimately, "there is nothing new under the sun" (1:9).

Ecclesiastes 1:12—6:9; An Investigation of Life

The author introduces himself: "I, the Teacher, when king over Israel in Jerusalem applied my mind to seek and to search out by wisdom all that is done under heaven . . . I saw [that] . . . all is vanity and a chasing after wind" (1:12–14). Wisdom brings vexation. Increasing knowledge increases sorrow.

Since pursing wisdom is pointless, the author considers that building projects might bring pleasure. He speaks of constructing houses and planting gardens, acquiring physical possessions as well as silver and gold. "Whatever my eyes desired I did not keep from them; I kept my heart from no pleasure, for my heart found pleasure in all my toil," yet this too, "was vanity and a chasing after wind, and there was nothing to be gained under the sun" (2:10–11).

It is also a vanity—pointless and absurd—to toil, because in the end one must "leave all to be enjoyed by another who did not toil for it" (2:21).

Consequently, eat, drink, and be merry, or as Ecclesiastes states it, "There is nothing better for mortals than to eat and drink, and find

---

9. Fox, *Ecclesiastes*, 3. The use of these words "senseless" and "absurd" are meant "not in the sense of ludicrous but in the sense of counter-rational, a violation of reason." Fox, *Ecclesiastes*, xix.

enjoyment in their toil." Yet, this too, has been ordained by God (2:24). "Whether we experience pleasure depends on God, not human efforts."[10] Far and beyond anything else in Ecclesiastes, it is the first nine verses of chapter 3 that are familiar to people. These particular sentences are analyzed in the Text Study at the close of this chapter, "For Everything There Is a Season." The section begins:

> "For everything there is a season, and a time for every matter under heaven." It then continues with thoughts such as: "a time to be born, and a time to die; a time to kill, and a time to heal; a time to weep, and a time to laugh; a time to mourn, and a time to dance; a time to seek, and a time to lose; a time to love, and a time to hate; a time for war and a time for peace." (3:1–4, 6, 8)

Ecclesiastes then repeats a familiar theme: what gain have the workers from their toil? Chapter 3 ends on a pessimistic, or at least cynical, note; for in place of justice the author finds wickedness, and in place of righteousness, again wickedness. God will judge both the righteous and the wicked, but all will die. "All go to one place; all are from the dust, and all turn to dust again" (3:20).

In chapter 4 Ecclesiastes turns to the importance and the value of companionship. "Two are better than one . . . if they fall, one will lift up the other . . . if two lie together, they keep warm . . . A threefold cord is not quickly broken" (4:9–12).

A number of the observations offered in chapter 5 reflect ideas spoken about earlier in the book of Proverbs. "Never be rash with your mouth, nor let your heart be quick to utter a word before God" (Eccl 5:2 [5:1 H]) has an affinity with the advice, "It is a snare for one to say rashly, 'It is holy,' and begin to reflect only after making a vow" (Prov 20:25). "Let your words be few" (v. 2 [1 H]) reflects the thought, "When words are many, transgression is not lacking, but the prudent are restrained in speech"(Prov 10:19). "Sweet is the sleep of laborers . . . but the surfeit of the rich will not let them sleep" (v. 12 [11 H]) echoes the thought, "Wealth is a ransom for a person's life, but the poor get no threats" (Prov 13:8).

Chapter 6 reflects the author's disquiet and unhappiness with the unfairness of life. Even if someone acquires "wealth, possessions, and honor, so that they lack nothing of all that they desire, yet God does not enable them to enjoy these things"—so that one is better off not having survived childbirth (6:2). Worse yet, someone else enjoys these gifts.

---

10. Ibid., 18.

Ecclesiastes 6:10—11:6; The Author's Conclusions

6:10-12; Introduction

Chapter 6 concludes with a kind of mute acceptance of the way of life. It is not even worthwhile discussing the matter, for "The more words, the more vanity, so how is one the better?" (6:11). This thought will be echoed later in the book. In the epilogue it states, "Of making many books there is no end, and much study is a weariness of the flesh" (12:12). Ecclesiastes' "outlook contrasts with that of Job, who believes that if he could confront God, there might be a change—and if not a change, at least an explanation; [Ecclesiastes] expects neither. Silence in the fear of God (6:10b-11; 5:5; 3:14b) is the only prudent behavior in a world in which humans can do little (6:10a; 3:14-15) and understand less (6:12; 3:11)."[11]

7:1—8:17; Humans Cannot Find Out What Is Good for Them to Do

Chapter 7 begins with a series of judgments on relative values. This matter is better than that matter. "A good name is better than precious ointment . . . It is better to hear the rebuke of the wise than to hear the songs of fools" (7:1, 5). Ecclesiastes then teaches that people should be joyful in the days of their prosperity, and reflective in the days of their adversity, realizing that God has made them all. He notes that there are righteous people who perish in their righteousness, and wicked who prolong their lives with evildoing. At the end of the day, you should fear God (see the Text Study section at the conclusion of this chapter, "To Err Is Human").

Ecclesiastes strikes a misogynist note in chapter 7. He warns against a woman who would set a trap for men, presumably seducing them. He says, "I found more bitter than death the woman who is a trap, whose heart is snares and nets" (7:26). In a similar manner, he shows disdain for women when he describes his search for a good person. Only one person in a thousand is worthy, and it is never a woman (7:28). "Ecclesiastes has no use for the contributions women are allowed to make to society."[12] This contrasts with the praise of the virtuous woman in Proverbs 31.

In chapter 8 Ecclesiastes muses on the exercise of royal privilege. Rulers have power, and they wield it. Consequently, one should be deferential and respectful to requests from the authorities. On the other hand, even

---

11. Ibid., 42.
12. Fontaine, "Ecclesiastes," 154.

royalty and rulers have their limits. "No one has power over the wind . . . or power over the day of death" (8:8) (NJPS/*TANAKH* translates "wind" [*ruah*] as "lifebreath.")

The author then returns to some familiar themes. Enjoy life as you can. "So I commend enjoyment, for there is nothing better for people under the sun than to eat, and drink, and enjoy themselves, for this will go with them in their toil through the days of life that God gives them under the sun" (8:15).

9:1—11:6; Humans Do Not Know What Will Come after Them

Death is the destiny of the righteous and the wicked, the good and the sinners. As long as someone lives, there is hope. "A living dog is better than a dead lion" (9:4). Death ends all. "The dead know nothing; they have no more reward, and even the memory of them is lost" (9:5).

Chance rules our lives. There are no guarantees, nor is there anything that we can do to ensure success. Clearly, "the race is not to the swift, nor the battle to the strong, nor bread to the wise, nor riches to the intelligent, nor favor to the skillful; but time and chance happen to them all" (9:11).

Chapter 10 contains a series of proverb-like sayings or observations. "Even when fools walk on the road, they lack sense, and show to everyone that they are fools." "Words spoken by the wise bring them favor, but the lips of fools consume them" (10:3, 12). These statements show familiarity with similar thoughts expressed in Proverbs (cf. Prov 13:16; 10:21, 32).

At the end of the day, it is impossible to "know the work of God, who makes everything" (11:5).

Ecclesiastes 11:7—12:8; Concluding Poem

These twelve verses divide into two sections. Ecclesiastes contrasts light/youth with darkness/death. The first four verses (11:7-10) focus on light, life, and youthfulness. Light itself is sweet, seeing the sun is good. Rejoice in your youth, and let your heart cheer you.

Rejoice in that special time, for as the next eight verses (12:1-8) explain, it will not be long before the sun and the light, the moon and the stars, will be darkened. Too soon, the doors on the street will be shut, "the silver cord [will be] snapped, and the golden bowl . . . broken . . . [as] the dust returns to the earth as it was, and the breath returns to God who gave it. Vanity of vanities, says the Teacher, all is vanity" (12:6-8).

Ecclesiastes 12:9–14; Epilogue

The closing verses of the book are an addendum; they serve as an epilogue. It speaks of the Teacher in the third person. There is a sense of distance from the previous chapters. The closing words come close to damning Ecclesiastes' advice with faint praise. "The Teacher sought to find pleasing words, and he wrote words of truth plainly." Yet the next verses explain, "The sayings of the wise are like goads" and further, there is a warning to be wary. Additionally, "Of making many books there is no end, and much study is a weariness of the flesh" (12:10–12) is not a ringing endorsement. Is this a different voice than the earlier chapters, or is this the same author, writing, so to say, tongue in cheek?

The book concludes with the sober advice to fear God and obey God's commandments, and a reminder that God brings every deed into judgment.

Ecclesiastes in the Christian Scriptures

In John's Gospel Jesus proclaims to the people, "I am the light of the world. Whoever follows me will never walk in darkness but will have the light of life" (John 8:12; cf. 1 John 2:10–11). This image that heralds the importance of light reflects Ecclesiastes' observation that "wisdom excels folly as light excels darkness. The wise have eyes in their head, but fools walk in darkness" (Eccl 2:13–14).

That humans cannot know God's ways, that they are "unsearchable" and "inscrutable" (Rom 11:33), is a hallmark of Ecclesiastes' teachings (Eccl 8:17; 11:5).

The observation in 1 Timothy that "we brought nothing into the world, so that we can take nothing out of it" (1 Tim 6:7), in addition to resonating with a statement in the book of Job, as noted in that chapter, also paraphrases the words, "As they came from their mother's womb, so they shall go again, naked as they came; they shall take nothing for their toil" (Eccl 5:15 [5:14 H]).

When James gives the prudent advice to "be quick to listen, slow to speak, slow to anger" (Jas 1:19), he offers similar thoughts to Ecclesiastes' suggestion to be "patient in spirit," and the admonition, "Do not be quick to anger" (Eccl 7:8–9).

Sin and sinners are the ways of humans. Paul claims that "both Jews and Greeks, are under the power of sin," and then he explains, paraphrasing Scripture, that "There is no one who is righteous, not even one . . . All have turned aside" (Rom 3:9–12; cf. 1 John 1:8–9). Although his words reflect thoughts expressed in Psalm 14:1-2; 53:1-2 (53:2-3 H), they also sound a great deal like Ecclesiastes' observation, "Surely there is no one on earth so righteous as to do good without ever sinning" (Eccl 7:20).

When John writes that the "wind blows where it chooses, and you hear the sound of it, but you do not know where it comes from or where it goes" (John 3:8), he echoes Ecclesiastes' statements about the futility of knowing God's ways, as well as the famous passages on the blowing of the wind (Eccl 1:6; 6:9; 11:4, 5). John also notes that there is a saying, "One sows and another reaps." This image is suggested earlier, although in a different context, for in Ecclesiastes the author points out that even if one is wealthy someone else will benefit (John 4:37; Eccl 6:2).

2 Corinthians states clearly that "all of us must appear before the judgment seat of Christ, so that each may receive recompense for what has been done in the body, whether good or evil" (2 Cor 5:10). This admonition parallels the closing words of Ecclesiastes, "The end of the matter . . . Fear God . . . For God will bring every deed into judgment, including every secret thing, whether good or evil" (Eccl 12:13-14).

Ecclesiastes in Rabbinic Literature

Ecclesiastes is one of the five "scrolls." During the Jewish liturgical year, on five holy days, in addition to the reading from the Torah and the Prophets (*Haftarah*), one of the five scrolls are read. Ecclesiastes is read at *Succot*/Booths/Tabernacles, the holy days that celebrate the autumn harvest.

The other four scrolls are Song of Songs (read at *Pesach*/Passover in the early spring), Ruth (read at *Shavuot*/Weeks/Pentecost in the late spring), Lamentations (read at *Tisha b'Av*, the ninth day of the Hebrew month of Av, in the midsummer), and Esther (read at *Purim* generally in late winter).

Midrash Ecclesiastes Rabbah. The midrash collection *Midrash Rabbah* (the Great Midrash) devotes a whole book to Ecclesiastes. *Midrash Ecclesiastes Rabbah* was not redacted earlier than the eighth century CE.

Solomon wrote Ecclesiastes. Solomon wrote the books of Proverbs, Ecclesiastes, and Song of Songs. He wrote the Song as a young man, Proverbs in his maturity, and Ecclesiastes in his elder years (*Midrash Song of Songs Rabbah* 1.1.10 end).

A controversial book—1. Several rabbis are disturbed at some of the advice found in Ecclesiastes. They suggest he is promoting heresy. "Need Solomon have said, 'What do people gain from all the toil at which they toil under the sun?' (Eccl 1:3). One might think that he means even studying Torah [literally, the Torah, but more widely, studying Judaism] has no gain. Nevertheless, they change their minds. If Solomon had said 'from all toil' and stopped there, one might have thought he meant even toiling in Torah. Solomon, however says 'the toil at which they toil.' For their toiling there is no gain, but for toil spent on Torah, there is a gain" (*Midrash Leviticus Rabbah* 28.1; *Pesikta de-Rab Kahana, Piska* 8.1; *Midrash Ecclesiastes Rabbah* 1.3.1).

A controversial book—2. The rabbis are likewise disturbed that Ecclesiastes offers the advice, "Rejoice, young man, while you are young . . . Follow the inclination of your heart and the desire of your eyes" (11:9). Did not Moses declare, do "not follow the lust of your own heart and your own eyes" (Num 15:39)? If people are to follow the inclination of their hearts and minds, they would act as if all restraint would be removed and there was neither justice nor judge. Solomon, however, continues, "but know that for all these things God will bring you into judgment" (Eccl 11:9). Therefore, the sages decide that Solomon speaks well (*Midrash Leviticus Rabbah* 28.1; *Pesikta de Rab Kahana, Piska* 8.1).

Repent while you can. Ecclesiastes' comment that "What is crooked cannot be made straight" (1:15) refers to the World to Come. One can repent in this world, but after one dies it is too late to repent (*Midrash Ruth Rabbah* 3.3 on 1.15). This notion disturbs some rabbis. They suggest that if one's sins are not too egregious, repentance is possible even in the World to Come (*Babylonian Talmud Rosh Hashanah* 16b–17a).

God will punish the wicked; no one will comfort them. The comment concerning "the tears of the oppressed—with no one to comfort them!" (4:1), in its biblical context, means innocents who are oppressed. "Rabbi Benjamin interprets the verse to refer to the hypocrites in regard to the Law . . . they wrap their prayer shawls around them; they put their phylacteries on their heads and they oppress the poor. Of them it is written, 'the tears of the oppressed—with no one to comfort them!'" "'It is mine to punish,' says God. As it is said, 'Accursed is the one who is slack in doing the work of the LORD' (Jer 48:10)" (*Midrash Ecclesiastes Rabbah* 4.1.1; cf. Matt 23:5).

Find a good study partner. The sages are aware that it is difficult to find a good study partner, someone with whom to learn. A good study partner proves the maxim, "Two are better than one, because they have a good reward for their toil. For if they fall, one will lift up the other; but woe to the one who is alone and falls and does not have another to help" (4:9–10) (*Sifre Deuteronomy, Piska* 305[13]).

---

13. See this title in the bibliography.

Knowledge and good deeds protect one. A person who is knowledgeable in Scripture, Mishnah, and good manners will not speedily sin, as it is written, "A threefold cord is not quickly broken" (4:12) (*Mishnah Kiddushin* 1.10).

Judge by results, not by promises. "The day of death [is better] than the day of birth" (7:1). Although this seems counterintuitive, the rabbis explain that when someone is born, none know what his deeds will be. Only when the person dies can one make a fair judgment about that life. "Rabbi Levi says, It is like two ships that sail upon the ocean. One leaves the harbor, and the other returns to it. People rejoice over the first, but not the latter. [They celebrate the leave-taking of the ocean voyagers.] . . . I take the opposite view. We should not rejoice over the ship leaving the harbor, for who knows what seas and winds it will encounter. People should rejoice over the ship returning from its ocean voyage, and that it has come back safely. Therefore, it is with humans. [Rejoice in what someone has accomplished, not in their unproved and unknown potential]" (*Midrash Exodus Rabbah* 48.1).

Who is the wise person? Ecclesiastes asks rhetorically, "Who is like the wise man?" Then he explains that "Wisdom makes one's face shine" (8:1). Who is a wise person? the rabbis ask. Someone who is the student of the wise. "Who knows the interpretation of a thing"—that is to say, the person can explain what he has learned. "Wisdom makes one's face shine"—when asked a question, the person is able to answer. The "hardness of one's countenance is changed" (8:1) when one is asked a question and is unable to answer it (*Pesikta de Rab Kahana, Piska* 4.4).

Beware the power of the ruler. Although the following passages in the Mishnah do not quote from this biblical book, they reflect the tenor of what Ecclesiastes writes when he says, "Keep the king's command . . . go from his presence . . . for he does whatever he pleases. For the word of the king is powerful, and who can say to him, 'What are you doing?'" (8:2–4). "Shemaiya says, 'Do not become overly familiar with the government'" (*Mishnah Avot* 1.10). Rabban Gamliel says, "Beware of rulers, for they befriend someone only for their benefit; they act friendly when it benefits them, but they do not stand by someone in their time of need" (*Mishnah Avot* 2.3).

Text Study

Ecclesiastes 1:2ff.; Familiar Passages

Ecclesiastes is one of the most quoted books in the Hebrew Bible.

1:2. "Vanity of vanities, all is vanity" (cf. 12:8). Alternately, "all was vanity and a chasing after wind" (cf. 2:11, 17, 23; 4:4, 16; 6:9 etc.).

1:9. "There is nothing new under the sun."

1:15. "What is crooked cannot be made straight" (cf. 7:13).

1:18. "For in much wisdom is much vexation, and those who increase knowledge increase sorrow."

2:24. "There is nothing better for mortals than to eat and drink, and find enjoyment in their toil" (i.e., "Eat, drink, and be merry") (Cf. 5:18; 8:15).

3:1. "For everything there is a season, and a time for every matter under heaven."

3:2ff. "A time to be born, and a time to die; a time to plant, and a time to pluck up what is planted; a time to kill, and a time to heal; . . . a time to seek, and a time to lose; . . . a time for war, and a time for peace."

3:11. "[God] has made everything suitable for its time."

4:9. "Two are better than one, because they have a good reward for their toil."

4:12. "A threefold cord is not quickly broken."

5:4-5. "Fulfill what you vow. It is better that you should not vow than you should vow and not fulfill it."

5:10. "The lover of money will not be satisfied with money; nor the lover of wealth, with gain."

7:20. "Surely there is no one on earth so righteous as to do good without ever sinning."

7:21. "Do not give heed to everything that people say."

9:11. "The race is not to the swift, nor the battle to the strong."

9:11. "Time and chance happen to them all."

10:14. "No one knows what is to happen, and who can tell anyone what the future holds?"

10:20. "Do not curse the king, even in your thoughts, or curse the rich, even in your bedroom; for a bird of the air may carry your voice, or some winged creature tell the matter" ("A birdie told me so").

11:1. "Send out your bread upon the waters, for after many days you will get it back."

12:7. "The dust returns to the earth as it was, and the breath [or the spirit] returns to God who gave it."

12:12. "Of making many books there is no end, and much study is a weariness of the flesh."

Ecclesiastes 3:1–15; For Everything There Is a Season

The opening verses of chapter 3, and their response are among the most familiar words not only of this book, but also of the entire Bible. The folksong "Turn, Turn, Turn" draws its imagery from this section.

The fifteen verses begin with the author's observation: everything has its proper time. Then come *seven* verses of doublets or pairs, stating the item and its opposite (born/die; break down/build up; seek/lose). Next come a further *seven* verses (the number seven is a favorite literary unit in the Bible), which address the implications of the opening principle. God has set a time for everything, but as mortals we have no way of knowing what is that "set time." Consequently, take life as it comes and enjoy yourself.

Verse 1. A season and a time. These words are used as synonyms. "'Time' here is not a specific moment in time but rather an occasion or situation that is *right* for something. For example, 'a time for war' means whenever the conditions demand and are ripe for entering into war . . . This does not imply that [these moments] . . . are predetermined and independent of human decision, but rather that certain occasions demand a certain type of response."[14]

Verse 2. Born . . . die. The time of our birth certainly is beyond our control, and most people do not choose the time of their death. The "time" referred to here suggests that the entity is ready for this stage. A child has been in utero for nine months and is fully formed, ready to be born. Conversely, someone has lived the length of his or her days, and so that person dies.

Verse 4. Weep/mourn (better: weep/wail); laugh/dance. There is a sense of connection with these couplets. One weeps and wails (mourns) at a funeral, or sad occasion, but then, when that period is over, there is a time for laughter and dancing.

---

14. Fox, *Ecclesiastes*, 20.

Verse 5. Throw away stones/gather stones; embrace/refrain from embracing. Here again there is a connection between the sections of the couplet. There is "an erotic significance" to the concept of throwing stones or gathering them. To throw stones "is used symbolically of sexual congress," which connects to embracing, as gathering stones refers to "abstinence" when one would not embrace.[15]

Verse 11. God has made everything suitable for its time, but humans have no way of knowing what constitutes that time frame. Seeking answers would be like chasing after wind.

Verse 12. Be happy . . . enjoy. Since one cannot know God's plans, or if God has specifically planned this, simply take life as it is, and be happy and joyful.

Verse 14. Whatever God does endures forever; nothing is added, nor is anything taken from it. How would Ecclesiastes deal with passages where God changes the Divine mind? Consider three examples: (a) God regrets creating humans—"The LORD was sorry that he had made humankind on the earth" (Gen 6:6). (b) Following the incident of the golden calf, God wants to destroy Israel and start over again with Moses. Moses argues on behalf of Israel. "And the LORD changed his mind about the disaster that he planned to bring on his people" (Exod 32:14). (c) When God sees that the Ninevites repent, God reverses the decision to destroy the city. "When God saw what they did, how they turned from their evil ways, God changed his mind about the calamity that he said he would bring upon them; and he did not do it" (Jon 3:10). Presumably, Ecclesiastes would argue that even the Divine reversal had been foreseen and planned.

Stand in awe before God. Ecclesiastes' God is an "unpredictable and aloof deity [that] provokes real fear and consternation, not only pious reverence."[16]

Verse 15. That which is already has been. These words echo Ecclesiastes' earlier teaching, "What has been is what will be, and what has been done is what will be done; there is nothing new under the sun" (1:9).

Ecclesiastes 7:20; To Err Is Human

There are righteous people, and there are wicked people, but even the righteous are not perfect. Ecclesiastes observed a few verses earlier that people should not overdo righteousness (7:16). Humans would be wise to accept

---

15. Gordis, *Koheleth*, 230. See also *Midrash Ecclesiastes Rabbah* 3.5.1; Matt 3:9.
16. Fox, *Ecclesiastes*, 24.

the fact that all of us are "a mixture of good and bad. Straining for perfection is presumptuous, a refusal to accept human limitations."[17] He continues by reminding the listener that one should not pay attention to "everything that people say . . . [for] your heart knows that many times you have yourself cursed others" (7:21–22). He does not suggest that people are inherently evil, but rather that realistically humans have both virtues and faults.

---

17. Ibid., 48–49.

9

Esther

Introduction

THE STORY OF ESTHER is set in ancient Persia (Iran). Esther is the title of the book and the name of its central character/heroine. Esther is a member of the Jewish community. They are the descendants of those Jews exiled when the temple was destroyed.

There are no historically verifiable characters in the work, therefore speculation for the time frame of the story varies. It may take place circa 350 BCE.

The narrative begins with a banquet in the capital city of Susa [Shushan], organized by King Ahasuerus. When his wife refuses to appear before the court, she is summarily dismissed from her role. After a while, the king decides to replace her. His advisors institute an empire-wide search.

In time, Esther becomes the new queen. Shortly thereafter, Esther's older cousin, Mordecai, uncovers a plot to assassinate the king and passes this information through Esther, who in turn passes it on to the king.

King Ahasuerus appoints a new chief official, Haman. All people bow down to Haman, but Mordecai refuses to give Haman this honor. In his fury, Haman retaliates and plans to wreak revenge not only on Mordecai but also on all of Mordecai's people, the Jewish community.

Mordecai learns of this plot. He goes to his cousin Esther, the queen, and asks her to intervene. At first reluctant to do so, she finally agrees. The climax of the narrative takes place at a banquet in Esther's own queenly apartments. Esther exposes Haman's plot. When Haman compromises himself, King Ahasuerus orders his execution. Mordecai is appointed chief official in his place, and the Jews are able to defend themselves successfully against their enemies.

Esther is the eighth book in the third section of the Hebrew Bible, the Writings/*Ketuvim* (see Introduction: "The Order of the Books of the Bible"). It follows Ecclesiastes and precedes Daniel. In the Christian Bible, Esther follows Ezra and Nehemiah and precedes Job.

The narrative plot of the book of Esther is full of conspiracy and deception. It is "is fast-paced and exciting, the story is well told . . . The book, however, had difficulty attaining canonical status in both Judaism and Christianity, not least because of the actions and character of its heroine, the Jewish woman Esther." A further controversy stems from the glaring fact of "the complete absence of any mention of God."[1] It is amazing that Esther was admitted into the canon. One commentary suggests that the book lacks many basic Jewish values, such "as kindness, mercy and forgiveness."[2]

Another controversial aspect of Esther is the fact that she is—as are other women—forced to become sex objects for the pleasure of the king. In contemporary times, Sidnie Ann White has written that "[many modern] women are . . . made uncomfortable by the actions of Esther—her entry into the king's harem and her lack of challenge to the status quo." Yet, to criticize Esther in this manner, fails to contextualize this narrative, for the "book must be accepted [and evaluated] in the cultural milieu that produced it."[3] Furthermore, Michael V. Fox argues, "the author of Esther is something of a protofeminist. This book is the only one in the Bible with a conscious and sustained interest in sexual politics . . . The book certainly does not align itself with the men's side in the conflict. Perhaps alone in the Bible, this

---

1. Crawford, "Esther," 201, 203. See "The Canonicity of the Book of Esther" in Moore, *Esther*, xxi–xxx.
See also Schonfield, "Esther: Beyond Murder"; and Zucker, "Importance of Being Esther."

2. The explanation then continues, in a self-righteous tone, "[In reality] the story evidences a vengeful, bloodthirsty, and chauvinistic spirit. Intrigue, deceit, and hatred abound regardless of whether the spotlight is on Haman, Esther, Mordecai, or on their enemies." *NOAB*, 612. For a more balanced view, see Moore, *Esther*, 74.

3. Crawford, "Esther," 203–4. See also "EXCURSUS: The Image of Woman in the Book of Esther," in Fox, *Character and Ideology*, 205–11. Esther has been interpreted as "classic stereotyping of how women shoulder their way to power." Too often the image of a self-assertive Vashti is contrasted with the shrewd strategy and subtlety of Esther, with neither description meant as a compliment. Maggay, "Power and Potential of Women," 268.

author is aware of female subservience and is cynical about the masculine qualities that require it."[4]

Authorship; Dating Esther; Historicity

The author of the book Esther is unknown.[5] Further, there is little consensus on when the book is composed. Speculation varies from the early fourth century BCE, or even earlier, to the Hellenistic period (c. 300 BCE) or even to the time of the Maccabees (c. 160 BCE).

Esther undoubtedly is a novella, a work of fiction. Although King Ahasuerus is sometimes associated with the Persian king Xerxes I, Xerxes did not have a queen named Vashti, much less a Jewish queen named Esther.

There are many reasons to doubt the factual basis for the book of Esther. Jon Levenson observes that "the historical problems with Esther are so massive . . . no evidence whatsoever for any of the key events of the book of Esther has ever turned up."[6]

1. There is no historical reference to a Persian queen named Esther.[7]
2. Queens come from noble Persian families; they are not selected from ethnic minorities.

---

4. Fox, *Character and Ideology*, 209.

5. Although Esther's author is unknown, it is clear that as "the story of Esther currently stands in the MT [Masoretic Text], its author was primarily concerned with telling a story which would provide the 'historical' basis for the festival of Purim, *both* days of it (9:16-19, 20-22, 26-28, 31).

". . . The establishment of Purim being the *raison d'être* of the book, the author's emphasis was more on plot and color than on personality or character. In fact, with the exception of Xerxes [Ahasuerus], who emerges as a hard-drinking, extravagant, and somewhat careless monarch with a nasty temper, all of the major characters seem rather two-dimensional. Neither Vashti nor Zeresh is a believable life-and-blood individual; they are merely tools the author uses to construct his story. Haman has no great stature or humanity, no redeeming qualities that enable the reader to identify with him or to pity him. The wisdom and goodness of Mordecai as well as the courage of Esther are asserted by the author more than proven. Beautiful and brave, Esther in the Hebrew account . . . seems to be a Jewish nationalist whose Jewishness is more a fact of birth than of religious conviction (4:16-17 notwithstanding). To say all this, however, is in no way to deny that the story is well told, its great popularity among Jews down through the ages certainly being proof of that.

"Nonetheless, the book has had its strong detractors almost from the time of its composition down to the present. In antiquity, a number of Jews and Christians contested its canonicity." Moore, "Book of Esther," 2:634-35.

6. Levenson, *Esther*, 23; See also Fox, *Character and Ideology*, 131-139; Moore, *Esther*, xxxiv-xlvi; Gladson, *Five Exotic Scrolls*, 326-33.

7. This point and the list that follows are based on Berlin, *Esther*, xvii.

3. Rulers, Persian or otherwise, do not choose their queens by using beauty contests; these are political alliances.
4. Esther enters the king's palace as a concubine; she ends as a proper queen.
5. Vashti, who is a proper queen, is treated like a concubine.
6. Monarchs are powerful rulers. While undoubtedly they delegate some of their decision-making to others, they do not leave important matters of state up to the whims of their nobles.
7. Part of the plot of Esther depends on a rule that says that once a ruler makes a decision, it cannot be revoked. To govern a country where nothing could be changed makes governing impossible.
8. Haman's decision and decree completely to annihilate completely the Jewish community is unlikely in tolerant Persia.
9. When Cyrus the Great defeats the Babylonians (c. 539/538 BCE), he allows, and even encourages, the Jews to return to Judea. No mention is made of this important fact.
10. An important part of the plot of the narrative depends on the improbability that Esther keeps her Judaism secret, and also keeps her connection to her cousin Mordecai secret. The story belies those issues.

Yet, on another level, Esther is a very serious book. Lillian R. Klein points out that there are political aspects to this book that highlight power and powerlessness. "As exiles, the Jews are in a 'dependent' position, one associated with females, whereas autonomy and power are associated with males. These male and female 'roles'—representing, respectively, honor and shame—not only permeate the text of Esther, but also are used pointedly to 'shame' the culture in which the Israelites are exiled and, by comparison, to 'honor' the Israelites."[8]

In a recent study, Jonathan Grossman challenges the idea that Esther is a preposterous parody. Rather he makes a strong case that there are numerous "concealed messages" throughout the book, messages that "contradict its revealed themes" and in particular its "lighthearted whimsy." He goes on to suggest that the book's author consciously chooses to "conceal his

---

8. Klein, *From Deborah to Esther*, 95. Klein adds: "Esther has been championed as an example of an enterprising woman. Nevertheless, the text demonstrates how she acts behind the mask of 'feminine shame.' Thus Esther epitomizes the book's message and manipulation of the honor/shame theme" (117). Honor and shame are applied to women and men. Klein, "Honor and Shame in Esther"; see also Grossman, *Esther*, 240–41. On power and shame see Day, *Esther*, 7–10.

messages," employing "satire, often peppered with irony and cynicism."⁹ Grossman offers many examples where events in the book, or language in the book, connect to other parts of the Bible.

Esther Is a Unique Book

Esther is a unique book in the Bible for many reasons. The most obvious is that, on a basic level of reading the text, it is a farce, a comedy. The heroes are larger than life; the villains likewise. While the place and setting of the story make sense in its context, nonetheless, exaggeration and excess are found in nearly every chapter. There are 127 provinces in Ahasuerus' empire. The celebratory banquet that begins the book lasts for six months! The gallows erected by Haman are 50 cubits, roughly 75 feet (25 meters) high. Many of the names of characters, whether they are the advisors, the eunuchs, or even Haman's sons, are simply unpronounceable. Further, the language is often elaborately fancy.

In terms of the text, as is the case for drinking wine at the frequent banquets, the rule "seems to be 'the more the better.' There are lots of 'alls' ('all the people who lived in the fortress Shushan [Susa],' . . . 'all the provinces,' 'all the women,' 'all the Jews,' 'all the king's servants,') and the story never uses one word if it can use two."¹⁰

Banquets are a frequent device in the book. There is a banquet at the beginning of the book and at its end. "More than just a structuring device, the banquet is the setting at which all the major events occur. Vashti loses her queenship at a banquet, Esther is made queen at a banquet, and, most important of all, Esther saves her people at a banquet."¹¹

Esther is unique in other ways. This is but one of two books in the Hebrew Bible that is named for a woman. Like Ruth (the other book), Esther plays a very prominent part. In Ruth, Naomi is a secondary but very pivotal character. The only person who has as much prominence in Esther is her cousin Mordecai. They are the dual heroes of the book.

1. Esther receives advice from Mordecai, but she works out the details of the plan.
2. She puts her life in danger when she goes to see the king unannounced.
3. She invites the king and Haman to a banquet not once but twice.

---

9. Grossman, *Esther*, 4, 11.
10. Berlin, *Esther*, xxvii.
11. Ibid., xxv.

4. She is the one who reveals the plot to annihilate her people.
5. She is the one who unmasks the villain.

While at the end of the book, technically, it is Mordecai who dictates the edicts that will allow the Jews successfully to defend themselves, it is Esther who makes the case to the king that this needs to be done. Ahasuerus then empowers both of them to do this.

The book of Esther is the most secular of the Bible's books. "The king of Persia is mentioned 190 times in 167 verses, but God is not mentioned once,"[12] although divine direction is hinted at in the line, "Who knows? Perhaps you have come to royal dignity for just such a time as this" (4:14). Esther is the only biblical book that addresses the origin of a festival, in this case Purim, the Festival of Esther. Yet this is a human-ordained, not divinely directed holy day.

Esther is also unique in the Bible because the story centers on the fact that a Jewish girl marries outside of the faith. Not only that, but she begins her royal connections as a concubine, where clearly she sleeps with the king before she marries him. Esther is secretive about her ethnic-religious origins. Further, there is no indication that Esther in any way follows the dietary traditions of Judaism. On the other hand, the plot, to say nothing of the drama of the story, requires this device of the beautiful and chaste orphan to move, so to say, from rags to riches, from near tragedy to full triumph.

Like the book of Daniel, there are several *additions* to this work, which appear in the Apocrypha (the Deuterocanonicals of the Roman Catholic, Greek, and Russian Orthodox Churches). "The purpose of the additions is to give a more specifically religious cast to the book as well as to the festival of Purim associated with it."[13] These additions attribute the deliverance of the people to God, and add some prayers for Esther and Mordecai. As noted earlier, the name of God does not appear in the Hebrew Scriptures version. In these additions, the words "God" or "LORD" appear more than fifty times.

---

12. Moore, *Esther*, xxxii. Carruthers (*Esther Through the Centuries*, 21) writes of Esther's "inherent religiosity."

13. Suter, "Rest of the Book of Esther," 282. The rabbis also add to the book of Esther through midrashim. See Bronner, "Esther Revisited"; and the section "Esther in Rabbinic Literature" below in this volume.

The Book of Esther

Divisions in the Book of Esther

Chapter 1

The narrative begins in the capital city of Susa. King Ahasuerus, who rules from India to Ethiopia (!), is just finishing hosting a very elaborate, six-month-long banquet. Then follows a weeklong banquet for the locals. Drinks are lavishly served in golden goblets. The king entertains the men, while Queen Vashti entertains the women at a separate banquet.

On the seventh day, "when the king was merry with wine," he commands his seven eunuchs to bring Queen Vashti to his festivities. She is to wear "the royal crown, in order to show the peoples and the officials her beauty; for she was fair to behold" (1:10–11). The queen refuses this invitation without giving a reason. The king is enraged.

Apparently incapable of reaching decisions on his own, the king consults his sages and officials. He is advised that the matter is very serious. The officials fear that Vashti's refusal "will be made known to all women, causing them to look with contempt on their husbands . . . the noble ladies of Persia and Media who have heard of the queen's behavior will rebel . . . and there will be no end of contempt and wrath!" (1:17–18). In short fashion Vashti is deposed, and a letter goes out "declaring that every man should be master in his own house" (1:22; see the Text Study at the conclusion of this chapter, "Vashti: A Woman Wronged").

Chapter 2

As the second chapter begins, King Ahasuerus is in a calmer frame of mind. His servants suggest that "beautiful young virgins be sought out for the king" and placed in the royal harem (2:2). One will be selected as the new queen. The plot thickens with the information that there is a Jew living in Susa who has adopted his orphaned cousin, Hadassah. Hadassah, also known as Esther, is young, fair, and beautiful. She is taken to the king's harem. She does not reveal her ethnic-religious origins. Preparations for their one night with the king take a full year. Each girl spends a night with the ruler, and comes back the next morning (2:12–14). When it is her turn, Esther spends a night with the king. "The king loved Esther more than all the other women . . . so that he set the royal crown on her head and made her queen instead of Vashti" (2:17). The king then gives a banquet in Esther's honor.

The chapter ends with the information that Mordecai overhears a plot to assassinate the king. Mordecai then passes this information on to Esther, who passes it on to the king in the name of Mordecai. The matter is investigated and found out to be true.

Chapter 3

King Ahasuerus appoints the arch villain Haman to the post of chief official. All people are instructed to bow down to Haman. Mordecai refuses to do this. Haman learns of Mordecai's slight. He then plans to wreak revenge for this rebuff. Learning that Mordecai is a Jew, Haman vows to annihilate all the Jews in Ahasuerus' kingdom. Haman goes to the king and protests that there "is a certain people" scattered among the kings' subjects whose "laws are different from those of every other people, and they do not keep the king's laws" (3:8). Consequently, Haman urges the king to issue orders to destroy them. Haman even offers to pay ten thousand talents into the king's treasury to see that this is done. The king agrees to this request, but he does not take Haman's bribe. Rather, the king tells Haman to do with them as he pleases. The inference is that Haman will pillage and plunder that community and then pocket their wealth.

Haman's statement, like all effective demagoguery, has a thread of truth to it. The Jewish community does have laws that are different from those of other people. That said, they are law-abiding subjects of the king. The chapter closes as a decree is sent to all the king's provinces that, at a set date in the future, the Jewish community is to be destroyed and plundered.

Chapter 4

Mordecai is mourning, wearing sackcloth and ashes. Esther learns about his distress and makes enquiries. Mordecai requests that she intervene with the king. She explains that she cannot just go to see the king; she needs to be summoned. If people come unannounced, they are put to death unless the king agrees to see them. Mordecai reminds Esther that she too will be affected by this decree. He adds, "Who knows? Perhaps you have come to royal dignity for just such a time as this" (4:14). Esther replies that she will go to see the king, even if it means she might perish.

Chapter 5

Three days later Esther visits the king. Fortunately, he is pleased to see her, and holding out the royal scepter, he asks her what she desires. Esther then invites the king and Haman to a banquet at her palace. At the banquet the king asks Esther what would be her desire. Demurely, she replies that she would ask that the king and Haman return the next evening for a second banquet. On his way home, Haman sees Mordecai and is renewed in his fury. When he arrives home, he complains to his wife. She suggests that he build gallows, and then have Mordecai hanged.

Chapter 6

That very same night, King Ahasuerus is unable to sleep. He has the royal records read out to him, presumably to lull him into sleep. Serendipitously—or some would say it was the hidden hand of God—the servant reads how Mordecai had saved the king's life when two men wanted to assassinate him. The king asks what honor was bestowed upon Mordecai for this act, and the servant explains that nothing was done.

Just at that moment, Haman arrives to seek the king's consent to hang Mordecai. Ahasuerus then asks Haman, "'What shall be done for the man whom the king wishes to honor?' Haman said to himself, 'Whom would the king wish to honor more than me?'" Thinking that he is the honoree, he suggests an elaborate ceremony where the person to be honored is dressed in royal robes and paraded through the city, with a noble official leading him. The official will proclaim, "Thus shall it be done for the man whom the king wishes to honor" (6:6, 9). The king is delighted with this advice. He orders Haman to follow through on his own excellent suggestion. Haman is to parade *Mordecai* throughout the city, and he does so (see the Text Study at the end of this chapter, "Turn-About"). Then Haman, dejected, hurries home. He tells his wife what happened, and she predicts disaster for Haman. Before he can answer her, messengers come reminding Haman that he is expected at the queen's banquet.

Chapter 7

This chapter serves as the dénouement, the climactic point of the book of Esther. In the midst of the feast, King Ahasuerus asks Esther a further time what she would want, even if it were half of the kingdom. Esther now is ready to speak her mind. "If I have won your favor, O king, and if it pleases the king, let my life be given me—that is my petition—and the lives of my people—that is my request. For we have been sold, I and my people, to be destroyed, to be killed, and to be annihilated. If we had been sold merely as slaves, men and women, I would have held my peace; but no enemy can compensate for this damage to the king" (7:3-4). Esther then identifies Haman as the villain. The king is appalled and flabbergasted. He storms out into the courtyard (see the Text Study at the end of this chapter, "Esther's Plea to the King").

Haman, understandably, is incredibly shocked. Even though the king has left the room, he remains with the queen and throws himself upon the couch where Esther is reclining. Just then, the king returns. He interprets Haman's actions as an assault upon the queen. As a note in NRSV explains, "To throw oneself as a supplicant at someone's feet was a common custom ... but even touching the queen's couch was a violation of harem law."[14] Haman is then taken and hanged on the very gallows he prepared for Mordecai.

Chapter 8

The king gives Mordecai the royal signet ring, and elevates him to the place held formerly by Haman. Queen Esther then asks the king to revoke his former order that called for the destruction of the Jews. He replies he cannot do this, for once the king issues a decree, it cannot be revoked. Nonetheless, new orders can be issued. In short order, Mordecai sends out letters in the name of King Ahasuerus that "allowed the Jews who were in every city to assemble and defend their lives, to destroy, to kill, and to annihilate any armed force of any people or province that might attack them ... and to plunder their goods" (8:11).

Chapter 9

Mordecai grows in power. The Jews successfully defend themselves against their enemies, but they do not plunder their enemies' goods. Mordecai sends out letters to the Jewish communities enjoining them to celebrate annually these days as a time when sadness was turned into joy. "Therefore these days are called Purim, from the word Pur" (9:26).[15] Esther follows up with a similar letter.

14. *NOAB*, 619.
15. A Pur is a dice or a lot. In chapter 3, at Haman's instigation Pur (dice) had been cast to determine the date when the Jewish community would be attacked (Est 3:7).

Chapter 10

Three short verses explain that King Ahasuerus was powerful, Mordecai advances in power, and that Mordecai intercedes for the welfare of his descendants.

Esther in the Christian Scriptures

The names of the book's central characters, Esther, Mordecai, Haman, and Ahasuerus, do not appear in the Christian Scriptures. Likewise, there is no direct quote from Esther found in those Scriptures. Connections between the book of Esther and the Christian Scriptures are more by way of inference than clear examples.

In Esther 4:1 Mordecai tears his clothes and puts on sackcloth as a sign of mourning. Matthew reproaches the citizens of a couple of towns on the Sea of Galilee (Lake Kinneret) for their having failed to repent. Had people in Tyre and Sidon acted similarly, they would have long repented "in sackcloth and ashes" (Matt 11:21).

Three times in the book of Esther, Ahasuerus asks the queen what she would like, even if it means half of his kingdom (5:3, 6; 7:2). In Mark's Gospel, King Herod (Herod Antipas) asks his daughter what she would like, even if it were half of his kingdom (Mark 6:23). When his daughter, Salome, seeks advice from her mother, her mother tells her to ask for the head of John the baptizer. She rushes back to the king and says she wants "the head of John the Baptist on a platter" (Mark 6:25).

In the Apocrypha, or Deuterocanonicals, there is a book titled the "Additions to Esther," or sometimes "Esther—the Greek Version."

Esther In Rabbinic Literature

Esther is one of the five "scrolls." During the Jewish liturgical year, on five holy days, in addition to the reading from the Torah and the Prophets (*Haftarah*), one of the five scrolls are read. Esther is read at Purim/Festival of Esther, which is celebrated generally in late winter.

The other four scrolls are the Song of Songs (read at *Pesach*/Passover in the early spring), Ruth (read at *Shavuot*/Weeks/Pentecost in the late spring), Lamentations (read at *Tisha b'Av*, the ninth day of the Hebrew month of *Av*, in the midsummer), and Ecclesiastes (read at *Succot*/Booths/Tabernacles, in the early autumn).

Midrash Esther Rabbah. The midrash collection *Midrash Rabbah* (the Great Midrash) devotes a whole book to Esther. This collection may have been compiled about the eleventh century CE, but it draws on earlier material. Most of the authorities quoted lived in the land of Israel around the fourth century CE. "The object of the Midrash is obviously to afford comfort to the Jews in a time of persecution by showing them how the Jews of Persia had undergone similar suffering and had been delivered. [The sages quoted in *Midrash Esther Rabbah*] unhesitatingly read the conditions of their own time into the Biblical text. Thus Ahasuerus's feat became a Roman banquet, and his soldiers the Praetorian Guard . . . [reflecting] Jewish conditions in Palestine under Roman rule."[16]

Reading the present into the past—1. "THE NOBLES (HA-PARTEMIM). Rabbi Eleazar says: The *partemim* are the two imperial legions of the king; for the king is not called Augustus [i.e., Cesar-emperor] unless they first proclaim him. And they [the legions] are the following. Rabbi Isaac says they are the Decumanian and Augustan legions [probably a reference to the Praetorian Guards, which frequently deposed and set up Emperors]. It was these which suggested to Nebuchadnezzar [the Babylonian king who ordered the destruction of the temple in Jerusalem in 586 BCE, but here a "code word" for Vespasian, who ordered the destruction of the temple in 70 CE] that he should go up and destroy the Temple" (*Midrash Esther Rabbah* 1.19).

Reading the present into the past—2. HAMAN SAID TO KING AHASUERUS, THERE IS A CERTAIN PEOPLE . . . NEITHER KEEP THEY THE KING'S LAWS (3:8). They observe neither Calends nor Saturnalia (Roman holidays, here transferred to Persia) (*Midrash Esther Rabbah* 7.12).

Embarrassing Vashti. TO BRING VASHTI THE QUEEN BEFORE THE KING WITH THE ROYAL CROWN (1:11). [At a royal banquet in chapter 1 in the book of Esther, the king wishes to show off the beauty of Queen Vashti. The guests said to him:] "Let her appear naked [so that we may see how beautiful she is.]" He replies to them, "Very well, let her appear naked . . . [wearing only the royal crown.]" She asks permission to wear at least as much as a girdle . . . but they would not allow her. He said to her, "it must be naked" [so she refused to obey the king's order] (*Midrash Esther Rabbah* 3.13).

Vashti's reply. QUEEN VASHTI REFUSED (1:12). [The rabbis credit Vashti with much greater sense and sensibilities than her husband, the king.] She remonstrates with him forcibly, saying: "If they consider me beautiful, they will want to enjoy me themselves, and kill you; and if they consider me

---

16. Simon, "Introduction," vii. Cf. Berlin, *Esther*, liii and n. 69.

plain, I shall bring disgrace upon you." But he is blind to her hints, and insensible to her good advice (*Midrash Esther Rabbah* 3.14).

A biased decision. AND MECUMAN ANSWERED BEFORE THE KING AND HIS PRINCES (1:16). [Mecuman is one of King Ahasuerus' advisors. He suggests that the queen be dismissed. According to the rabbis, he was biased in his decision. When Mecuman says:] VASHTI THE QUEEN HAS NOT DONE WRONG TO THE KING ALONE (1:16), the rabbis explain, He felt snubbed because the queen did not invite [Mecuman's] wife to the women's banquet. Another rabbi says, basing his opinion on the words, THAT THE KING GIVE HER ROYAL ESTATE UNTO ANOTHER THAT IS BETTER THAN SHE (1:19), [Mecuman] had a daughter whom he desired to marry into the royal house (*Midrash Esther Rabbah* 4.6).

Esther is very beautiful. Four women are surpassingly beautiful, and Sarah is one of these. The other three women are Rahab (the prostitute mentioned in Josh 2:1), Abigail (one of David's wives; 1 Sam 25:3) and Queen Esther (Est 2:7, 15) (*Babylonian Talmud Megillah* 15a).

Explanation of names. Why is Esther called Hadassah? Esther means "the hidden one," for she remains hidden fast in her chambers; but she comes forth into the world when there is need to give light to Israel. As for her name Hadassah, of which it is written, "Mordecai had brought up Hadassah [myrtle], that is Esther" (2:7), it is given to her because of her righteousness. Mordecai, too, is called *Hadas*, or "myrtle," this being a name for righteous men, as in the verse, "I saw a man ... standing among the myrtle trees in the glen" (Zech 1:8) (*Midrash on Psalms*, Ps 22.3).

Means justify the ends. Mordecai walks every day before the court of the women's house (2:11). He thinks to himself: How is it possible that this righteous maiden should be married to an uncircumcised man? It must be because some calamity is going to befall Israel and they will be delivered through her (*Midrash Esther Rabbah* 6.6).

The Mordecai-Esther-Ashasuerus triangle. The biblical text explains that Mordecai treated Esther, who was his young cousin, like a daughter (Hebrew: *bat*; 2:7). A talmudic rabbi puns on this word, and says, read not daughter (*bat*) but as a wife (lit. "house," *bayit*). In short, Mordecai married Esther (*Babylonian Talmud Megillah* 13a).[17]

---

17. Walfish suggests that the "idea that Mordecai and Esther were a married couple has had a long history in Jewish tradition, originating in the LXX [Septuagint], flourishing in the Talmud and continuing on into the commentaries of the sixteenth century and beyond." Walfish, "Kosher Adultery," 135.

Esther recites Psalm 22:11 (22:12 H). "Do not be far from me, for trouble is near and there is no one to help." When did Esther recite these words? At the time when Ahasuerus decrees "to destroy, to kill, and to annihilate all Jews" (3:13). At that time Esther comes into the king's house without permission, as it is says, "Esther . . . stood in the inner court of the king's palace" (5:1). [At first the king is upset, for she had come without permission, but then apparently he is mollified when she says,] "Do not be far from me, for trouble is near and there is no one to help" (*Midrash on Psalms*, Ps 22.24).

Divine intervention. NOW IT HAPPENED ON THE THIRD DAY, THAT ESTHER PUT ON (5:1). Esther puts on her most beautiful robes and richest ornaments . . . She puts on a smiling face, concealing the anxiety in her heart. Then she comes to the inner court facing the king and she stands before him . . . when he lifts his eyes and sees Esther standing in front of him he is furiously angry because she is breaking his law and coming before him without being called . . . when the queen perceives how angry the king is, she is overcome and her heart sinks . . . But our God sees and has mercy on his people, and he notes the distress of the orphan who trusts in him, and he gives her grace in the eyes of the king and invests her with new beauty and new charm. Then the king rises in haste from his throne, and runs to Esther and embraces her and kisses her . . . He also says to her: "Why when I saw you did you not speak to me?" Esther replied: "My lord the king, when I beheld you I was overcome by your high dignity" (*Midrash Esther Rabbah* 9.1).

Defeating Haman. Mordecai and Esther are hungry for the word of God. They take Haman's power away not with weapons and a shield, but with prayers and supplications before God (*Pesikta Rabbati*, Piska 18.3).

Mordecai and Esther equated with light and fire. Isaiah said: "The light of Israel will become a fire, and his Holy One a flame; and it will burn and devour his thorns and briers" (Isa 10:17). The rabbis explain that "the light of Israel" means Mordecai, "His holy one" means Esther, and "will burn and devour his thorns and briers" means that Haman and his sons will be devoured (*Midrash on Psalms*, Ps 22.2).

Another talmudic rabbi even suggests that not only were Mordecai and Esther married, they remained intimate even after she married Ahasuerus—clearly labeling Esther as an adulteress (and Mordecai as a knowing and willing procurer, and adulterer). He bases his thought on the line, "Esther obeyed Mordecai's bidding, as she had done when she was under his tutelage" (Est 2:20). The sage explains, "She used to rise from the lap of Ahasuerus and bathe and sit in the lap of Mordecai." (*Babylonian Talmud Megillah* 13b.)

An alternative view is that Mordecai was married, and since Esther's mother died in childbirth, Mordecai's own wife suckled Esther. (*Midrash on Psalms*, Psalm 22.23.)

Out of darkness, light. "Scripture says, 'The people who walked in darkness have seen a great light' (Isa 9:2 [9:1 H]). This verse alludes to the generation of Mordecai. No day was more dark and evil for the people of Israel than the one at Shushan the castle, when it was decreed 'to destroy, to kill, and to annihilate all Jews . . . in one day' (Est 3:13). But they saw a great light: A redeemer rose up for them and saved them. And who was he? Mordecai. Of him it is written, 'Mordecai went out from the presence of the king, wearing royal robes of blue and white' (Est 8:15). And what followed? [The next verse reads:] 'For the Jews there was light and gladness' (Est 8:16)" (*Midrash on Psalms*, Ps 22.15).

Text Study

Esther 1: 9–22; Vashti: A Woman Wronged

Queen Vashti, the wife of King Ahasuerus, is a minor heroine in this narrative. Unfortunately for her, the plot requires her dismissal from royal favor in order to create the situation where Esther can become queen in her stead. When analyzed carefully, it is clear that Vashti is a strong-willed, honorable, and moral woman. A strong case can be made that she is punished for those very qualities. On the face of it, her punishment is undeserved.

Verse 9. Just as the king is entertaining his guests, so Vashti entertains a banquet for the women. In the preceding lines, it is clear that the king's banquet is lavish and the wine is free-flowing. Vashti's banquet, apparently, was more sedate.

Verses 10–11. The king and his guests are drunk. They had been drinking for a week. "Merry with wine" is what this line says, but in verses 7–8 it is clear that "royal wine was lavished according to the bounty of the king. Drinking was by flagons, without restraint." The king then sends seven of his eunuchs to approach the queen, telling her to wear the royal crown. The biblical text does not indicate what they said to her. Did they say, as the rabbinic midrash suggests, that she is to wear the crown, but *only* the crown and nothing else? (see "Embarrassing Vashti" and "Vashti's Reply" in the section on Esther in Rabbinic Literature).

Verse 12. Vashti refuses to appear before a group of drunken, and probably unruly, strangers. She is in a very tenuous and difficult situation. There is no way that she can maintain her honor, and/or her husband's honor, and still be deferential to his request. The biblical text is silent on what she does—or does not—say in reply to the king's request. Again, there is no way to know if (or not) the eunuchs report honestly to the queen what the king said, much less what the queen said in reply. As the rabbis suggest, she does try to reason with him, but it is to no avail. Ahasuerus has a quick temper. He goes from drunk to nasty drunk in an instant. "At this [the queen's refusal] the king was enraged, and his anger burned within him."

Verses 13–18. There is no attempt to listen to Vashti's thoughts. She is condemned by the king's advisors. Then Mecuman (who may have had his own reasons for badmouthing Vashti; see "A Biased Decision" in the section on Esther in Rabbinic Literature) warns that Vashti's example will not only become known, but exploited by the noblewomen of Persia and Media, who "will rebel against the king's officials, and there will be no end of contempt and wrath!" (v. 18). This claim is preposterous. To credit it as real would mean that Vashti would have been enormously popular with the women of the realm, and that reports of her disobedience concerning the king's request would cause havoc throughout the empire! It also suggests that officials of the empire, to a man, were ruled by—indeed, were at the mercy of—their wives.

Esther 6:1–10; Turn-About

Verses 1–6. The opening verses of the chapter finds the king unable to sleep. His solution is to listen to the "book of records, the annals" (v. 1). The inference is that listening to this will soon cause him to grow drowsy and fall asleep. Amazingly, what he hears has the opposite effect. He learns of a plot—of all things, a conspiracy against his own life—and that the plot was foiled. Self-centered King Ahasuerus wants to know how generously the crown has rewarded the person who saved his life. He is appalled to learn that nothing has been done.

At that exact moment, who appears suddenly at his chambers? His chief official, Haman. Haman's purpose in seeing the king is to ask his consent to hang Mordecai on specially built gallows (vv. 4–5). When the king asks what should be done for a person whom the king wishes to honor, Haman, certainly no less self-centered than Ahasuerus, thinks that the king means him, Haman.

Verses 7–9. Haman suggests that the honoree should be dressed in royal robes, placed on one of the royal steeds, and paraded by an important official throughout the city, with the official proclaiming the person's high honor.

Verse 10. Turn-about! The monarch is delighted with this suggestion, and instructs Haman to do this for Mordecai the Jew.

Esther 7:1–4; The Second Banquet; Esther's Plea to the King

Verses 1–2. Haman has barely time to get home from parading Mordecai, when the king's eunuchs arrive and hurry him off to the banquet that Queen Esther prepared (6:14). Now the king and Haman are at the second banquet drinking wine. In a merry mood, the king asks Esther what she would request.

Verse 3. This is the dénouement. Esther is about to spring the trap she has set for Haman. She begins slowly. At first, she asks merely that her life be saved, and her request is that likewise her people's lives should be spared.

Verse 4. Then she figuratively delivers the death blow to Haman. Similar to much of the dialogue in the book of Esther, this is a long speech, with many dependent clauses. She begins with what appears to be, on the face of it, a strange statement. "We have been sold, I and my people, to be destroyed, to be killed and to be annihilated." This is the first time that Esther "reveals" that she is a Jew, although she does not make that specific connection. Ahasuerus is unaware of her ethnic-religious origin, and it is clear that Haman likewise is in the dark about this. Then Esther says, in effect, that if she and her people merely had been sold as slaves she would not have bothered to bring this to the king's attention.

Irony and understatement fill Esther's statement. She implies that the king would not have noticed the absence of his queen, and that her enslavement would not have merited his attention.

The final clause is difficult to translate: "but no enemy can compensate for this damage to the king" (NJPS/*TANAKH*: "for the adversary is not worthy of the king's trouble"). The *alternative* translation offered in the NIV is the clearest in revealing Esther's intent: "but the compensation our adversary offers cannot be compared with the loss the king would suffer."

To place this into its context, Esther subtly reminds King Ahasuerus that Haman offered to pay a bribe to the king to have the privilege to destroy and annihilate "a certain people," who, Haman infers, are traitors. "They do not keep the king's laws, so that it is not appropriate for the king to tolerate them" (3:8). "To sell the Jews into slavery implies that they are being wrested away from the sovereignty of the king and given over to the sovereignty of another power. This is a treasonous offense. If this is what Haman had proposed, then he is a traitor to the king. The king, of course, had not understood Haman's proposal in that light . . . Haman may have wished to be king [see ch. 6] . . . in Esther's account, Haman's plan has ostensibly become a way to deprive Ahasuerus of a group of his subjects, including his queen . . . a power grab by Haman against the king. Esther is framing Haman as a traitor. And how sweet is the irony, for . . . Haman had framed the Jews as traitors."[18]

18. Berlin, *Esther*, 67.

10

Daniel

Introduction

THERE ARE TWELVE CHAPTERS in Daniel. The first six are narratives set in the courts of ancient Babylon (what is today the country of Iraq) or Persia (modern-day Iran). They are presented in the third person. In these chapters, Daniel and/or his companions "undergo various trials because of their piety and strict observance of Jewish customs and practice." Chapters 7–12 contain four visions, one each in chapters 7, 8, and 9, and then a longer vision spanning chapters 10–12. These latter chapters "contain, in the first-person form, four apocalypses or visions granted to the same Daniel for the purpose of sustaining faith and loyalty during the perilous times to come."[1]

The word Daniel means either "God is my judge" or "God has judged/vindicated."

There are some small differences in versification between the Hebrew Bible and many Christian Bibles.

Daniel is the ninth book in the third section of the Hebrew Bible, the Writings/*Ketuvim* (see Introduction: "The Order of the Books of the Bible"). It follows Esther and precedes Ezra and Nehemiah. In the Christian Bible Daniel is one of the "major prophets" (see the reference to Daniel as a prophet in Matt 24:15). Consequently, in the Christian Bible Daniel follows Ezekiel and precedes Hosea.

---

1. Hartman and Di Lella, *Book of Daniel*, 3.

Authorship; Dating Daniel; Historicity

There are ten sections to this book. The first six stories, which correspond to the first six chapters, bear similar broad themes. It is probable that they have one author. The latter four episodes, described in chapters 7–12, are very different in content and suggest another author, or possibly multiple other authors.² Most scholars suggest that this is a book composed late in the biblical period, parts of which stem from the second century BCE.³ The apocalyptic visions, which make up the latter four narratives, probably stem from the period of Antiochus Epiphanes (Antiochus IV), the ruler of the Seleucid Empire (more or less modern Syria). Antiochus is the ruler who persecutes the Jews of Judea in the middle of the second century (c. 168–64 BCE). His Jewish opponents are the Maccabees. Through their successful efforts Jerusalem is regained and the temple rededicated. This is the basis for the Jewish holy day of Hanukah (Ḥanukah, Chanukah).

> Antiochus IV Epiphanes (175–64 [BCE]) ... figures prominently as the archvillain in Daniel 7–12. Antiochus was a despot of the worst sort, eccentric and unpredictable, ferocious and tyrannical ... Antiochus had a penchant for luxury, flashy spectacles, and magnificent buildings. [A historian termed] ... Antiochus as *epimanes* (Greek for "madman") rather than as (theos) *epiphanes* "(God) manifest," a title [Antiochus] assumed in 169 [BCE]. When Antiochus ascended the throne he was faced with many problems—money, a lack of cohesion in his kingdom, and pesty neighbors ... who kept pressing him. To solve his financial crisis he plundered temples and shrines, including the Jerusalem Temple. To unify his domain he insisted on total Hellenization, even in religion. To keep his neighbors in check he engaged in repeated military operations, many of which are alluded to in Daniel 11.⁴

---

2. Ginsberg, "Book of Daniel," 1284–86. Goldingay discusses the book's origin, authors, and theological significance. Goldingay, *Daniel*, 326–34. The first six chapters are "*about* Daniel and his companions," and the second six chapters "fictitiously claim to be *by* Daniel." Craven, "Daniel and Its Additions," 191 (emphasis original).

3. "The ostensible setting of the book of Daniel is in the Babylonian exile at the courts of Babylonian, Median, and Persian kings. Critical scholarship has established that the book actually comes from the 2d century B.C.E. The tales in chaps. 1–6 are older, and may have had lengthy prehistories ... In their present form, however, the tales can be no earlier than the Hellenistic age ... Since there is no clear allusion to Antiochus Epiphanes, a date in the late 3d or early 2d century B.C.E. is most likely." Collins, "Book of Daniel," 2:33.

4. Hartman and Di Lella, *Book of Daniel*, 39–40.

In their written form, the first six tales probably predate the persecution of Antiochus. They may well have been told in some kind of oral form before this. That said, they are not from the seventh and sixth centuries BCE, which is the purported time of the narratives. It is likely that they were written during the third century BCE. These dates are deduced from the particular use of language, certain references to customs in the Persian court, and the use of certain Aramaic words.

The book of Daniel purports to be history. It mentions kings and kingdoms, and frequent mention is made of four world empires, which will succeed each other, and all of which will precede the fifth and final empire, which will be established by God and last for all time. The difficulty with these descriptions is that they do not reflect historical fact. There are further problems. The book does not follow a logical historical order. "Chapters 1–4 are set in the reign of Nebuchadnezzar, in chap. 5 the king is Belshazzar, and in chap. 6 Darius the Mede. Chapters 7 and 8 revert to the reign of Belshazzar, followed in sequence by Darius in chap. 9 and Cyrus of Persia in chap. 10." In addition, apart "from the book that bears his name, Daniel does not appear as a historical personality of the exilic period in any biblical book."[5]

The authors of Daniel are not concerned with rigorous scientific history, as we would commonly use that term today. They are writing history with a theological purpose. That goal is to point to the establishment of God's final empire. In the latter chapters, the authors want to give hope to the persecuted, to instill the courage to believe that the tyranny of the present will be followed by the eventual reign of peace. "Many conservative Christians however continue to defend the view that the whole book was composed in the sixth century [BCE] and that Daniel was a historical person."[6]

Daniel Is a Unique Book

Resurrection

The book of Daniel is exceptional among the Hebrew Scriptures because it alone attests to the notion of physical resurrection of dead bodies. The key line is 12:2. The preceding verse sets the context for the allusion to resurrection. Daniel is told, "At that time Michael, the great prince, the protector of

---

5. Collins, "Book of Daniel," 2:29. While the "carefully plotted" narratives are "full of historical errors" this does not "diminish their theological significance . . . for narrative is a powerful instrument for theological reflection." Newsom, "Daniel," 293.

6. Collins, "The Book of Daniel," 206. Lucas writes that "an excessive concern with the historicity of the stories might lead us to miss the truth they are intended to convey." Lucas, *Daniel*, 27.

your people, shall arise. There shall be a time of great anguish ... But at that time your people shall be delivered, everyone who is found written in the book" (12:1). Then comes the specific line suggesting resurrection: "Many of those who sleep in the dust of the earth shall awake, some to everlasting life, and some to shame and everlasting contempt" (12:2; see the Text Study at the conclusion of this chapter, "Resurrection").

Discrete Stories

As noted earlier, there are ten separate sections to the book of Daniel. Among all of the books of the Hebrew Bible and the Christian Scriptures, Daniel is unique in that any one of these sections "could have existed independently of any of the others and would have been virtually as intelligible or unintelligible" as they are now found in the book. "Or put differently, any one or more of the sections could have been lost and the remaining sections would not have suffered in any significant way at all."[7]

Aramaic

Although most of the book is written in Hebrew, the central section is written in Aramaic (1:1—2:4a in Hebrew; 2:4b—7:28 in Aramaic; 8:1—12:13 in Hebrew).[8]

Apocalyptic

Apocalyptic literature is literature that mysteriously reveals some kind of secret about future events. These secrets often are revealed by angels or by some kind of supernatural figures. The word "apocalyptic" derives from the Greek *apokalypsis*, which means "revelation" or "uncovering." Although there are apocalyptic-like elements in the prophets Ezekiel (chs. 38–39) and Zechariah (chs. 9–14), true apocalyptic writing is found in Daniel (chs. 7–12).[9] The following elements, common to apocalyptic literature, are all

---

7. Hartman and Di Lella, *Book of Daniel*, 9.

8. Davies, *Daniel*, 35–39. Biblical Hebrew sentences generally divide into two segments, divided by something like a comma. The first part is designated the a section (1a, 2a, 3a) and the second part the b section (1b, 2b, 3b).

9. Hartman and Di Lella also suggest Dan 2:13–45 is apocalyptic writing. They present a list of apocalyptic writing in the Hebrew Scriptures, the Christian Scriptures, and other ancient writings. Hartman and Di Lella, *Book of Daniel*, 62–63.

found in Daniel: *pessimism* about the state of the world; *dualism* between forces of good and evil, and a coming battle; *determinism* in some kind of divine plan; *confidence in divine intervention*; a *cosmic* viewpoint; *intermediate beings*, often angels and demons; belief in the *fulfillment of previous prophecies*; and hope in *resurrection* and a *new world order*.[10]

Lists

A feature of the book of Daniel is that there are long and elaborate lists of items. For example, mention is made of "the satraps, the prefects, and the governors, the counselors, the treasurers, the justices, the magistrates, and all the officials of the provinces." In similar fashion, the narrative mentions "the sound of the horn, pipe, lyre, trigon, harp, drum, and entire musical ensemble" (3:3, 5).

Additions to Daniel

There are three books that are known as the Additions to Daniel. They are part of the Apocrypha (Deuterocanonicals). They constitute part of the Septuagint* translation of the Bible. Although not part of the Hebrew Scriptures (Masoretic Text) or the Protestant version of the Christian Bible, in the Roman Catholic Bible they form part of the text of Daniel.

The specific books are *The Prayer of Azariah and the Song of the Three Jews* (Hananiah, Mishael, and Azariah), *Susanna*, and *Bel and the Dragon*. The first of these stories is placed between Daniel 3:23 and 3:24. Consequently, in the Roman Catholic Bible these additional verses are 3:24–90. In a Hebrew Bible or Protestant version, 3:91–97 = 3:24–30. In the Septuagint and Roman Catholic Bible, *Susanna* and *Bel and the Drago*n follow 12:13.

The Book of Daniel

Divisions in the Book of Daniel

Chapter 1

The first chapter of Daniel sets the stage of why Daniel and his companions (Hananiah, Mishael, and Azariah, subsequently renamed Shadrach, Meshach, and Abednego, even as Daniel is renamed Belteshazzar; v. 7) are living in

---

10. Boadt, *Introduction the Old Testament*, 447.

Babylon. They are part of the concessions wrested from King Jehoiakim by the Babylonian ruler, Nebuchadnezzar. The intent of King Nebuchadnezzar is that these youths from royal families, all of whom are handsome and without physical defect, would be trained in the life, literature, and language of the Chaldeans (Babylonians). Presumably, they would then become envoys back to Judah. They would be both bilingual and bicultural. The Babylonians mean to treat Daniel and his companions well. They are fed royal rations. Yet Daniel demurs, for he wants to follow the dietary requirements of his religious tradition. The four eat a vegetarian diet and thrive.

"To these four young men God gave knowledge and skill in every aspect of literature and wisdom; Daniel also had insight into all visions and dreams" (v. 17). The book reports that when it comes to matters of "wisdom and understanding," they are "ten times better than all the magicians and enchanters" in the kingdom.

Chapter 2

Nebuchadnezzar's difficult dreams are the subject matter of the second chapter. He cannot sleep. The king appeals to his wise men and magicians for the interpretation of these nightmares. The king seeks answers, but places a terrible burden on these advisors. First tell me what I dreamt, and then tell me the meaning of it. The magicians, enchanters, and other wise men claim that this is an impossible task. The king then threatens to tear them from limb to limb if they do not comply. The ruler flies into a violent rage and orders their execution.

Just before this sentence can be carried out, Daniel makes enquiries why the matter is so urgent. He then asks permission to see the king; Daniel wants to provide an interpretation for him. Daniel goes home, implores his companions to join him in prayer concerning the mystery. God reveals the secret to Daniel, and verses 20–23 contain Daniel's prayer of thanks to God.

Daniel meets with King Nebuchadnezzar. The king asks Daniel if he is able to tell him the dream, and its explanation. Daniel says, "there is a God in heaven who reveals mysteries" (v. 28). Then, while he claims no special insights for himself, he explains that God has provided answers for the king. In this, Daniel speaks like a latter day Joseph (cf. Gen 41:16, 25).

In verse 28 the phrase "end of days" is actually an "idiomatic expression meaning 'a future time.'"[11]

Daniel describes the dream as featuring a great statue made up of many materials (gold, bronze, iron, etc.), which frightens the king. Then a stone

---

11. *NOAB*, note to Dan 2:28, 1129.

strikes the statue and destroys it piece by piece. The stone then turns into a great mountain and fills the earth. Daniel praises Nebuchadnezzar lavishly. "You, O king, [are] the king of kings—to whom the God of heaven has given the kingdom, the power, the might, and the glory, into whose hand he has given human beings, wherever they live, the wild animals of the field, and the birds of the air, and whom he has established as ruler over them all" (vv. 37–38). Nonetheless, after you shall arise several kingdoms, until a fourth kingdom comes to crush all that came before it.

Nebuchadnezzar recognizes Daniel's wisdom, and promotes him to high office. Daniel requests that his companions Shadrach, Meshach, and Abednego also be honored.

Chapter 3

This chapter contains the familiar narrative of the three (four) figures in the fiery furnace. King Nebuchadnezzar erects a golden statue sixty cubits high and six cubits wide (roughly ninety feet by nine feet, or thirty meters by three meters). At the dedication ceremony, the king explains that anyone who refuses to bow down before the statue summarily will be executed.

At this time, several people come forward and point out that there are "certain Jews whom you have appointed . . . They pay no heed to you . . . They do not serve your gods and they do not worship the golden statue that you have set up" (v. 12). These words are similar to the accusation that Haman makes against the Jewish community in the book of Esther ("There is a certain people . . . they do not keep the king's laws"; Est 3:8).

To his credit, Nebuchadnezzar takes the time to check out the validity of this accusation. He asks them directly if they worship his gods and bow down to his golden statue. Nebuchadnezzar then explains the consequences of disobedience. He warns them that if they fail to bow down before the statue, they will be thrown into a furnace of burning fire.

The three companions, Shadrach, Meshach, and Abednego, nobly reply that they prefer martyrdom to apostasy. "O Nebuchadnezzar, we have no need to present a defense to you in this matter. If our God whom we serve is able to deliver us from the furnace of blazing fire and out of your hand, O king, let him deliver us. But if not, be it known to you, O king, that we will not serve your gods and we will not worship the golden statue that you have set up" (vv. 16–18).

Rulers do not like to be overruled. Nebuchadnezzar is so furious and "filled with rage . . . that his face was distorted" (v. 19). Ordering the fire to be heated seven times more than its normal custom, he has the three thrown into the fire, still wearing their tunics, trousers, and hats.

When peering into the furnace, the king is amazed. The three are unconsumed by the fire, and a fourth figure appears to be with them. They are saved by someone/something "walking in the middle of the fire [with them] and they are not hurt; and the fourth has the appearance of a god" (lit. "a son of the gods"; "a divine being," NJPS/*TANAKH*; v. 25). The three are brought out of the fire, Nebuchadnezzar praises the God of these men "who has sent his angel and delivered his servants who trusted in him" (v. 28). The king then promotes Shadrach, Meshach, and Abednego in the province of Babylon.

Chapter 4

One day King Nebuchadnezzar, who is living at home, has a strange and utterly terrifying dream. He consults with his wise men, magicians, enchanters, Chaldeans, and advisors, but to no avail. Then he sought the advice of Daniel, called Belteshazzar after Nebuchadnezzar's own god (v. 8; v. 5 Aramaic]).[12] He describes the dream to Belteshazzar (Daniel). The king imagined a large tree located at the center of the earth. Its foliage is abundant, and animals graze near it, birds nesting in its branches. "[F]rom it all living things were fed" (v. 12; v. 9 Aramaic). Then a holy watcher comes down from heaven and orders the destruction of the tree, leaving but its stump. The watcher continues and says that the king's mind is to "be changed from that of a human, and let the mind of an animal mind be given to him. And let seven times pass over him." The purpose of this exercise is that "all who live may know that the Most High is sovereign over the kingdom of mortals" (vv. 16–17; vv. 13–14 Aramaic).

Daniel explains that the king is the tree itself! Although he has known greatness, Nebuchadnezzar will be brought low. He shall be driven from human society, and dwell with wild animals. Nebuchadnezzar's kingdom will only be restored to him when he acknowledges that heaven is sovereign (vv. 25–26;vv. 22–23 Aramaic]).

---

12. As mentioned in the Introduction, occasionally there are differences in versification between Christian translations of the Bible and the Masoretic (traditional Jewish) edition of the Hebrew Bible. The NRSV translation generally is followed by the Hebrew tradition in brackets and marked with an "H" for Hebrew (e.g., Exod 20:17 [20:14 H]). In Daniel the middle chapters are written in Aramaic, not Hebrew. Consequently, when there is a difference in versification, instead of the letter "H" there follows the word "Aramaic" (e.g., Dan 4:16–17 [4:13–14 Aramaic]).

Daniel then has the audacity to say to King Nebuchadnezzar, "O king . . . atone for your sins with righteousness, and your iniquities with mercy to the oppressed, so that your prosperity may be prolonged" (v. 27; v. 24 Aramaic]).

Nebuchadnezzar apparently does not heed Daniel's advice. One day, a year later, he is walking on the roof of his royal palace. He brags about his power. Suddenly a voice comes from heaven chastising him. He then goes mad for a period. He becomes disheveled and unkempt. Finally sanity is returned to him, and at the end of the chapter he praises the Ruler of heaven.

Chapter 5

The chapter features the familiar episode known variously as the incident of the "Writing on the wall," or "Belshazzar's feast." This chapter narrates events during the life of King Belshazzar, purportedly the son of King Nebuchadnezzar (vv. 2, 11). This is a historical inaccuracy. Belshazzar was the son of, and coregent with, Nabonidas. The author of Daniel does not feel bound to follow a strict historical standard. He wants to tell a tale of religious significance and pedagogic value; adhering to an accurate picture of the facts is less important.

Belshazzar is hosting a large banquet. Under the influence of the wine he is drinking, he commands that the servants bring the vessels of gold and silver that his father had taken from the temple in Jerusalem. He wants his guests to drink wine from them. They do so. Then they praise the gods of gold, silver, bronze, iron, wood, and stone. In the next moment, "the fingers of a human hand appeared and began writing on the plaster of the wall of the royal palace, next to the lampstand" (v. 5). Quite reasonably, Belshazzar is terrified. The "king's face turned pale, and his thoughts terrified him. His limbs gave way, and his knees knocked together" (v. 6). He seeks advice, and even promises to reward richly anyone who can read the writing. When no one comes forward, the queen provides the possible solution: summon Daniel, who has "an excellent spirit, knowledge, and understanding to interpret dreams, explain riddles, and solve problems." Daniel is brought forward. He is told that if he interprets the writing, he will be rewarded. Daniel spurns these gifts but agrees to help. Daniel reminds Belshazzar that Nebuchadnezzar had been punished for his arrogant spirit, being driven mad (see ch. 4). Although Belshazzar knew this, he too had not only refused to humble his heart, he had the nerve to praise false gods, the gods of silver, gold, bronze, iron, wood, and stone. Daniel interprets the event, predicting the fall of the Babylonian Empire. "That very night Belshazzar, the Chaldean

[Babylonian] king, was killed. And Darius the Mede received the kingdom" (vv. 30–31; 5:30—6:1 Aramaic) (see the Text Study at the close of this chapter, "The Writing on the Wall").

Chapter 6

This is the familiar narrative of Daniel in the lions' den. At the close of chapter 5, Darius the Mede overthrows the Babylonian Empire. King Darius sets up 127 satraps (governors; cf. Est 1:1 with 127 provinces in Persia), with Daniel as one of these leaders. Daniel excels in his work, and the king plans to make him senior governor. The other satraps are jealous of Daniel; they seek out a pretext against him. They go to Darius and propose that if anyone prays for thirty days to anyone, human or divine, instead of King Darius, that person should be "thrown into a den of lions" (v. 7; v. 8 Aramaic]). Darius gives this order. While he is aware of this decree, Daniel "continued to go to his house, which had windows in its upper room open toward Jerusalem, and to get down on his knees three times a day to pray to his God and praise him, just as he had done previously" (v. 10; v. 11 Aramaic]). Predictably, Daniel soon is brought before the king. Although Darius tries to avoid the consequences, in short order Daniel is cast into a lions' den. The king is upset, and he goes to his palace. Sleepless, he fasts all night. The next morning, filled with dread, he goes to the den. He finds that Daniel has been saved, for God has sent an angel to shut the lions' mouths so that they would not hurt him. Daniel is returned to power, his accusers and their families are thrown to the lions, and Darius ends up praising God.

Chapter 7

Beginning with chapter 7, the book of Daniel takes on a new characteristic. The final chapters are apocalyptic writing. Chapters 7–12 contain four visions, one each in chapters 7, 8, and 9, and then a longer vision spanning chapters 10–12. The first three visions are nearly the same length, twenty-seven to twenty-eight verses, and the final vision, over the cumulative verses of the three chapters, is about three times the length of its predecessors.

Chapter 7 is at the center of Daniel, and connects the first six chapters with the latter five. Linguistically it continues the Aramaic, which began in chapter 2. Chapter 7 returns to the reign of King Belshazzar of Babylon. This time Daniel dreams. His vision is one of four terrible and terrifying beasts. Daniel explains, "my spirit was troubled within me, and the visions of my head terrified me" (v. 15). An angel/attendant explains the meaning of the visions to Daniel. The four beasts represent four kingdoms. In the fourth kingdom the ruler "shall speak words against the Most High" and in punishment, "his dominion shall be taken away, to be consumed and totally destroyed . . . [and it] shall be given to the people of the holy ones of the Most High" (vv. 25-27) (see the Text Study at the close of this chapter, "Apocalyptic Writing").

Chapter 8

Another vision of Daniel, again in the realm of King Belshazzar, features a ram and a male goat. Daniel is in Susa, the winter capital of the Persian kings (cf. Est 1:2). The ram has two horns, representing the Median-Persian Empire. It is powerful and no beasts can stand up to its might. A male goat then appears from the west (v. 5) and successfully defeats the ram. The angel Gabriel (v. 16) provides an explanation: "As for the ram that you saw with the two horns, these are the kings of Media and Persia. The male goat is the king of Greece" (i.e., Alexander the Great; vv. 20-21).

The goat in turn is succeeded by four prominent figures. These refer to the successors of Alexander.

Gabriel then explains to Daniel that eventually "a king of bold countenance shall arise, skilled in intrigue. He shall . . . cause fearful destruction . . . He shall destroy . . . the people of the holy ones. By his cunning he shall make deceit prosper . . . in his own mind he shall be great . . . he shall . . . even rise up against the Prince of princes. But he shall be broken, and not by human hands" (vv. 23-25). "The name of Antiochus IV Epiphanes, the . . . king of Syria, is not mentioned anywhere in this chapter, but there is not the slightest doubt that he is the one meant in the description . . . whom the angel identifies as a king 'brazen-faced and skilled in trickery' [NRSV, "a king of bold countenance shall arise, skilled in intrigue"] (vss. 23-25)."[13]

Chapter 9

Daniel has a third apocalyptic vision. This occurs in the realm of Darius the Mede, a son of Ahasuerus. "*Ahasuerus* means Xerxes, a fictitious parent for a fictitious Darius."[14] It expounds a vision of the prophet Jeremiah, who is specifically named. Daniel makes confession and acknowledges that

13. Hartman and Di Lella, *Book of Daniel*, 235; see also Goldingay, *Daniel*, 217-18.
14. *NOAB*, 1141.

the people have been unfaithful to the covenant with God as articulated by Moses. Therefore was Jerusalem destroyed, and "all this calamity has come upon us" (v. 13).

As Daniel continues and seeks God's favor, suddenly once again the figure of Gabriel appears, bringing wisdom and understanding. Gabriel explains that while Jeremiah had spoken of seventy years (see v. 2), this really means seventy times a week of years (i.e., 70 years x 7 = 490 years; v. 24).[15] Eventually desolations shall befall the desolator.

Chapters 10–12 are linked into one vision. Chapter 10 serves as the prologue, the vision itself comprises chapter 11, and finally chapter 12 provides an epilogue.

Chapter 10

Daniel sees an angel-like figure. He falls into a trance, with his face to the ground. Although not named, this figure probably again is Gabriel, who tells Daniel that another angel, "Michael, one of the chief princes," is involved and together they will assist Daniel (vv. 13, 21). He urges Daniel to be strong and courageous.

Chapter 11

Beginning in chapter 11, the angel interprets the vision to Daniel. There will be three kings, and then a fourth. "A warrior king shall arise, who shall rule with great dominion and take action as he pleases" (v. 3). Yet, in time, his kingdom shall be broken and divided. There will be terrible conflict between various kings.

A king shall arise (a veiled reference to Antiochus IV Epiphanes, i.e., the self-proclaimed "evident god"), a ruler who "shall act as he pleases. He shall exalt himself and consider himself greater than any god, and shall speak horrendous things against the God of gods. He shall prosper until the period of wrath is completed . . . Yet he shall come to his end, with no one to help him" (vv. 36, 45).

---

15. Ibid., 1142.

Chapter 12

Finally, in chapter 12 the narrative explains that at an appointed time, "Michael, the great prince, the protector of your people, shall arise. There shall be a time of anguish . . . But at that time your people shall be delivered" (v. 1). Daniel is urged to keep the matter secret until the proper time.

Daniel in the Christian Scriptures

The Gospel writer Matthew calls Daniel a prophet (Matt 24:15).

According to N. T. Wright, "Jesus made the book of Daniel thematic for his whole vocation. He understood it to be referring to the great climax in which YHWH [God] would defeat the fourth world empire and vindicate his suffering people. He projected the notion of evil empire on to the present [Roman dominated] Jerusalem regime, and identified himself and his movement with people who were to be vindicated. This provided him with a messianic self-understanding."[16]

Wright further explains that the book of "Daniel . . . is an obvious source for first-century reflection on the way in which the fate of nation and martyr hang together."[17]

The apocalypse in 7:13 explains that Daniel sees that

> "One like a son of man" ascends to the throne of the Ancient of Days . . . Daniel is using this imagery to assure the readers that the persecution of Antiochus . . . will come to an end with glorious divine victory . . .
> The New Testament applies "Son of Man" to Jesus. The heavenly origins of the "Son of Man" figure are evident in the association with angels (Mt 13:41; 16:27; 24:31; 25:31; Mk 8:38; 13:27, 41; Lk 9:26) and the exercise of judgment.[18]

Daniel 2:34-35 speaks of a stone that is cut out supernaturally. The stone then crushes the multi-material statue. In Luke 20:18 (cf. Matt 21:44) reference is made to a stone; everyone who falls on it will be broken to pieces, and it will crush anyone on whom it falls.

Daniel's phrase referring to "signs and wonders" (Dan 4:2; 3:32 Aramaic]) is spoken by Jesus in John's Gospel (John 4:48).

---

16. Wright, *Jesus and the Victory of God*, 598–99.
17. Ibid., 585.
18. Perkins, *Reading the New Testament*, 42.

Idols of various materials, silver, gold, bronze, iron, wood, and stone (Dan 5:23) are reflected by a similar reference in the book of Revelation (Rev 9:20).

When the author of Hebrews 11:32-34 writes of "prophets—who through faith . . . shut the mouths of lions, quenched raging fire," these are oblique references to episodes in Daniel (Daniel in the lions' den, Dan 6; the companions in the fiery furnace, Dan 3.)

Four winds of heaven stirring up the sea (Dan 7:2) has a companion figure of four winds of the earth being held back so they cannot blow on earth or sea (Rev 7:1).

As beasts arise from the sea in Daniel (Dan 7:3), so does one arise from the sea in Revelation (Rev 13:1). Daniel's beasts have the animal qualities of lions, eagles, bears, leopards and birds' wings (Dan 7), so in Revelation these beasts have characteristics of leopards, bears, lions, and dragons (Rev 13). These beasts devour or conquer (Dan 7:7, Rev 13:7; 12:17). Further, they are boastful (Dan 7:8; Rev 13:5).

As books of judgment are opened in Daniel (Dan 7:10), so they are opened in Revelation (Rev 20:12).

Daniel in Rabbinic Literature

Daniel was a prophet. Christianity regards Daniel a prophet. As noted earlier, Matthew specifically refers to Daniel as a prophet (Matt 24:15). In Christian tradition, the book of Daniel is part of the section of the prophets, following Ezekiel and preceding Hosea. In the Hebrew Scriptures Daniel is not part of the prophets, but rather part of the Writings (see the Introduction at the beginning of this chapter).

That said, there are Jewish sources that regard Daniel as a prophet. The *Mekilta* explains that God spoke to prophets "outside of the land of Israel." In addition to Ezekiel, Daniel is mentioned by name, with reference to Daniel 8:2 and 10:4 (*Mekilta de Rabbi Ishmael, Pisha* 1.58-59; 65-66[19]).

Daniel was not a prophet. On the other hand, there is a tradition that Daniel was a particularly wise man, but he is not termed a prophet (*Babylonian Talmud Yoma* 77a). *Babylonian Talmud Megillah* 3a states specifically that Daniel was not a prophet.

Daniel saved non-Jewish wise men of Babylon. Israel is likened to sand (1 Kgs 4:20), and the nations of the world to lime (Isa 33:12). If sand [Israel] were not put in lime, the lime [the non-Jewish world] would not last. Thus, if

---

19. See the title in the bibliography.

there were no Israel, the nations would not endure. Except for Joseph, Egypt would have starved. Except for Daniel, the wise men of Babylon would have perished (*Pesikta Rabbati, Piska* 11.5).

Why Daniel was punished. Daniel was punished because he gave advice to the evil king Nebuchadnezzar (*Babylonian Talmud Baba Batra* 4a).

Daniel prayed three times a day. How many *Tefillot* [prayers] is one obligated to pray in a day? One does not pray more than the three *Tefillot* which our ancestors of the world instituted. Abraham instituted the morning *Tefillah* [prayer], as stated (in Gen 19:27): NOW ABRAHAM WENT EARLY IN THE MORNING UNTO THE PLACE WHERE HE HAD STOOD (*'MD*) BEFORE THE LORD. Isaac instituted the *Tefillah* of the *minha* (the *Tefillah* in the afternoon), as stated (in Gen. 24:63): NOW ISAAC WENT OUT TO BOW DOWN . . . IN THE FIELD TOWARD EVENING. Jacob instituted the evening *Tefillah* as stated (in Gen. 28:11): WHEN HE CAME TO A CERTAIN PLACE. Now it is written about Daniel (in Dan 6:10 [6:11 Aramaic]) AND THREE TIMES A DAY [HE KNELT ON HIS KNEES]. But <the text> did not explain at what hour (*Midrash Tanhuma, Genesis, Miqqets* 10.11, Gen 43:14ff., part I).

The word *Tefillah* refers to the three formal daily prayers. At each service there is a section, the Standing Prayer (*Amidah*). This midrash provides a direct link to the term "stood" (*'-m-d* [*ayin-mem-dalet*]) in the biblical text in Genesis 19:27.

God appears in many forms. At the Sea of Reeds, God appeared as a mighty warrior (Exod 15:3), and in the book of Daniel as an ancient one (Dan 7:9). Nonetheless, God is still the same God. Hence it says, "See now that I, even I, am he [i.e., unchanging]; there is no god besides me" (Deut 32:39), and "I, the LORD, am first, and will be with the last" (Isa 41:4) (*Mekilta, Shirata* 4.20–31).

God cast truth to the earth. Prior to creating humans, the angels debate with God about the wisdom of this endeavor. Some say, create humans. Others say no. Righteousness comes before God and says, Let humans be created, because they will do loving deeds. Truth then counters, Let humans not be created, because they will lie. What does God do? God takes hold of Truth and casts it to the ground, as it says, God "cast truth to the ground" (Dan 8:12). The angels are appalled, and say to God, How can you do this to your angel of Truth, let Truth arise from the earth. So we read in the Psalms, "Truth springs up from the earth" (Ps 85:11 [85:12 H, NJPS/*TANAKH*]).[20] (*Midrash Genesis Rabbah* 8.5)

20. NRSV: "Faithfulness [Heb. *emet*, usually translated "truth"] will spring up from the ground."

Some are bound for eternal damnation. The School of Shammai says, There will be three groups on the Day of Judgment—one of these is thoroughly righteous, one of these is thoroughly wicked, and one of these is intermediate. The thoroughly righteous will forthwith be inscribed definitively as entitled to everlasting life; the thoroughly wicked will be inscribed definitively to Gehinnom, as it says, "Many of those who sleep in the dust of the earth shall awake, some to everlasting life, and some to shame and everlasting contempt" (12:2) (*Babylonian Talmud Rosh Hashanah* 16b end; cf. *Pesikta de-Rab Kahana*, Piska 24.3).

Praise of righteous judges. It is written, "Those who are wise shall shine like the brightness of the sky" (12:3). These are judges that give a just and truthful judgment (*Babylonian Talmud Baba Batra* 8b).

Praise for the righteous. That same verse continues, "[Those who . . .] lead many to righteousness, like the stars [shall shine] forever and ever" (12:3). As among the stars there is no enmity, jealousy and contention, so too with the righteous. (*Sifre Deuteronomy*, Piska 47). Those who collect moneys for charity, are likewise called righteous ["righteous/righteousness" and "charity" both derive from the Hebrew root *tz-d-q, tzadeh-dalet-quf*] (*Babylonian Talmud Baba Batra* 8b).

That which shall be in the Time to Come, has been done here. Rabbi Aha, citing Rabbi Simeon bar Hilfa, says: All that the Holy One will do in the Time to Come, He has anticipated and done in part by the hand of the righteous in this world . . . The Holy One says "Kings shall be your foster fathers, and their queens your nursing mothers, With their faces to the ground they shall bow down to you" (Isa 49:23). Has he not already brought about these things? Was not Nebuchadnezzar a king, and to whom did he bow down? To Daniel, as Scripture says, "Then King Nebuchadnezzar fell on his face, [and] worshipped Daniel" (Dan 2:46) (*Pesikta de-Rab Kahana*, Piska 9.4).

Daniel is a direct descendant of Ruth and David. Ruth is told that six special sons would be her descendants, people filled with blessings: David, the Messiah, Daniel, Hananiah, Mishael, and Azariah (Shadrach, Meshach, and Abednego) (*Babylonian Talmud Sanhedrin* 93b).

Daniel is connected to the book of Esther. Daniel is the same person as Hatach in the book of Esther (*Babylonian Talmud Baba Batra* 4a).

Daniel is a subject of Psalm 64. The rabbis suggest that when David wrote Psalm 64, God told him what would happen to Daniel, and the difficulties he would face in Babylon. "To the leader. A Psalm of David. Hear my voice,

O God, in my complaint; preserve my life from the dread enemy" (Ps 64:1 [64:1–2 H]) (*Midrash on Psalms*, Ps 64).

Even the stone over the lion's den was miraculous. "A stone was brought and laid on the mouth of the den" (6:17; 6:18 Aramaic). But whence stones in Babylon? This stone flies from the Land of Israel and comes to rest at the mouth of the den. Rabbi Huna, in the name of Rabbi Yose, interprets the word *stone* as meaning that an angel, in the likeness of a lion, comes and sits at the mouth of the den. And the proof? The verse "My God sent his angel and shut the lions' mouths so that they would not hurt me" (6:22; 6:23 Aramaic) (*Midrash on Psalms*, Ps 64).

What Daniel prays in the lions' den. Daniel recites the creedal statement Sh'ma ("Hear, O Israel: The LORD is our God, the LORD alone"; Deut 6:4) (*Midrash on Psalms*, Ps 64).

Text Study

Daniel 5:1–13, 24–29; The Writing on the Wall

The famous "writing on the wall" takes place at the celebratory feast of King Belshazzar (see description of ch. 5 above). Belshazzar of Babylonia has invited a thousand of his nobles to a sumptuous banquet. They drink wine from vessels of gold and silver stolen from the temple in Jerusalem. Suddenly and mysteriously, "the fingers of a human hand appeared and began writing on the plaster of the wall of the royal palace, next to the lampstand" (v. 5). The monarch is horrified and feels overwhelmed. When none of his own advisors can determine the meaning, the queen suggests that they seek the advice of Daniel, who has "an excellent spirit, knowledge, and understanding to interpret dreams, explain riddles, and solve problems" (v. 12). Daniel interprets the strange writing. He predicts the collapse of the Babylonian Empire. "That very night Belshazzar, the Chaldean [Babylonian] king, was killed. And Darius the Mede received the kingdom" (vv. 5:30–31; 5:30—6:1 Aramaic).

Daniel explains to Belshazzar that God has sent this strange message. "And this is the writing that was inscribed: MENE, MENE, TEKEL, and FARSIN [MENE MENE TEKEL UPHARSIN; NJPS/*TANAKH* translation]. This is the interpretation of the matter: MENE, God has numbered the days of your kingdom and brought it to an end; TEKEL, you have been weighed on the scales and found wanting; PERES, your kingdom is divided and given to the Medes and Persians" (vv. 25–28).

The words themselves actually represent weights. *Mene* is a mina, *Tekel* is a shekel, and *Parsin* is two half-minas. The words can also be understood to be verbs, meaning respectively, to number, weigh, and divide.[21] In verse 26ff. Daniel takes the words as verbs, not as nouns, and then puns on them. Daniel explains that the time of Belshazzar's reign is "numbered," meaning limited. He has been "weighed" up and found to be wanting. Consequently his empire is to be divided, that is, given over to the Medes and the "Persians" (*Peres* is close to the word *Paras* in Aramaic, meaning Persian).

Daniel 7:1–28; Apocalyptic Writing

The word "apocalyptic" derives from the Greek *apokalypsis*, meaning "revelation" or "uncovering." As noted earlier in this chapter, there are certain elements that are common to apocalyptic writing. Many can be seen in this chapter.

Pessimism concerning the state of the world. In Daniel's dream vision he sees four great and terrible beasts coming out of the sea (v. 2ff). These beasts cause havoc. One is told to "devour many bodies!" (v. 5). Another beast had "great iron teeth and was devouring, breaking in pieces, and stamping what was left with its feet" (v. 7). Daniel is told that these four destructive beasts represent four kingdoms (v. 17).

Dualism between forces of good and evil, and a coming battle, is another characteristic of apocalyptic writing. The first eight verses are filled with descriptions of terrifying beasts, representing the forces of evil. The "Ancient One" to whom "was given dominion and glory and kingship, that all peoples, nations, and languages should serve him" (vv. 13–14), and his thousands of attendants, are the forces of good. One segment of the beasts contests the role of the holy ones, and prevails over them. Finally, however, the Ancient One comes and the time arrives when "the holy ones gained possession of the kingdom" (v. 22).

That there is such a kind of divine plan that will come about addresses the characteristic of *determinism*. That one can have *confidence in divine intervention* is evident in the explanation given to Daniel.

Daniel approaches "one of the attendants" of the heavenly court "to ask him the truth concerning all this," and that intermediate being gives him "the interpretation of the matter" (v. 16). As that special being explains, the heavenly "court shall sit in judgment, and his [the evil one's] dominion shall be taken away, to be consumed and totally destroyed." The *new world order* shall be realized for the "kingdom and dominion . . . shall be given to the people of

21. *NOAB*, 1136.

the holy ones of the Most High; [and] their kingdom shall be an everlasting kingdom, and all dominions shall serve and obey them" (vv. 26-27).

Daniel 12:1-2; Resurrection

The book of Daniel is unique in the Hebrew Scriptures; it is the only source that makes a direct reference to a time of resurrection. It provides "the explicit promise of resurrection for the righteous."[22]

"At that time Michael, the great prince, the protector of your people, shall arise. There shall be a time of great anguish . . . But at that time your people shall be delivered, everyone who is found written in the book. Many of those who sleep in the dust of the earth shall awake, some to everlasting life, and some to shame and everlasting contempt" (vv. 1-2).

Resurrection in Daniel is not a broad concept having universal application. It is very limited in scope. Those resurrected are the righteous, and more specifically those righteous Jews who stood up to the Antiochan persecutions, who resisted the lures of Hellenization.

> Prior to the time of our author, the normative doctrine of retribution was simply this: faithful observance of the Law brought prosperity in the present life and length of days to nation and individual; sin brought adversity and early death (cf. Deuteronomy 28). Rewards and punishments after death were not even thought of. Because after death, all men and women—saints and sinners alike—went to Sheol, the abode of the dead, and because the dead were believed not to rise again (Job 14:12), Sheol cannot be understood as a place of retribution. In Sheol, all of the dead, regardless of their loyalty or disloyalty to the Covenant, shared alike a dark, listless, dull subsistence separated from God.[23]

The idea of resurrection is taken up by, and becomes a hallmark of, the rabbis of the Talmudic period. Just who would be resurrected, and the connections between suffering and eternal reward, is the subject of a fine book by David Kraemer, *Responses to Suffering in Classical Rabbinic Literature* (see bibliography).

---

22. Kraemer, *Responses to Suffering*, 27.
23. Hartman and Di Lella, *Book of Daniel*, 309.

11

Ezra

Introduction

JEWISH TRADITION CREDITS EZRA as being the person who, through his enormous efforts following the Babylonian Exile, reestablishes Judaism in the land of Israel. In that sense, some characterize Ezra as a second Moses. That said, "unlike Moses, Ezra's authority to promulgate and administer the Torah in Jerusalem was not derived from a Divine Revelation. Ezra arrived at Jerusalem as a Persian commissioner with a royal letter placing 'the Law of thy God' on the same compulsory level as the law of the king, and threatening the offender of Mosaic precepts with death, banishment, confiscation of goods and imprisonment [cf. Ezra 7:11, 26]."[1]

King Darius of Persia sends Ezra to Judah with enormous powers. His role is to teach and enforce the laws of Moses. Technically, Ezra's position is "a scribe skilled in the law of Moses that the LORD the God of Israel had given" (Ezra 7:6). More specifically, this is "Ezra's official title as a commissioner of the government. He was 'Royal Secretary for the Law of the God of Heaven' (i.e., the God of Israel) or, to modernize somewhat, 'Minister of State for Jewish Affairs' with specific authority in the satrapy of Abar-nahara ["Across the River," i.e., west of the Euphrates]."[2]

Ezra is the tenth book in the third section of the Hebrew Bible, the Writings/*Ketuvim* (see Introduction: "The Order of the Books of the Bible"). It follows Daniel and precedes Nehemiah and Chronicles. In the Christian

---

1. Elias Bickerman, *From Ezra to the Last of the Maccabees*, 9–10.
2. Bright, *History of Israel*, 386.

Bible Ezra is one of the historical books; it follows Chronicles and precedes Nehemiah and Esther.

Scholars often present Ezra and Nehemiah as one unit, and originally it was considered one book.[3] The books of Ezra and Nehemiah connect closely. Not only do they cover a parallel period and similar geographical locale, but the closing narrative of Ezra, chapters 7–10, which addresses Ezra's mission, continues in Nehemiah 8–9. In this volume, each of these biblical books has its own chapter. This chapter on Ezra should be read in conjunction with the chapter on Nehemiah.

"The Bible connects the mission of Ezra with that of Nehemiah. But there was a significant difference. Nehemiah's activities centered, for the most part in political aspects of the community, specifically in building projects . . . The fulfillment of the congregation in its cultic sense was basically the purpose of Ezra's coming."[4]

Ezra's name is part of the institution known in rabbinic literature as the Great Assembly (or the Great Synagogue, *Kenneset HaG'dolah*). It is assumed that he was one of its leaders. The Great Assembly is vital in the chain of tradition that connects the biblical period to the time of the rabbis.[5]

Ezra's contribution is that he almost single handedly brings the Torah (the Pentateuch) and the Torah tradition from Babylon to Jerusalem. "It is highly probable that Ezra was responsible for the editing and introduction of the Pentateuch in its present form. The latter aspect of his work is demonstrated by the events related in Nehemiah viii–x."[6] (See the Text Study section at the end of this chapter, "Ezra and the Torah.")

Through Ezra's enormous efforts, the face and faith of Israel change. "The distinguishing mark of a Jew would not be political nationality, nor primarily ethnic background, nor even regular participation in the Temple

---

3. Myers, *Ezra-Nehemiah*, xxxviii.
Though there are debates where to establish the exact boundaries, and questions about the dating of certain sections, the following five divisions are commonly accepted among scholars:
    1. The Nehemiah memoirs include most of Neh 1:1—7:5, and 13:4–31.
    2. The Ezra memoirs include at least Ezra 7:27—9:15.
    3. Aramaic documents, Ezra 4:7–24a; 4:24b—6:18; 7:12–26.
    4. Lists and genealogies, Ezra 2 paralleled by Neh 7; Ezra 8:1–14.
    5. Other Hebrew sources and material.
Eskenazi, *In an Age of Prose*, 13.

4. Myers, *Ezra-Nehemiah*, lvii; see lvii–lix, lxii for a more detailed description of Ezra's achievements.

5. *Mishna Avot* 1.1; Moore, *Judaism in the First Centuries*, 29–36.

6. Myers, *Ezra-Nehemiah*, lxxiv.

cult (impossible for Jews of the Diaspora), but adherence to the law of Moses. The great watershed of Israel's history had been crossed, and her future secured for all time to come."[7]

The majority of the book of Ezra is written in Hebrew (1:1—4:7; 6:19—7:11; 7:27—10:44), although there are sections in Aramaic. "The Aramaic of Ezra (iv 8-vi 18, vii 12-26) is that prevailing in the official documents of the Persian empire."[8]

The events described in Ezra-Nehemiah, some of which clearly predate him, span over one hundred years. They take place in stages.

Geo-Political Background

538 BCE and Thereafter

King Nebuchadnezzar of Babylonia exiled the Jews both before and after the destruction of the temple in Jerusalem in 586 BCE. According to biblical sources (2 Chr 36:22-23; Ezra 1:1-4; 6:2-5), Cyrus of Persia (who defeats the Babylonians), in the first year of his reign (538 BCE), issues a decree permitting the exiles to return to Jerusalem. Cyrus not only permits the rebuilding of the temple, he even returns the golden vessels taken by Nebuchadnezzar.

Cyrus' benevolent policy with the nations that he vanquishes is unique. Other countries, such as Assyria and Neo-Babylon, displaced those they conquered, relocating them within the empire. Instead, Cyrus encourages the repatriation of these forced refugees. Cyrus returns captive peoples to their homes, the condition that they retain their allegiance to him. He urges them to rebuild their communities and to reconstruct their sanctuaries. He provides financial aid. They can rule themselves as long as they remain loyal to him. In Cyrus' own words, "I returned to (these) sacred cities . . . the sanctuaries of which have been ruins for a long time . . . and established for them permanent sanctuaries. I (also) gathered all their (former) inhabitants and returned (to them) their habitations."[9]

Among these "[former] inhabitants . . . returned [to] . . . their habitations" were those people from the kingdom of Judah, who, over fifty years earlier, were forced into exile by the Babylonians. These particular captive

---

7. Bright, *History of Israel*, 390. See also Cohen, *Beginnings of Jewishness*.
8. Myers, *Ezra-Nehemiah*, lxiii.
9. Pritchard, Editor, *Ancient Near Eastern Texts*, 208; see also Meyers and Meyers, *Haggai, Zechariah 1-8*, xxix-xl; Meadowcroft, *Haggai*, 42-5; Matthews and Benjamin, 207-9.

peoples who return to Judah become known as the Jews. "During the Babylonian exile, the Judean exiles retained their communal identity. After their return to Jerusalem, . . . they came to be called by the name *Yehudi* [Jew; plural *Yehudim*]. The word became synonymous with the 'descendants of Abraham.' . . . Hence, *Jew* developed into a common appellation . . . from which the word *Judaism* was derived to designate the faith of the Jew."[10]

Those who return find a land much smaller in territory than the one that they or their family had left. Judah (Judea) is not large. It constitutes an area about twenty-five to thirty-five miles long, from Bethel and Ai in the north to Beth Zur in the south, and about the same distance broad, from Jericho in the east to Lod in the west. It includes the plateau between the Salt Sea and the lowland in the west. In Nehemiah some specific outlying towns are mentioned: Bethel and Ai, Jericho, Lod, and Beth-zur (Neh 7:32, 36–37; 3:16). It is about a thousand square miles, a good part of which is desert land.[11] By comparison, it is a bit smaller than the state of Rhode Island. The Edomites, a neighboring tribe, have moved into southern Judah. There are conflicts with this group and others as well, over territory and other matters. In addition, internal tensions divide those who choose repatriation. Work to rebuild the temple and to resettle the land begins under the leadership of Sheshbazzar in 538 BCE (Ezra 1:8). The prophecies and promises of Second Isaiah and Ezekiel were inspiring. Isaiah said, "Violence shall no longer be heard in your land, devastation or destruction within your borders." "They shall build up the ancient ruins, and shall raise up the former devastations; they shall repair the ruined cities, the devastation of many generations. Strangers shall stand and feed your flocks, foreigners shall till your land and dress your vines" (Isa 60:18; 61:4–5). Ezekiel prophesied that the mountains of Israel would yield produce and bear fruit, the towns resettled and the ruined sites rebuilt (Ezek 36:8, 10). Reality is considerably grimmer and great difficulties face these refugees.

Furthermore, *not all those who could return to Judah actually choose to do so.* For several reasons a significant group decides to continue residing in Babylon. A full generation grows up there. They are unwilling to return to what is in all likelihood a less sophisticated and certainly more difficult life in Judah. They have made a new life. The choice to return is a dangerous venture; the success of that idea is unknowable.[12] While many Jews elect to stay in Babylonia, a number do return in this period.

10. "Jew" in Werblowsky and Wigoder, *Oxford Dictionary of the Jewish Religion*, 369 (emphasis original). See also Cohen, *Beginnings*.

11. Bickerman, *From Ezra to the Last of the Maccabees*, 11.

12. Meyers and Meyers, *Haggai, Zechariah 1–8*, xxxvii; see also Josephus, *Antiquities*, 11.1.

522 (520?) BCE and Thereafter

A second effort takes place about 522 (520?) BCE. Through the leadership of Zerubbabel, a grandson of exiled King Jehoiachin, there is a further attempt to rebuild the temple. Jeshua (Aramaic for Joshua), the son of Jehozadak (Jozadak), a priest of the Zadokite lineage, joins Zerubbabel. They serve respectively as the official governor and as high priest, holding commissions under Cyrus's successors, Cambyses (530/529–22 BCE) and Darius (522–486 BCE) (cf. Ezra 3:2ff.; Hag 1:12.)

"Evidence seems to indicate that the people who returned were poor and not very well organized, though doubtless invested with religious zeal. They appear to have rebuilt the altar first (Ezra iii 2, 3) so as to carry on at least a modicum of worship, such as the celebration of the regular festivals and the daily sacrifices (Ezra iii 4–6a)."[13]

In the second year of their return, they lay the foundations of the temple (Ezra 3:8) (520 [518?] BCE). Their efforts, however, are opposed by local inhabitants from Samaria (the Samaritans). These locals refuse to allow them to rebuild. The issue is not the rebuilding as such, but rather that those doing the rebuilding regard these Samaritans as ritually impure. Hence, the returning refugees reject their help.

In addition, there may be some indifference on the part of those returning, because they are busy with building their homes, as well as some issues with crop failure (see Zech 8:10ff.).

This is the period of the prophets Haggai and Zechariah. According to Ezra, the two men work together in common purpose (Ezra 5:1; 6:14). Haggai and Zechariah support and encourage Zerubbabel and Joshua in rebuilding the temple in Jerusalem.

Haggai demands that the people resume the work of rebuilding the temple. Although local opposition continues (Ezra 4:1–5; 5:2—6:15), after several years they complete a small structure about 515 BCE.

450 BCE

The next stage, according to the text of Ezra, begins during the reign of King Artaxerxes I of Persia. Ezra brings a codification of the Torah. He attempts to deal with problems brought on by Jewish men marrying local (non-Jewish) women.

---

13. Myers, *Ezra-Nehemiah*, xxvi–xxvii.

425 BCE and Thereafter

Finally, a fourth stage places Nehemiah coming from Persia twice to rebuild the walls of Jerusalem. In these endeavors, he overlaps the work of Ezra. Nehemiah may also have returned to Jerusalem early in the fourth century.

Nonetheless, there are difficult textual problems in Ezra-Nehemiah. It is possible that Ezra actually follows the period of Nehemiah.

In the Septuagint, the book titled *1 Esdras* contains a paraphrase of 2 Chronicles 35-36 (basically the final years of the southern kingdom of Judah), the whole of the book of Ezra, and Nehemiah 7:38—8:12, plus a tale about the bodyguards of King Darius of Persia.[14] *1 Esdras* is part of the Apocrypha (Deuterocanonicals). Called *3 Esdras* in the Latin Vulgate*, it often appears in Roman Catholic Bibles after the New Testament.

The Title

Ezra is the chief character in this book. He is a priest and scribe (a kind of secretary). He appears in the latter half of this book and in the book of Nehemiah.

> Ezra is referred to as priest in Ezra 7:1-5, 11, 12, 21; 10:10, 16 and in Nehemiah 8:2, 9; 12:26, and he performed priestly functions (Ezra 7:10, 25: 8:21; 9:6ff., 10:6; Neh. 8:1ff., 6).
>
> The scribal office attributed to him is equally important. He is termed scribe (from the Hebrew root *spr*) at least ten times (Ezra 7:6, 11, 12, 21; Neh. 8:1, 4, 9, 13; 12:26, 36). Ezra was apparently an important person in Babylon before he assumed the role of religious leader of the Jewish community in Jerusalem.[15]

Authorship; Dating Ezra; Historicity

Although the author of Ezra is unknown, one theory is that it was written by the same person who authored Chronicles. It is possible that this person actually was Ezra himself. Another possibility is that Ezra, Nehemiah, and Chronicles were written by authors from the same school of thought. Some scholars speak of the Ezra-Nehemiah-Chronicles narratives. One of the

---

14. *NOAB*, "Introduction to the Apocryphal/Deuterocanonical Books," xiii; see also the introduction to 1 Esdras.

15. Myers, "Ezra," 1105.

characteristics of Chronicles, the listing of names and census numbers, is also found in Ezra.

The relationship between Ezra-Nehemiah and Chronicles remains an unsettled scholarly question. On balance, although there are some similarities, these works appear to have different authors. "Consequently, if by the Chronicler one means the person or group responsible first and foremost for Chronicles, then a different person or group must be deduced for Ezra-Nehemiah."[16]

The dating for the writing of Ezra, in any case, is about 400 BCE.[17]

To what extent is this narrative of Ezra actual history?[18] One of the difficulties of Ezra (Ezra-Nehemiah) is that it does not conform to the known sequence of historical events. The first six chapters of Ezra precede the time of Ezra-Nehemiah. Chapters 7–10 are contemporary to Ezra.

The primary concern of the post-exilic* community is to reestablish the nation of Judah. To do this required an energetic and sound religious structure. To achieve this end, in terms of the books of Ezra and Nehemiah, much of the historical material is dealt with in a sermonic manner. References to contemporary events are often dictated by the theme rather than by historical sequence.[19]

Regretfully, the books of Ezra and Nehemiah lack any sense of what today would be considered an adequate, coherent, or even "chronological skeleton or a systematic chronological framework."[20] They have been characterized as "complicated mixtures of history, tradition, invention,

---

16. Eskenazi, *In an Age of Prose*, 33.

17. "Because Ezra and Nehemiah recount the rebuilding of the Temple and the work of Ezra and Nehemiah after their return to Judah, it is universally granted that the books were composed in Palestine.

"The date for the present shape of the books must be later than the events they recount: the dedication of the Temple in 515 B.C.E., the return of Ezra in 458 B.C.E. (or 398 B.C.E.) . . . and the governorship of Nehemiah, 445–33 B.C.E., and his second visit to Jerusalem, no later than 424 B.C.E. How many years elapsed after these dates until the basic shape of the books evolved depends on the compositional theory presupposed." Klein, "Books of Ezra-Nehemiah," 2:732.

18. "The account of the activities of Ezra . . . conventionally, called his Memoir . . . contains narratives in the first person (7:27—9:15), as well as in the third person (Ezra 7:1–26; Neh 8, 9:1–5 [partim]). While the first-person narrative probably comes from Ezra himself, it is unclear whether the third-person perspective results from the recasting of Ezra's account by an editor (who [may have been] . . . the Chronicler) . . . or whether there was an independent third-person source." Ibid., 2:733.

19. Myers, "Book of Ezra and Nehemiah," 1115.

20. Japhet, "Periodization between History and Ideology II," 491–92; see also Eskenazi, "The Structure of Ezra-Nehemiah," 642.

and folklore combined into ideologically driven, usually analysis-resistant narratives"[21] and "theologized historiography."[22]

The Book of Ezra

Divisions in the Book of Ezra

Chapter 1

King Cyrus of Persia sends out a written edict stating that God has charged him with the task of (re-)building a house in Jerusalem. Those exiled by the Babylonians may now go back and build the temple. Cyrus will assist in this endeavor with gifts of gold, silver, goods, and animals (vv. 1–4).

Cyrus authorizes that the "vessels of the house of the LORD that Nebuchadnezzar had carried away from Jerusalem" be released to the care of Sheshbazzar, the prince of Judah, who then brought them to Jerusalem (v. 7).

Chapter 2

This chapter features a long list of those who chose to return to Jerusalem. This record includes leaders, temple officials, servants, a number of people who decide to accompany those exiled even though they cannot establish their ethnic connections to Judah, as well as a list of animals. The list includes priests and Levites. This census is paralleled in Nehemiah 7:6–73a.

Chapter 3

It is clear that nearly two decades have passed. The chapter mentions specifically Jeshua son of Jozadak as one of the priests who is working with Zerubbabel son of Shealtiel (v. 2). As indicated earlier, Jeshua is Aramaic for Joshua (cf. Hag 1:1; Zech 6:11).

They set up the altar and begin festive worship, "But the foundation of the temple of the LORD was not yet laid" (v. 6). These temple foundations finally are set in place and there is a great celebration. This joyous occasion, however, is not without its sad side. Some of those present, in their youth, had seen the temple that was destroyed by the Babylonians. These people

---

21. Schwartz, *Imperialism and Jewish Society*, 20–21. See also Davies, *Ezra and Nehemiah*, ix–xiii; Clines, *Ezra, Nehemiah, Esther*, 25–31.
22. Davies, *Ezra and Nehemiah*, 128.

wept because the "new edifice was not so splendid as the former Temple of Solomon . . . It was a mighty achievement for the Jewish community, nonetheless, and was destined to become the center and bulwark of its life in the post-Exilic era."[23]

Chapter 4

Conflicts arise between some local inhabitants and those who came from Babylonia. The local inhabitants approach Zerubbabel and explain that they had been resettled in this area by Esarhaddon of Assyria in the seventh century BCE. They claim to worship the same God. The text describes these locals as *"adversaries"* (vv. 2, 1). Zerubbabel and Jeshua firmly reject their request to join in the rebuilding of the temple. The locals then place obstacles in the way of the building and threaten the builders. They bribe local officials and write an accusation against the inhabitants of Judah and Jerusalem to King Artaxerxes of Persia (vv. 4–7).

The local, non-Jewish inhabitants suggest in their letter that if the building succeeds and the city and its walls are rebuilt, the Persian king will lose his power over Judah (v. 16). Their petition is successful, and the building project is temporarily suspended.

Chapter 5

There are specific reference to the prophets Haggai and Zechariah, and to the authorities Zerubbabel and Jeshua.

There is an investigation by Tattenai, the governor of the province. He travels to Jerusalem to see what is taking place. He interviews the builders. Then Tattenai sends a report to King Darius, explaining that building is taking place, and will continue to do so subject to the king's pleasure.

Chapter 6

Darius replies. After due investigation, proof is found that supports the building project. Darius orders that the building continue uninterrupted. It is completed and dedicated during the sixth year of the reign of Darius (515 BCE). The returned exiles then keep the festival of Passover, and celebrate with great joy.

---

23. West, *Introduction to the Old Testament*, 410.

Chapter 7

This is Ezra's first appearance. Many years have gone by. It is now the middle of the fifth century BCE. The text traces Ezra's priestly ancestry back to the time of the high priest Aaron, brother of Moses. The text explains that Ezra "was a scribe skilled in the law of Moses that the LORD the God of Israel had given." Further, Ezra went with the full knowledge and approval of the king of Persia (v. 6). As mentioned in the beginning of this chapter, in effect Ezra's title was "Minister of State for Jewish Affairs," with specific authority in the satrapy of Abar-nahara ("Across the River," i.e., beyond the Euphrates).

The trip from Babylon to Jerusalem takes a full four months.

Ezra 7:11–26 lays out Ezra's commission. He has authority to make purchases, act in a priestly function, and to appoint magistrates and judges.

The chapter ends (vv. 27–28) with a first-person account by Ezra, blessing God for the good fortune that has befallen him. This is the beginning of the Ezra memoirs. It is curious that while Ezra is clearly associated with the "law of Moses," the book of Ezra does not feature Ezra reading from the Torah. That will only take place in the book of Nehemiah (see the Text Study section at the close of this chapter, "Ezra and the Torah").

Chapter 8

Even though the previous chapter mentions that Ezra has arrived in Jerusalem, a catalog is featured here of all those personnel who accompany Ezra. It includes mention of a farewell service that takes place in Babylon before they depart.

The priestly list in this chapter follows the Aaronide line, whereas in chapter 2 they follow the Zadokite line.

Chapter 9

The issue of exogamy (marriage with people outside of one's own group)

> became a major component in the reforms of Ezra and Nehemiah. Two entire chapters in Ezra (9 and 10) are devoted to this subject (see also Neh 9:2; 10:30; 13:3, 23–27, 28). The guilty parties included members of the priests (Ezra 10:18–22), the Levites (Ezra 10:23–24), and the laity (Ezra 10:25–43) . . . Given this situation, Ezra's reform had as its goal a separation of Israel from everything that induced contamination. His goal . . . was the purification of the people according to a priestly ideal of

separation from all that is unclean. For Ezra it was impossible to make consonant with each other this penchant for intermarriage and God's call to his people to be holy.[24]

Ezra is fixated on a sense of ritual ethos, of ritual purity. He is "concerned with a ritualized ethnicity, reinforced by a sense of the impurity of those who did not adhere to its particular praxis and modes of purity."[25]

Ezra is in Jerusalem. He faces problems with a Jewish population that has married local, possibly (ethnically and/or religiously) non-Jewish women.

The problem is set out clearly in the first two verses. Difficulties are widespread and are found at every level. Officials approach Ezra and tell him that the "people of Israel, the priests, and the Levites have not separated themselves from the peoples of the lands with their abominations" (vs. 1). They have married local women, perhaps divorcing their Jewish wives to do so, and married their sons to local women. "Thus the holy seed has mixed itself with the peoples of the lands, and in this faithlessness the officials and the leaders have led the way" (v. 2). Ezra is appalled. Much of chapter 9 is Ezra's fervent prayer to God in his sense of chagrin and sorrow at the situation he faces (see the Text Study section at the conclusion of this chapter, "Divorcing Foreign Wives").

Ezra prays, "And now, our God, what shall we say after this? For we have forsaken your commandments" (v. 10). Ezra then purports to quote from the prophets, lessons that the people were not to intermarry with the local populace when they took possession of the land. There are no specific prophetic statements attesting this, but these ideas are suggested in Leviticus 18:24–30 and Deuteronomy 7:3.

> Intermarriage with the "peoples of the lands" was fraught with dire consequences for the struggling community, especially since it involved the ruling families of the Jews . . .
>
> Part of Ezra's concerns arose from his feeling for the . . . purity of Israel as the people of Yahweh. The maintenance of the true relationship between Yahweh and his people could be achieved only through [endogamy] . . . Israel was a holy people, chosen by a holy God (Lev xi 44; Isa vi 13) . . . Israel had been set apart for Yahweh (Deut vii 6) as his servant (Isa xlii 1) to be a light to the nations (Isa xlii 6), which could not be done by watering down its faith through compromise.[26]

---

24. Hamilton, "Marriage," 4:564–65.

25. Fishbane, *Biblical Interpretation in Ancient Israel*, 114.

26. Myers, *Ezra-Nehemiah*, 77–78. There was "a danger that the distinctive elements of the Jewish faith would be watered down, perhaps beyond the point of recognition, by assimilation to the surrounding cultures." Williamson, *Ezra, Nehemiah*, 160.

Ezra's prayer and confession ends with a statement that he understands that God might well turn from Israel forever if matters do not change.

Chapter 10

There is an immediate response to Ezra's prayer sermon. Shecaniah son of Jehiel, presumably a prominent figure among the officials and leaders who have taken foreign wives, comes forward and pledges to change. He states, "We have broken faith with our God and have married foreign women from among the peoples of the land, but even now there is hope for Israel in spite of this. So now let us make a covenant with our God to send away all these wives and their children, according to the counsel of my lord and of those who tremble at the command of our God; and let it be done according to the law" (vv. 2–3).

Ezra implores "the leading priests, the Levites, and all Israel" to swear to this, and they do.

Ezra speaks of his being "ashamed and embarrassed" with those who have intermarried (9:1–15, see 10:6). It is however, Shecaniah son of Jehiel, not Ezra himself, who speaks of those "who married foreign women [*nashim nokhriyot*]." It is Shecaniah who states that these wives and their children are going to be sent away/divorced (vv. 2–3). The text does not define "foreign women." Whether they were sent away is unknown. Indeed, only descendants of Jeshua's (Joshua's) priestly family explicitly agree (vv. 18–19).

Who are these "foreign wives"? Are they Judeans? Are they ethnically different, racially different, and/or religiously different? If so, how different? How did they define the "other"? We do not know.

Within three days the people of Judah and Benjamin assemble at Jerusalem and pledge to follow Ezra's command. Although there is some limited opposition, the new order prevails. Within a period of about three months the transition is complete. A long list of those who had married foreign wives (vv. 18–43) concludes with the final verse in the book: "All these had married foreign women, and they sent them away with their children" (v. 44).

Ezra in the Christian Scriptures

In the opening genealogies of the Gospel of Matthew there is series of names that includes "after the deportation to Babylon . . . Salathiel the father of Zerubbabel" (Matt 1:12), who is same Zerubbabel who works with Jeshua (Joshua) son of Jozadak in Ezra 3. Luke, in his genealogy, also mentions Zerubbabel son of Shealtiel (Luke 3:27).

Zerubbabel and Jeshua's distance from, and fear of, their non-Jewish neighbors (Ezra 3:3) as well as their direct rejection of the local inhabitants (Ezra 4:3), although not specifically stated, is inferred by the contrast with Jesus' conversations with the Samaritan woman in John's Gospel (John 4:9).

Ezra has a strong reaction at hearing the report about the Israelite leadership marrying foreign women. He tears his garment and his mantle as a sign of his distress. When Jesus speaks to the high priest and tells him that he "will see the Son of Man seated at the right hand of Power," the high priest, according to Matthew's account, "tore his clothes and said, 'He has blasphemed!'" (Matt 26:64–65; cf. Ezra 9:3).

Ezra laments that in the past Israel's kings and priests were handed over to other rulers, and were killed, or sent into captivity, with others being plundered and put to shame (Ezra 9:7). Luke predicts that a similar fate awaits the people of contemporary Jerusalem (Luke 21:24).

Ezra in Rabbinic Literature

Great praise for Ezra. Rabbi Jose suggests that if Moses had not preceded him, Ezra would have been worthy of receiving the Torah for Israel (*Babylonian Talmud Sanhedrin* 21b).

Ezra writes Chronicles, and Nehemiah finishes it. Ezra writes the book known by his name. He writes the book of Chronicles up to his own time, and Nehemiah finishes the rest of it (*Babylonian Talmud Baba Batra* 15a).

When Ezra leaves for the land of Israel—1. Ezra does not leave for the land of Israel until he has finished writing his own genealogy in Chronicles (*Babylonian Talmud Baba Batra* 15a).

When Ezra leaves for the land of Israel—2. Ezra does not leave earlier for the land of Israel because he does not want to intrude on the priesthood of Joshua son of Jehozadak (*Midrash Song of Songs Rabbah* 5.5.1).

When Ezra leaves for the land of Israel—3. Ezra does not leave for the land of Israel because he is studying Torah with Baruch son of Neriah. Baruch son of Neriah is the scribe of the prophet Jeremiah (Jer 36:4, 10). The midrash assumes that Baruch went into exile to Babylonia, and is still living at the time of Ezra (*Midrash Song of Songs Rabbah* 5.5.1).

Torah study is paramount. The study of Torah is superior to the building of the temple, for as long as Baruch son of Neriah is alive, Ezra would not leave him to go up to the land of Israel (*Babylonian Talmud Megillah* 16b).

Ezra takes people of doubtful lineage to Israel. Ezra consciously takes a group of people of doubtful lineage with him from Babylonia to Israel. He does not want them to be a burden in Babylon (*Babylonian Talmud Kiddushin* 69b).

Ezra pronounces God's unspoken name. "Then Ezra blessed the LORD, the great God" (Neh 8:6). Rabbi Joseph says in the name of Rab, He magnified him by [pronouncing] the Ineffable Name[27] (*Babylonian Talmud Yoma* 69b).

Ezra sets the Hebrew calendar. After Ezra the Hebrew calendar is set (*Babylonian Talmud Betza* 6a).

Ezra is extremely well-versed in the Torah. Rabbi Zera and Rabbi Hananel say: Even if a person is as well-versed in the Torah as Ezra, he must not read it from memory and write it. (The person must not write a scroll from memory, but copy it from another scroll) (*Midrash Genesis Rabbah* 36.8).

Ezra reestablishes Torah in Israel. In ancient times, when the Torah was forgotten in Israel, Ezra comes up from Babylon and reestablishes it (*Babylonian Talmud Sukkah* 20a).

Diacritical dots in the Torah. In the Hebrew of the Torah, over certain words there are diacritical dots (see for example Gen 33:4). According to rabbinic tradition, Ezra affixes these dots because he has some doubts about the meaning of those particular words (*Avot de Rabbi Natan*, ch. 34[28]).

Ezra is highly self-disciplined. Ezra dominates and controls his urge toward evil (*Midrash Song of Songs Rabbah* 4.4.3).

Ezra determines when the Torah should be read. Ezra ordains that the Torah should be read on Mondays and Thursdays in addition to the Sabbath; that there should be three readers; and that ten verses are to be read (*Babylonian Talmud Baba Kama* 82a; see also *Babylonian Talmud Megillah* 31b).

Ezra and Malachi. Rabbi Joshua bar Korha says, Malachi is the same as Ezra, and the Sages say that Malachi is his proper name (*Babylonian Talmud Megillah* 15a).

Ezra and Nehemiah. Ezra is supreme in Torah; Nehemiah in worldly affairs. Each balances out the strengths of the other (*Babylonian Talmud Gittin* 59a; *Sanhedrin* 36a).

27. Lit. "the Distinguished Name," generally understood to be the Tetragrammaton, YHWH. Traditionally Jews do not pronounce this name but say instead Adonai, Lord, or Eternal.
28. See this title in the bibliography.

Prepare your heart for prayer; God will hear. Rabbi Samuel bar Naḥmani says: When you prepare your heart for prayer, you will be sure that your prayer will be heard by God, for it is said . . . "For Ezra had set his heart" (7:10) and "The king granted him all that he asked, for the hand of the LORD his God was upon him" (7:6) (*Midrash on Psalms*, Ps 108.1).

God is lenient with wrongdoers. The Rabbis teach: When God makes someone pay for his iniquities, God does not make him pay in full, as it is said, "You, our God, have punished us less than our iniquities deserved and have given us such a remnant as this" (9:13) (*Midrash on Psalms*, Ps 30.4; cf. *Midrash on Psalms*, Ps 62.4).

Ezra's descendants. Being a descendant of Ezra is a matter of high honor (*Babylonian Talmud Berakhot* 27b).

Ezra's disciple. Hillel the Elder is praised highly as a "Disciple of Ezra" (*Babylonian Talmud Sotah* 48b).

Rejoicing in the days of the Great Assembly. The Great Assembly (Great Synagogue) with which Ezra is associated, the rabbis understand as the link between the biblical period and the post-biblical period of the rabbis themselves. People rejoice at the time of the Great Assembly. The proof is, "They offered great sacrifices that day and rejoiced . . . The joy of Jerusalem was heard far away" (12:43) (*Tanna Debe Eliyyahu*, ER, p. 94, ch. 18 (210–11).

Text Study

Ezra 9:1–3; 10:2–5; 9–14, 44; Divorcing Foreign Wives

Ezra 9–10 was and remains a controversial set of chapters. After reading these passages, many modern readers, influenced by the sensibilities of the twenty-first century, find themselves questioning Ezra's thinking. How could he demand that these men arbitrarily divorce their wives and send them and their children away? Is this not narrow-minded thinking? Where is Ezra's sense of compassion?

The problem with criticizing Ezra for these acts is that it is judging him by today's standards, when he lived 2500 years ago. Ezra is better understood within the context and milieu of his own day.

The issue of exogamy in Ezra-Nehemiah comes as some of the exilic community returns to Judah from Babylon, two generations after the original Cyrus (539 BCE) returnees. Years earlier, following Jerusalem's destruction by the Babylonians in 586 BCE, while a small number of Judahites escape to Egypt, the vast majority of Judah, including the leadership class, is exiled to Babylon. Relatively few people remain in Judah. No doubt, with a limited gene pool available, there is some exogamous marriages. During the Babylonian Exile itself, while it is very likely that there is a greater degree of endogamy among those who lived in Babylon, it is probable that there too is some degree of exogamy.

Ezra and Nehemiah worry about marrying "others" (Ezra 9:12; 10:1–17; Neh. 13:1–3, 23–27). These "foreign wives" in Ezra could be Judeans who have not been in exile and therefore might follow different religious practices from the Babylonian Judahites.

Those people who returned from Babylon—either initially in the years immediately following the Cyrus decree, and certainly those two generations later who come with Ezra/Nehemiah—establish some form of social solidarity when they live as a minority community in Babylon. By contrast, those remaining in Judah (and other proximate diaspora communities) may have created syncretistic changes in priestly rules and other religious/cultural rules. It is likely that the Jews coming from Babylon (Persia) have different rituals and cultures than those who remained in the land.[29]

What is the impact in terms of acceptable marriage partners? *"It is clear that Ezra conceived of this group* [i.e., those women who would be acceptable wives] *as consisting only of former exiles (Ez. 9:4)."*[30] Yet, clearly those Judeans who remain in Israel believe if they married Judean wives they have married within the group. The returning exiles apparently think of themselves as more legitimate descendants than those who stayed in Judah. This is the sense of the seeming exclusivist position of Ezra-Nehemiah. As Tamara Cohn Eskenazi has written, the "question of intermarriage looms large in texts that depict Judah in the fifth century B.C.E., when . . . conditions of the fledgling, newly restored Jewish life in Judah are still precarious." She goes on to write of the "struggle to define and maintain a distinct identity in the midst of a more diverse population made the question of legitimate citizenship a bone of contention."[31]

When Ezra requires that the leaders of the community divorce their foreign wives, his concern is simply: what are the most likely conditions that will insure the future of the Jewish community? As noted earlier in this chapter, "Intermarriage with the 'peoples of the lands' was fraught with dire consequences for the struggling community, especially since it involved the ruling families of the Jews."

---

29. Smith, *Religion of the Landless*, 188–90.
30. Smith-Christopher, "Mixed Marriage Crisis," 247 (emphasis original).
31. Eskenazi and Frymer-Kensky, *Ruth*, xli.

The very purity of Israel, as the people of God, was threatened. God had chosen Israel as God's special servant to be a light to the nations. This "could not be done by watering down its faith through compromise."[32]

When the Israelite tribes were living amongst themselves on the lands of Israel/Judah, endogamous marriage and the continuity of Israel-the-people (i.e., the Jews) was assured. Conditions, however, changed. With the destruction and forced exile of the northern kingdom, a serious threat to Israel's future as a people emerges. Yet, Judah remains viable and the temple continues to stand in Jerusalem, a symbol of the religion and the people. Following the Jerusalem temple's destruction in 586 BCE, with the subsequent Babylonian Exile and early refugee Jewish settlement in Egypt, it is clear to some people that new strategies are needed to maintain the continuation of Israel-the-people.

As Cohen explains, "In these new circumstances marriage with outsiders came to be seen as a threat to Judean (Jewish) identity and was widely condemned. The Judaeans sensed that their survival depended upon their ideological (or religious) and social separation from the outside world."[33]

Ezra acts neither arbitrarily nor capriciously when he demands in-marriage. Deuteronomy makes it very clear. "When the LORD your God brings you into the land that you are about to enter . . . Do not intermarry with them [the native population] giving your daughters to their sons or taking their daughters for your sons, for that would turn your children from following me, to serve other gods . . . For you are a people holy to the LORD your God, the LORD your God has chosen you out of all the peoples on earth to be his people, his treasured possession" (Deut 7:1, 3–4, 6).

Marrying people with a different theology means syncretism: the worship of many gods—paganism. Israel is a small community. If it does not protect itself and isolate itself, it will be swallowed up by the larger society. The very survival of a group that is committed to the worship of the one God depends upon drastic action. It would have been too easy to succumb to and be absorbed by the syncretism of its stronger and more powerful neighbors.

These concerns with mixed marriage may have been religious and/or ethnic in nature, but it is also possible that there were socioeconomic factors. Marriage with "outsiders spells loss of land to the Jewish province . . . Ezra-Nehemiah's preoccupation with separation of foreign wives implies . . . [that women could] inherit land from their husbands or fathers . . . [therefore,

---

32. Myers, *Ezra-Nehemiah*, 77–78. On the other hand, a different view is offered in the book of Ruth. There the author shows that "a non-Israelite could become a faithful worshiper of the LORD. This would counter the books of Ezra and Nehemiah, both of which consider intermarriage wrong (see Ezra chs 9 and 10; Neh 10.30)." *NOAB*, 332.

33. Cohen, *Beginnings*, 261.

these] foreign women pose an economic threat; without such rights they would not represent a loss of land to the community."[34]

The report in Ezra and in Nehemiah does not concern itself with the welfare of these divorced women, nor does it indicate whether or not they protest this matter. Further, it "is noteworthy that, although the prohibition against marrying outsiders applies to both men and women, Ezra 9 does not mention any Judahite women marrying foreigners."[35]

Ezra's insistence on in-marriage is not unique for that time.

> The opposition to intermarriage with other peoples was . . . no new thing . . . Nor is there anything particularly Jewish in the restriction of marriage to the members of a people, citizens of a state, or even to a class of citizens in the state. In Rome, marriage was confined to members of the patrician families . . .
>
> In Athens, Pericles put through a law that only those both of whose parents were Athenian citizens should be reckoned as Athenians . . . the proceedings in Ezra 10 appear tame by comparison . . . it is a matter of self-preservation, and nothing more.[36]

Ezra 7:14; Nehemiah 8:1-3, 13-18; 10:29; Ezra and the Torah

Nehemiah explains that Ezra brought "the book of the law of Moses [*sefer Torat Moshe*] which the LORD had given to Israel" (Neh 8:1; cf. Ezra 7:14). Ezra reads the book to the people, who are spellbound by his words. The next day the people make preparations for the festival of *Succot*/Booths/Tabernacles. As the book of Leviticus commands, they make booths and dwell within them (Lev 23:40-43; Neh 8:14-18). During the time of this seven-day festival, Ezra reads from the "book of the Law of God" (Neh 8:18). Next Ezra prays for the people, and finally the people vow to "walk in God's law, which was given by Moses the servant of God" (Neh 10:29).

What exactly Ezra brought from Babylon remains a mystery. What constitutes this "book of the law of Moses"? Is it solely the book of Leviticus? The context suggests that Ezra reads Leviticus 23, the festival cycle. Is it Deuteronomy, which also has a chapter mentioning the festival cycle (ch. 16), or is it a much larger document?[37] Most scholars believe that Ezra's

---

34. Eskenazi, "Ezra-Nehemiah," 197-98.
35. Ibid., 197.
36. Moore, *Judaism in the First Centuries*, 19-20.
37. "Much attention has been focused on the 'book of the law' of which Ezra was a scribe (Ezra 7:6, 12, 21). Artaxerxes sent Ezra to make inquiries on the basis of this law (Ezra 7:14) and to teach it to those who did not know it (Ezra 7:25). The Ezra story

"book of the law of Moses" is the same document that is now regarded as the Torah (the Pentateuch).[38]

Ezra's very purpose in being in Jerusalem is to apply the law of the God of Israel. This is specifically stated in his orders when he leaves Babylon (Ezra 7:14).

When Ezra reads from this scroll, it is likely that he reads from selected parts. The text explains that he reads "from it." The people "told the scribe Ezra to bring the book of the law of Moses . . . Accordingly, the priest Ezra brought the law before the assembly, both men and women . . . He read from it" (Neh 8:1–3).

---

concludes with his festive reading from the law (Nehemiah 8). The Bible says nothing about Ezra writing or compiling this book, and the text seems to presuppose that it was already known before Ezra's arrival (cf. Ezra 7:25; . . . Since the law is identified as the law of Moses in Ezra 7:6 and Neh 8:1; 13:1, the present text of Ezra-Nehemiah suggests that this law was the Pentateuch.

"Numerous modern scholars have shared this opinion . . . Others thought the law book of Ezra was only the priestly writing . . . or some form of Deuteronomy . . .

"Texts like Ezra 9:2 seem to allude to Deuteronomy (7:1, 3; 23:3) while Neh 8:14–15 is best construed as an interpretation of Deut 16:15 and Lev 23:33–43 . . . If the Pentateuch was complete by the time of Ezra, there seems to be no reason to deny that his law book was the Pentateuch in its present form, or something very much like it." Klein, "Books of Ezra-Nehemiah," 2:737. Williamson, *Ezra, Nehemiah*, xxxvii–xxxix.

38. Myers, *Ezra-Nehemiah*, lxxiv. It "was doubtless the latest recension of the Pentateuch" (153).

12

Nehemiah

Introduction

THE BOOKS OF EZRA and Nehemiah often are featured as one unit. These books are closely connected, although according to Sara Japhet they "*appear to be independent of each other.*"[1]

They cover a similar period and a similar geographical locale. Also, the closing narrative of Ezra (chs. 7–10), which addresses Ezra's mission, continues in Nehemiah 8–9. In this volume, each of these biblical books has its own chapter. It would be beneficial to read this current chapter on Nehemiah in conjunction with the chapter that precedes it on Ezra.

The Bible connects the mission of Ezra with that of Nehemiah. Each man has his role to play. Nehemiah concerns himself largely with the rebuilding of Jerusalem, physically and politically in terms of its governance. Ezra's activities center largely on the cultic organization of the congregation in Jerusalem.

Nehemiah is the eleventh book in the third section of the Hebrew Bible, the Writings/*Ketuvim* (see Introduction: "The Order of the Books of the Bible"). It follows the Ezra and precedes Chronicles. In the Christian Bible, Nehemiah is one of the historical books; it follows Chronicles and Ezra and precedes Esther and Job.

---

1. Japhet, *From the Rivers of Babylon*, 245 (emphasis added).

On two occasions Nehemiah serves as the governor of Judah (Judea), probably in the mid-fifth century BCE. "Nehemiah's activity is set in the reign of a Persian ruler Artaxerxes. It appears probable that this is Artaxerxes I (465–24 B.C.). If so, Nehemiah's first governorship began about 445 and lasted until 433 (Neh. 2:1; 13:6); his second began at an unspecified date after this . . . however, the possibility that Nehemiah belongs to the reign of Artaxerxes II (405/4–359/58) cannot be ruled out."[2]

It is not clear whether Nehemiah precedes Ezra in Jerusalem, or Ezra precedes Nehemiah, or if the two were contemporaries. Ezra briefly mentions that someone named Nehemiah accompanies Zerubbabel and Jeshua (Jeshua is Aramaic for Joshua; cf. Ezra 2:2; Hag 1:1–4; 2:1–4; Zech 1:1; 3:1; 6:15) and several others from Babylon. This would have been in (522?) 520/518 BCE. This Nehemiah, therefore, is not the same person as the author of the book of Nehemiah. Other than this, there is no mention of a person named Nehemiah in Ezra's account. The book of Nehemiah mentions the person of Ezra several times, but the two men never appear in dialogue.

Nehemiah is deservedly praised for his "seriousness of purpose" and "superb leadership qualities" in organizing "the community for the work he came to do (ch. iii) and the way he handled the impending threats of disruption to that work (iv 15ff.)." Nehemiah demonstrated courage and a resolute will, especially as a layperson in standing up to "the compromising tendencies of the high priest Eliashib (xiii 4–9) and to hold in check the commercial interests that threatened to undermine the religious obligations of the new community (xiii 15–22)."[3]

The thirteen chapters of Nehemiah are written in the first person, so there is a sense of immediacy and personal connection to the events. Parts of Nehemiah read like a memoir.

In the Apocrypha (Deuterocanonicals), *Sirach* lauds Nehemiah in glowing terms for being instrumental in the rebuilding of Jerusalem (but does not even mention Ezra): "The memory of Nehemiah also is lasting; he raised our fallen walls, and set up gates and bars, and rebuilt our ruined houses" (Sir 49:13). Likewise, the book of 2 Maccabees, also part of the Apocrypha (Deuterocanonicals), praises "Nehemiah, who built the temple and the altar, offered sacrifices" (2 Macc 1:18, cf. 19–36).

---

2. Ackroyd, "Book of Nehemiah," 694; see also Allen and Laniak, *Ezra, Nehemiah, and Esther*, 8.

3. Myers, *Ezra-Nehemiah*, lxxvi. For a more detailed description of Nehemiah's accomplishments, see Myers, *Ezra-Nehemiah*, liii–lvi; and West, 414.

Geo-Political Background

The name Nehemiah means "God comforts" or "God consoles." It is made up of the root words *naḥam* (*n-ḥ-m*, *nun-ḥet-mem*, "comfort, console") and *ya* (*y-h*, *yud-hey*, one of the names of God). Nehemiah is a layperson, in contrast to Ezra, who is a priest.

Nehemiah is a noted figure in the Persian court of Artaxerxes. As mentioned in the chapter on Ezra, the Persians had conquered Babylonia, integrating it into the Persian Empire some years earlier (c. 539 BCE).

The narrative of Nehemiah focuses on the success of this seminal figure, despite serious opposition from nearby governments, to rebuild Jerusalem and once again to establish a temple in it. Unlike the book of Ezra, which covers many decades, some that precede Ezra himself, the book of Nehemiah is a first-person account of his own achievements and those of his compatriots.

Nehemiah's activities center basically on practical and political matters. His focus is on building up the physical structures in Jerusalem, which have the effect of protecting the Jews living there from the threat posed by hostile neighbors. Nehemiah is a religious person and he tries to achieve some social reforms, but he is not a recognized authority in Jewish law. This is Ezra's expertise.

Authorship; Dating Nehemiah; Historicity

There is no way to pinpoint with accuracy the author of Nehemiah. That is also true of the book of Ezra and the following book of Chronicles.

Some scholars argue that all three works probably share the same author, but that is vigorously debated.[4] Today, "most modern scholars recognize that Ezra-Nehemiah is a distinct work with its own literary and theological coherence."[5] One of the characteristics of Chronicles, the listing of names and census numbers, is also evident in Nehemiah.

The date of its composition is about 400 BCE or later,[6] probably during the Persian period prior to the time of Alexander.

---

4. "A principal issue in research on Ezra and Nehemiah is whether the books were once part of a longer Chronicler's history, or whether they formed from the beginning an independent work. The question has not been finally resolved in recent studies." Klein, "Books of Ezra-Nehemiah," 2:732. See Klein, *1 Chronicles*, 2–6.

5. Eskenazi, "Ezra-Nehemiah," 192. The interested reader might also consult the article on Ezra-Nehemiah in the *Anchor Bible Dictionary*, Klein, "Books of Ezra-Nehemiah."

6. Williamson, *Ezra, Nehemiah*, xxxvi.

What can one say about the historicity of the events portrayed in Nehemiah? The fact that the book does not whitewash the failures of the community, nor does it deny the frustrations of and opposition to Nehemiah, suggests either that this is a first-hand account or that it was written by someone who had access to first-hand information.

> Because Ezra and Nehemiah recount the rebuilding of the Temple and the work of Ezra and Nehemiah after their return to Judah, it is universally granted that the books were composed in Palestine.
>
> The date for the present shape of the books must be later than the events they recount: the dedication of the Temple in 515 B.C.E., the return of Ezra in 458 B.C.E. (or 398 B.C.E.) . . . and the governorship of Nehemiah, 445–33 B.C.E., and his second visit to Jerusalem, no later than 424 B.C.E. How many years elapsed after these dates until the basic shape of the books evolved depends on the compositional theory presupposed.[7]

To acknowledge that Nehemiah has a contemporary ring to it, and that the book does not ignore the failures of the Jewish community of his time, however, does not in itself mean that this is a history in the contemporary sense. To repeat some observations made in the chapter on Ezra,

> The primary concern of the post-Exilic community is to reestablish the nation of Judah. To do this required an energetic and sound religious structure. To achieve this end, in terms of the books of Ezra and Nehemiah, much of the historical material is dealt with in a sermonic manner. References to contemporary events are often dictated by the theme rather than by historical sequence.[8]

Regretfully, the books of Ezra and Nehemiah lack any sense of what today would be considered an adequate, coherent, or even "chronological skeleton or a systematic chronological framework."[9] They have been characterized as "complicated mixtures of history, tradition, invention, and folklore combined into ideologically driven, usually analysis-resistant narratives"[10] and "theologized historiography."[11]

---

7. Klein, "Books of Ezra-Nehemiah," 2:732.

8. Myers, "Book of Ezra and Nehemiah," 1115.

9. Japhet, "Periodization between History," 491–92; see also Eskenazi, "Structure of Ezra-Nehemiah," 642.

10. Schwartz, *Imperialism and Jewish Society*, 20–21. See also Davies, *Ezra and Nehemiah*, ix–xiii; Clines, *Ezra, Nehemiah, Esther*, 16–31.

11. Davies, *Ezra and Nehemiah*, 128.

The Book of Nehemiah

Divisions in the Book of Nehemiah

Broadly, the book of Nehemiah divides into three sections. The first seven chapters detail his commission and first governorship. The intermediate section, chapters 8–10, feature Ezra, plus related material. The last three chapters include further organizational work in Jerusalem, and Nehemiah's second governorship. As noted earlier, Nehemiah is written in the first person, giving the narrative a sense of immediacy.

Chapter 1

This opening chapter and the beginning of chapter 2 (1:1—2:8) detail Nehemiah's commission from King Artaxerxes. Nehemiah is attending the ruler in Susa, the winter capital of the Persian monarchs. He is a cupbearer to the king, an important official in the royal household (v. 11). While in Susa, Nehemiah receives a report from his brother, who has come with certain men from Judah. They report that Jerusalem is defenseless; its walls have been broken down, and its gates have been destroyed by fire. Nehemiah, a religious man, offers a heartfelt prayer to God asking for help in the mission he intends to undertake.

Chapter 2

It is clear that several months have transpired. Nehemiah received the news in early winter, and now it is spring. One day, when he carries the wine to the king, it is obvious that the cupbearer is visibly upset. Artaxerxes discerns that Nehemiah is deeply saddened, and then asks him what is of such concern. Nehemiah replies to the king, "May the king live forever! Why should my face not be sad, when the city, the place of my ancestors' graves, lies waste, and its gates have been destroyed by fire?" (v. 3). When the king asks Nehemiah what he would like to do, Nehemiah replies that he wants to be sent to Judah to repair the city. The narrative then explains that Nehemiah negotiates his time away, but also that he receives a royal commission to achieve his goals. Verse 6 notes that the queen was sitting beside the king. Queens generally were not present at public banquets, so this is exceptional in itself. "The queen of Artaxerxes was Damaspia. She may have had something to do with the king's decision, for the influence of women was strong during Artaxerxes' reign."[12]

---

12. Myers, *Ezra-Nehemiah*, 98 n. 6.

The rest of chapter 2 (vv. 9-20) finds Nehemiah in Jerusalem (see the Text Study at the conclusion of this chapter, "Setting Out; Inspecting Jerusalem"). It is clear that he is on an official visit, because the king has sent officers and cavalry to accompany him. After a few days respite, during the darkness of the night hours, Nehemiah, accompanied by a few men, does a secret reconnaissance of Jerusalem, inspecting the broken walls of the city. Soon thereafter Nehemiah announces his plans to rebuild the city wall (v. 17). His news is well received by the Jewish inhabitants. Yet when some of the local governors, Sanballat the Horonite, Tobiah the Ammonite, and Geshem the Arab (Arabian), learn of these plans, they challenge Nehemiah and accuse him of rebellion against the king (v. 19).

Chapter 3

This is a long and detailed list of the repairs, naming specific workers, and the work that they accomplish. Quite a large area is covered. It is clear that this work takes some time, and requires careful planning. An intriguing detail lists among the builders, "Shallum son of Hallohesh, ruler [or supervisor] of half of the district of Jerusalem . . . and his daughters" (Neh 3:12). Women clearly, are involved in this building project.

Chapters 2, 3 and 12 present a rich list of the topography of Jerusalem (see reference in this note).[13]

The success of the rebuilding effort angers the aforementioned local governors.

Chapter 4

Sanballat and his associates initially disparage the work of the Jews. Then, when it is clear that the builders are making good progress, they plot to stop Nehemiah and his forces. This requires defensive action; guards are set out day and night (v. 9 [v. 3 H]). Nehemiah shares fascinating details of the protective measures needed for building the walls. The work force divides into builders and defenders armed with "spears, shields, bows, and body armor." The builders carry swords. Since the work is spread out, Nehemiah organizes an alarm system, using trumpets. Ready at moment's notice, Nehemiah notes that he and his entourage sleep in their clothes (vv. 16-23 [vv. 10-17 H]).

---

13. Ibid., 116-20; see 118 for a sketch of the walls of Jerusalem.

Chapter 5

Nehemiah faces additional problems. The Jewish populace of Jerusalem faces economic privation. Money is limited, and taxes are burdensome. They have to mortgage their fields, and subject their children to slavery. It is clear that much of the Jewish population is in debt to their fellow Jews. A small group of wealthy residents of Jerusalem are causing economic hardship, exacting unfair interest from their coreligionists. Nehemiah is angry when he learns of these matters (v. 6). He considers his options and then brings "charges against the nobles and officials," calling "a great assembly to deal with them." Nehemiah tells them what they are doing is wrong. He demands that this wealthy group restore to the people "this very day, their fields, their vineyards, their olive orchards, and their houses, and the interest on money, grain, wine and oil that [they] have been exacting from them" (v. 11). These mortgage holders agree to restore what they have taken, and to demand no more. Nehemiah calls for the priests to exact an oath that the mortgage holders will do as they have said.

The text then inserts a small detail that personalizes the narrative. Nehemiah writes, "I also shook out the fold of my garment and said, 'So may God shake out everyone from house and from property who does not perform this promise. Thus may they be shaken out and emptied.' And all the assembly said, 'Amen,' and praised the LORD. And the people did as they had promised" (v. 13). What Nehemiah did was to take "his sash or girdle in the folds of which he carried personal belongings and shook it out; at the same time he pronounced a penalty for failure to comply with the oath, which was, in effect a curse. When he had shaken his girdle out, he held it up empty, signifying the fate of the man who failed to carry out his promise."[14]

The rest of chapter 5 explains that Nehemiah serves twelve years as Persian governor in Jerusalem. He states that, unlike former governors, he neither profits from his office nor does he exploit it. He claims to have paid out of his own funds for his upkeep and that of his entourage. The chapter concludes with a short prayer that God should remember his actions for good.

Chapter 6

The governors in the areas around Judah, Sanballat, Tobiah, and Geshem the Arab, want to meet with Nehemiah. Since the gates of Jerusalem have yet to be hung, Nehemiah puts them off repeatedly, claiming that he is engaged and cannot take time off to meet.

---

14. Ibid., 131. This description reads like an ancient version of a "fanny pack."

Sanballat then accuses Nehemiah of formulating a rebellion against the Persian Empire. He suggests that the true purpose for rebuilding Jerusalem's walls is that they intend to secede and that Nehemiah intends to become an independent ruler (v. 6). Nehemiah replies that none of this is true; that Sanballat is inventing these accusations out of his own mind.

Nehemiah has detractors among the Jewish leaders of Jerusalem. The text explains that someone wants to meet with Nehemiah secretly, in the temple, with the doors closed. This would compromise Nehemiah, for it violates religious tradition. Nehemiah refuses to participate.

This chapter mentions that among those opposed to Nehemiah was the female prophet Noadiah (v. 14). "The mention of this mysterious female prophet together with such highly placed officials suggests that her status was comparable to theirs and that she, like them, was a prominent person. The importance of this reference to Noadiah the prophet is highlighted when one realizes that the Hebrew Bible names only four women as prophets. The other three are preexilic (Miriam, Deborah and Huldah). With Noadiah there is evidence that the prophetic office was open to women in the postexilic period. The basis of her disagreement with Nehemiah remains unknown."[15]

Chapter 7

Nehemiah explains that the doors of Jerusalem are set in place, and that he has appointed his brother, Hanani, to be in charge over Jerusalem, along with Hananiah, the commander of the citadel. They are responsible for security. To that end, the gates are not to be opened until sunrise, and they are to be closed at sunset. Guards are always to be in place (vv. 1–3).

The rest of the chapter, for over sixty verses, primarily provides a list of those people who had returned to Jerusalem from Babylon (a list very similar to that one in Ezra 2). The chapter then ends with a statement that a variety of people came and settled in their towns. This list includes "the priests, the Levites, the gatekeepers, the singers, some of the people, the temple servants, and all Israel" (v. 73 [v. 72 H]). This is followed by a link sentence to chapter 8, explaining that this is now the seventh Hebrew month.

Chapter 8

Ezra reads "the book of the law of Moses, which the LORD had given to Israel" (v. 1). The previous link sentence is a connecting verse based on Ezra 3:1.

---

15. Eskenazi, "Ezra-Nehemiah," 199.

Reading the book of the law, the Torah, the Pentateuch, is quite purposely set for the seventh month. Solomon had dedicated the temple in the seventh month (1 Kgs 8:2). According to Leviticus, the seventh month is the time for the celebration of major holy days: Atonement (what would become the High Holy Day of Yom Kippur) and the festival of *Succot*/Booths/Tabernacles.

The people listen to Ezra's reading. Both men and women are present. A group of Levites stand next to Ezra. There also is a translation of what Ezra reads, so that all will understand (vv. 7-8). Although the matter is not absolutely certain, Ezra seems to read the text in Hebrew, and the Levites then translate this into Aramaic, which is the common language of the people listening. This way they fully comprehend what Ezra is reading. There are thirteen Levites (or representatives of Levitical families) mentioned. With Ezra this makes for fourteen people, double the biblically significant number of seven. Seven is associated with God (seven days of the week, seven-branched candelabra, etc.). There is a sense here that God's benign influence, and probably divine approval, if not actual divine intervention, is present here. "Seven is an ethereal number in the Bible; its supernatural power and influence is evoked over and over again."[16]

Verses 13-18 explain that the people keep the festival of *Succot*/Booths/Tabernacles, concluding with the biblically ordained eighth day of solemn assembly.

Chapter 9

This chapter divides into two sections. The opening verses (1-5) state that the people assemble before Ezra. They are mourning their past sins, and the iniquities of their ancestors. The "people of Israel" that assemble before Ezra are fasting; they are dressed "in sackcloth and with earth on their heads" (v. 1). They listen to the reading of the book of the law, make confession, and worship God (for a discussion of what Ezra read, see the Text Study at the conclusion of the chapter on Ezra, "Ezra and the Torah").

The chapter continues with a long penitential prayer spoken by Ezra (vv. 6-37) (see the Text Study section at the conclusion of this chapter, "Ezra's Penitential Prayer"). The author of this "prayer psalm drew upon a wide knowledge of the theology and traditions of his people, skillfully weaving into it elements of instruction, exhortation, and confession. As such it is prophetic rather than priestly."[17]

16. Reis, "Uncovering Jael and Sisera," 45. See also Reis, *Reading the Lines*, 73, 82, 157-58, 185.

17. Myers, *Ezra-Nehemiah*, 169-70; see 167-69 for a detailed listing of the sources and influences on Ezra's words.

This prayer psalm divides into several sections. Verse 6 addresses God as the creator and preserver of the heavens and the earth. Ezra then lauds God for choosing Abraham, finding his heart faithful, and making a covenant with Abraham to give to him and his descendants the sacred land (vv. 7–8). God saw the distress of the Israelites in Egypt, performed signs and wonders there, and divided the sea before them. God led them to Mount Sinai, and made known to Israel the sacred Sabbath, giving them statutes and commandments (vv. 9–15).

Regrettably, the "ancestors acted presumptuously and stiffened their necks and did not obey [God's] commandments." They wanted to return to Egypt, but God is a deity who is "ready to forgive, gracious and merciful, slow to anger and abounding in steadfast love," and so God forgave them (vv. 16–17). Even when they built the golden calf, God forgave them and did not forsake them. Eventually God "brought them into the land . . . [and God] subdued before them the inhabitants of the land . . . And they captured fortress cities and a rich land, and took possession of houses filled with all sorts of goods, hewn cisterns, vineyards, olive orchards, and fruit trees in abundance" (vv. 23–25).

Sadly, again the people were disobedient and rebelled and did evil before God. There were cycles of rebellion and forgiveness (vv. 26–31). The final verses of Ezra's prayer (vv. 32–37) are a plea for God's help. It is summarized in the lines that say, "You have been just in all that has come upon us, for you have dealt faithfully and we have acted wickedly"; nonetheless, "we are in great distress," so please help us (vv. 33, 37).

Chapter 10

This chapter lists the names of Nehemiah and many officials, priests, and Levites who affirm the covenant to pledge themselves to a life of reform. This commitment begins with the closing verse of the previous chapter, which is the opening verse of chapter 10 in the Masoretic Text (9:38 [10:1 H]).

Highlights of this formal pledge include commitment to walk in God's law, to observe and do all the commandments; not to give their daughters to the peoples of the land; not to take their daughters for their sons; not to purchase anything on the Sabbath; and finally to observe the sabbatical year (vv. 29–31 [vv. 30–32 H]).

They also commit themselves to support the temple monetarily: to bring the first of their produce to the temple; likewise the firstborn of herds and flocks, as prescribed by the Torah; to provide tithes; and generally not to neglect the house of God (vv. 32–39 [vv. 33–40 H]).

Chapter 11

There is a kind of lottery set up to determine which residents from the outlying areas will need to move to Jerusalem. One tenth of the people are required to do so, which causes some upheaval. The names of various groupings are listed: first lay leaders, then priests, Levites, and finally other groups. The chapter closes with an inventory of the towns in Judah and Benjamin.

Chapter 12

The chapter divides into three parts. The first section (vv. 1–26) is a set of genealogies or a census list of people who came from Babylon to Jerusalem with Zerubbabel and Joshua. The next seventeen verses (27–43) describe the dedication of the walls of Jerusalem. Noteworthy is that many Levites were living in areas outside of Jerusalem; they have to be brought there. Finally, there are some details about temple revenues and how, once again, all Israel supply regular portions for various personnel in Jerusalem (vv. 44–47).

Chapter 13

This final section in Nehemiah begins with three verses that hearken back to issues raised earlier in Ezra, which appear again at the close of chapter 13, the matter of close connections to non-Jews. This involves the expulsion of certain people from the community (see the Text Study in Ezra, "Divorcing Foreign Wives"). In this case, the matter concerns Moabites and Ammonites. The Torah reference, although not specified here, is Deuteronomy 23:3–6.

After Nehemiah accomplishes his mission in Jerusalem, he returns to Persia. In his absence, and without his strong guiding influence, the people slip back to some of their former habits. Nehemiah, however, returns for a second tour of duty. He finds that Eliashib the priest (possibly the high priest, although this is not certain) has allotted a room for Tobiah the Ammonite (cf. 2:19) in the temple precincts. This is doubly egregious because this is a room designated for temple supplies, and further, Tobiah is an Ammonite. Nehemiah reverses that decision. He has the room purified and restored to its proper purpose.

Levites in Nehemiah's absence have not been given their proper allotments. Nehemiah straightens out this matter as well. In verse 14, like verses 22 and 31 in this chapter, Nehemiah asks that God remember these righteous acts and credit them to him for goodness. A similar statement appears earlier (5:19).

Sabbath observance has grown lax in Nehemiah's absence. There is extended economic activity and dealings with food markets on the Sabbath, contrary to laws prohibiting this. Nehemiah orders that this cease immediately. He reminds the people that it is just for these kinds of Sabbath violations that Israel had been punished in the past (cf. Jer 17:19–27; Ezek 20:12–24).

Marriage with foreign women appears as a concern towards the close of chapter 13. Nehemiah is quite adamant in his opposition to this practice. As noted in the chapter on the book of Ruth, Ruth may have been written in part to present the view that not all marriages with foreigners were disastrous for Israel.[18]

The book ends with a summary of his latest acts and the aforementioned brief prayer to God. "Thus I cleansed them from everything foreign, and I established the duties of the priests and Levites . . . Remember me, O my God, for good" (vv. 30–31).

> The line "Remember me, O my God, for good" (Neh 13:31) and similar expressions in Neh 13:14, 22, and [31], whatever their function in the Nehemiah Memoir, call attention in the canonical context to the virtue of Nehemiah, wall-builder and reformer of the community. At the same time, Nehemiah 13 reminds the reader that even the best intentions of the perfect community under ideal leadership (see the ceremonies in Nehemiah 8–10) can fail and the people can lapse into sin. While the people confessed in chap. 9 that God's saving goal for them had not yet been achieved, the final chapter of Nehemiah concedes that the behavior of the restored community, too, is never fully perfected and often in need of reform. The real circumstances in which people live—still under Persian rulership and in imperfection—set limits to the salvation that God gives in fulfillment of his promises. The author leaves unresolved the relationship between the present and the future in the divine plan of salvation.[19]

---

18. The author of the book of Ruth "wished to show that a non-Israelite could become a faithful worshipper of the LORD. This would counter the books of Ezra and Nehemiah, both of which consider intermarriage wrong (see Ezra chs 9 and 10; Neh 10.30). Like the books of Jonah and Isaiah chs 40–55, Ruth affirms that the concern of the LORD extends beyond the people of Israel to people of every nation." *NOAB*, 332.

19. Klein, "Books of Ezra-Nehemiah," 2:741.

Nehemiah in the Christian Scriptures

Ezra's prayer to God, which acknowledges God as the creator of heaven and earth (Neh 9:6), is echoed in a human prayer in Acts and an angelic one in Revelation (Acts 4:24; Rev 10:6).

Ezra's prayer refers to God's providing food for the Israelites in the desert (Neh 9:15), and at Capernaum the crowds come to Jesus and mention that God provided manna for the people in the desert (John 6:31).

Nehemiah 10:37 is the list of what the people obligate themselves to do, including bringing the first of the dough, fruit, wine, oil, and so on. In his message in Romans, Paul uses the image of dough and first fruits. "If the part of the dough offered as first fruits is holy, then the whole batch is holy" (Rom 11:16).

Toward the close of Ezra's prayer, recognizing the distressful condition of those in Jerusalem, he says, "Here we are, slaves to this day—slaves in the land that you gave to our ancestors to enjoy its fruit and its good gifts" (Neh 9:36). That memory of servitude, much less the servitude in Egypt, is denied by the people when they say to Jesus, "We are descendants of Abraham and have never been slaves to anyone" (John 8:33). Jesus, however, is speaking metaphorically, and replies, "Very truly, I tell you, everyone who commits sin is a slave to sin" (John 8:34).

N. T. Wright suggests that

> the great majority of Jesus' contemporaries believed that they were still in exile, in all the senses that really mattered. They would have shared the view expressed by Ezra and Nehemiah: though we are back in our own land, we are still slaves ["Here we are, slaves to this day—slaves in the land that you gave to our ancestors to enjoy its fruit and its good gifts" (9:36)]. In so far as Jesus' work offers a sense of location and condition, it represents the long-awaited news that the slaves were at last being freed. The meek would inherit the land; the hungry and thirsty would be satisfied [Matt 5:5f.; Luke 6:21]."[20]

Nehemiah in Rabbinic Literature

Nehemiah is a prophet. Nehemiah can be considered a prophet, because he is guided by the holy spirit (*Babylonian Talmud Berakhot* 13a).

---

20. Wright, *Jesus and the Victory of God*, 445.

Nehemiah is Zerubbabel. Punning on the word *zerua* ("born," lit. "sown") in Babylon (*Babel*), the rabbis say Nehemiah was Zerubbabel (*Babylonian Talmud Sanhedrin* 38a).

Nehemiah narrates the book of Ezra. The whole subject matter [of the book] of Ezra is narrated by Nehemiah son of Hachalia; why then is the book not called by his name? Rabbi Jeremiah bar Abba says: Because he claims merit for himself (i.e., he was immodest), as it is written, "Remember for my good . . . all that I have done" (5:19) . . . Rabbi Joseph says: Because he spoke disparagingly of his predecessors, as it is written, "The former governors . . . laid heavy burdens . . . of silver" (5:15). Moreover, he spoke thus even of Daniel, who was greater than he (because Daniel alone saw a vision; Dan 10:7) (*Babylonian Talmud Sanhedrin* 93b).

Nehemiah sets Sabbath prohibitions. Certain rulings set by Nehemiah concerning the Sabbath are confirmed by the Mishnah (Neh 13:15) (*Babylonian Talmud Shabbat* 123b).

Nehemiah and Chronicles. While Ezra begins the book of Chronicles, Nehemiah completes it (*Babylonian Talmud Baba Batra* 15a).

Although Israel rebels, God does not forsake them. Balaam rhetorically tells Balak, "How can I curse whom God has not cursed?" (Num 23:8). The proof comes from Nehemiah. "Even when they had cast an image of a calf for themselves and said, 'This is your God who brought you up out of Egypt,' and had committed great blasphemies, you [God] in your great mercies did not forsake them in the wilderness" (Neh 9:18–19) (*Midrash Numbers Rabbah* 20.19).

Each person has strengths. Ezra was supreme in Torah; Nehemiah in worldly affairs. Each balanced out the strengths of the other (*Babylonian Talmud Gittin* 59a; *Sanhedrin* 36a).

A liturgical connection. Part of Ezra's prayer praising God as creator, preserver, and redeemer is part of the liturgy of the traditional morning service (9:6–11) (see the Text Study at the end of this chapter, "Ezra's Penitential Prayer").

Text Study

Nehemiah 2:9-20; Setting Out; Inspecting Jerusalem[21]

Verse 9. Chapter 2 begins with Nehemiah approaching King Artaxerxes and getting consent to go to Judah. There is no description of Nehemiah's journey, but the text notes that he was supported with army officers and cavalry.

Verse 10. Appropriately, Nehemiah informs the local officials of his presence. They are displeased that someone has taken up the cause of the people of Israel.

Verses 11-16. Nehemiah pauses three days before he begins his clandestine night reconnaissance of Jerusalem. He wants to get his bearings and be settled in before his inspection. Nehemiah takes but a few people with him. He mentions that he took along the animal that he rode, probably a donkey. He leaves by the Valley Gate and returns by that structure as well. He inspects the "walls of Jerusalem that had been broken down and its gates that had been destroyed by fire" (v. 13, see also vv. 3-5). Several specific structures are mentioned in addition to the Valley Gate: the Dragon's Spring, the Dung Gate, the Fountain Gate, and the King's Pool. Although the book of Nehemiah is rich in topographical information about ancient Jerusalem, there is not a scholarly consensus that identifies all of these places.

In verse 14 there is a note that there is not even enough clearance for Nehemiah's animal to pass through the debris.

Nehemiah is chary and cautious. He does not inform the local non-Jewish officials that he is planning this inspection. He also keeps his plan from the "Jews, the priests, the nobles, the officials and the rest that were to do the work" (v. 16). The Jews in this verse refers to the common people, for clearly the priests, nobles, and the officials also were Jewish.

Verses 17-18. Nehemiah now informs the local citizens of Judah what he plans to do, and they enthusiastically support his ideas for the rebuilding.

Verses 19-20. When the non-Jewish Persian-appointed officials (Sanballat the Horonite, Tobiah the Ammonite official, and Geshem the Arab) learn of Nehemiah's plans, they oppose his reconstruction efforts, suggesting that he is formulating rebellion. He replies that the "God of heaven" will give Nehemiah and his supporters success, and that Sanballat, Tobiah, and Geshem, as outsiders, "have no share or claim or historic right in Jerusalem."

---

21. As noted earlier, for a sketch of Jerusalem, see Myers, *Ezra-Nehemiah*, 118.

Nehemiah 9:6–37; Ezra's Penitential Prayer

Ezra's prayer divides into several uneven sections, but there are seven divisions—an appropriate number for a priest.

i. *Verse 6.* God alone creates the heavens and the earth, and all that is in them; God preserves these entities as well.

ii. *Verses 7–8.* God chooses Abraham, brings him to the land, finds his heart faithful (presumably a reference to Gen 22, the binding of Isaac), and promises this land to Abraham and his descendants. God fulfills divine promises and is righteous.

iii. *Verses 9–15.* God sees the distress of the ancestors in Egypt, performs signs and wonders against Pharaoh and his courtiers, divides the Sea of Reeds so that the Israelites pass through on dry land, leads them by a pillar of cloud by day and a pillar of fire by night, comes to them at Mt Sinai, gives them the sacred commandments including the Sabbath, and feeds them in the desert.

iv. *Verses 16–23.* In recounting the failures of the ancestors in the desert, their rebelliousness, presumptuous, and stiff-necked behaviors, Ezra points his finger at his own contemporaries. Nonetheless, God shows the ancestors steadfast mercy, and sustains them in the wilderness for forty years, multiplying their descendants like the stars of heaven, and bringing them to the land that they are about to possess.

v. *Verses 24–25.* The ancestors possess the land, subdue the local inhabitants, and take possession of "all sorts of goods, hewn cisterns, vineyards, olive orchards, and fruit trees in abundance."

vi. *Verses 26–31.* "Nevertheless they were disobedient and rebelled against you and cast your law behind their backs" (v. 26). They kill the prophets sent by God. God gives them into the hands of their enemies, who make them suffer. They cry out to God, and God saves them from their distress. Again they are presumptuous and rebellious. Still, God does not forsake them.

vii. *Verses 32–37.* Ezra describes God as great, mighty, and awesome, keeping covenant and steadfast love. Ezra speaks of the hardships brought by the Assyrian kings (presumably including the Babylonians as well). Ezra praises God as being "just in all that has come upon us" (v. 33) but acknowledges that the people have "acted wickedly" by not heeding the commandments or keeping God's laws. Ezra concludes by saying that here they are now, "slaves to this day—slaves in the land that you gave to our ancestors to enjoy its fruits and its good gifts," and that the people again "are in great distress" (vv. 36–37).

Several things are notable in this address. Ezra recounts the failings of the people's past, but also that each time God brings relief. Therefore, there is an expectation that once again God will redeem them. Ezra also reminds the people that their acting wickedly is, regretfully, repeated behavior.

What is interesting, however, is what Ezra does not say, or more particularly, whom Ezra does not mention. While Abraham is named, conspicuously missing are the names of Isaac, Jacob, and Joseph. There are no women's names. Moses is mentioned, but only once (v. 14). Joshua and the names of all the judges are missing; indeed the word "judge" does not appear. While the kings of the desert experience, Sihon of Heshbon and Og of Bashan, are noted, incredibly, neither David nor Solomon appear, nor does Hezekiah or Josiah. While the generic term "prophets" appears, Isaiah, Jeremiah, Ezekiel, Amos, Hosea, and Micah all are absent by name.

13

Chronicles (1 and 2)

Introduction

THE CHRONICLER WRITES A history of Israel, but it is history with a purpose. He did not want merely to recall the events described in Samuel and Kings, although he repeats much of the same data. This author is living in a country that is nominally a vassal of the Persian Empire, and is ruled by a governor appointed by Persia. There is no present Israelite monarch, nor does there seem to be any chance there will be another in the foreseeable future. Living at the time of the close of the fifth century BCE, or perhaps toward the beginning of the fourth century (c. 400 or thereafter), the Chronicler understood that the

> political aspect of the Davidic line had come to an end and there was no hope of re-establishment, at least not so far as he could see. Hope for Israel lay in the fortification of the religious institutions that survived the tragic experiences of 597 B.C. and the long years of Exile . . .
>
> Despite the fact that it had almost ceased to exist, the Davidic house was important for the Chronicler. So was his kingdom. Hence the Davidic monarchy receives full treatment and David himself is given quite extensive coverage . . . His chief concern . . . was Jerusalem and the Jewish community, with the Davidic line on the throne of Judah only an important episode . . .
>
> [Consequently he took] hold of the Davidic institutions—Jerusalem, the temple, the cultus—through which the people of the Lord could operate as a community once more.[1]

1. Myers, *1 Chronicles*, xxx–xxxi. Thanks to my friend and colleague Rabbi Dr.

The term cult, or cultus, in this context is used as a synonym for the religion/religious rites of Judaism of that day.

As Sara Japhet explains, the goal of Chronicles "is a comprehensive expression of the perpetual need to renew and revitalize the religion of Israel."[2] For example, in 1 Chronicles 23, the numbers of Levites far exceeds that which is found in the Torah. The Chronicler seeks to portray these levitical orders as broadly as possible, both in terms of their numbers and their organization.[3] The Levites' obligations include such traditional tasks as guarding the priests and the tent of meeting against any kind of lay intrusion. Yet, in addition duties include responsibility for "ritual cleanliness, 'the purity of all sacred objects' (v. 28), and for maintaining a system of balanced measures (v. 29)." The Levites likewise have responsibility for the temple gates. In addition to merely guarding, "the Levites are responsible for the musical liturgy: 'to give thanks and to praise Yhwh' every morning and evening and during the festivals (vv. 30–31). Such a mandate for the Levites was previously established by David vis-à-vis the ark ([1 Chr] 16:1–38)."[4]

The Judeans are living under Persian suzerainty; they understand that a call for the reestablishment of a Davidic dynasty would have been regarded as seditious.

> What then becomes of the Davidic monarchy? Here it would seem the Chronicler is offering an interpretation of that monarchy. Its true function is to be seen in relation to the temple and its worship, and as the expression of a united people . . . The loss of the kingship led to a renewed understanding of its more ultimate meaning . . . less political interpretation . . . With this non-political interpretation of the monarchy, the Chronicler shows himself to be sensitive to the situation in which the Jewish community found itself . . . a repeated emphasis on the providential care which is evident in the activity of the Persian rulers. Cyrus decreed the rebuilding of the temple; when it was questioned, Darius confirmed it even more generously (Ezra I, 6).[5]

Moshe Reiss for valuable exchanges of ideas about Chronicles. See Moshe Reiss and David J. Zucker, (2013) "Chronicles as Revisionist Religious History," *The Asbury Journal*: Vol. 68: No. 2, p. 120–33.

2. Japhet, *I and II Chronicles*, 49. "The Chronicler shaped his material to highlight the continuity within the community of faith." Childs, *Introduction to the Old Testament*, 655. For the Chronicler, the "sanctity of the new Temple was no less than the sanctity of the Tabernacle that Moses constructed in the desert." Kalimi, *Reshaping of Ancient Israelite History*, 226.

3. Japhet, *I and II Chronicles*, 412.

4. Knoppers, *1 Chronicles 10-29*, 825.

5. Ackroyd, *Israel Under Babylon and Persia*, 299–300.

The Chronicler certainly is aware of, and has before him, the narratives of Samuel and Kings.[6] The Chronicler did not regard Samuel-Kings as canonical or immutable. "On the contrary, these books served him as raw material to be manipulated as he saw fit: he adapted them, adding to them and deleting from them in accordance with his ideological-theological outlook, his literary and historiographical methods, and his linguistic and stylistic taste."[7] He borrows heavily from 1 Samuel 25 (late in the reign of Saul, c. 1001 BCE), 2 Samuel (the reign of David, c. 1000–961 BCE), and both books of Kings, beginning with the reign of Solomon and then moving on to the destruction of Jerusalem by the Babylonians in 586 BCE. He also writes a bit about life during the exilic, and post-exilic periods. While the primary sources are Samuel and Kings, the Chronicler also relies on some records in Genesis, Numbers, and Nehemiah.[8] Further, it is clear that the Chronicler has sources of information independent of what is now in the Hebrew Bible.

Originally, the current two books of Chronicles were one book. By the sixteenth century CE, with the advent of printed Hebrew Bibles, the books were divided into two sections, following the precedent of the Septuagint and Vulgate translations.

The two books of Chronicles are collectively the twelfth and thirteenth—and coincidentally, the final—books in the third section of the Hebrew Bible, the Writings/*Ketuvim* (see Introduction: "The Order of the Books of the Bible"). They follow Ezra and Nehemiah. In the Christian

---

6. For the Chronicler, "the most frequently used canonical source is the Samuel-Kings corpus from the Deuteronomistic History," however, the "Chronicler's use of Samuel-Kings is, of course, selective. For his depiction of David he utilized those materials ... that would enhance David's qualifications as builder of the temple or highlight his position as a victorious and powerful king. Thus he omitted most of the narrative commonly known as the History of David's Rise (1 Samuel 16–2 Samuel 5), in which David gradually gained ascendancy over Saul and kingship over all Israel, and almost all of the Succession Narrative (2 Samuel 9–20; 1 Kings 1–2) ... These omissions are probably not the cover-up they are sometimes portrayed to be, since the Chronicler could have presupposed that his readers already knew these stories. Rather, the Chronicler selected only those passages for his account of David that fit his positive agenda. Similarly, passages about the northern kingdom were omitted unless interaction with the south required their inclusion (e.g., 2 Chr 18:2–34, the joint campaign of Ahab and Jehoshaphat). At times his selective citations ignored the original context." Klein, "Book of 1–2 Chronicles," 1:996.

7. Kalimi, *Reshaping of Ancient Israelite History*, 7; see also 409.

8. The exact dating of the rulers of Judah and Israel are notoriously difficult to ascertain. The dates in this chapter follow the suggestions in *NOAB*, based on the research of Albright, "Chronology Tables of Rulers," 338–39.

For a detailed description of parallel sources for Chronicles, see Myers, *1 Chronicles*, xlix–lxii.

Bible, 1 and 2 Chronicles are part of the section of the historical books. They follow Kings and precede Ezra, Nehemiah, and Esther.

Scholars sometimes speak of the Ezra-Nehemiah-Chronicles narratives.[9]

The Chronicler and the Deuteronomists

Theologically, the Chronicler considers God in a similar way as the Deuteronomistic historians. God is an active deity, vitally interested and involved in the life of the people of Israel.[10]

Yet, the Chronicler differs from the Deuteronomists (Deuteronomistic historians) in several ways (see the sections on "Deuteronomistic History" in the chapters on Judges and Kings in the companion volume *The Bible's PROPHETS*). He presents a different viewpoint from the Deuteronomists because his worldview is shaped by conditions that the earlier group was unable to envision. The Deuteronomists conclude their work 150–200 years earlier (c. 550 BCE, as opposed to the Chronicler's day, c. 400–350 BCE). The writings of the Deuteronomists were edited in the Exile in Babylon, before the fall of that empire.

The Deuteronomists hope for a political and religious restoration led by a descendant of David. That is their expectation, but they know it is not in the near future. The Chronicler, by way of contrast, feels that hope for Israel is directly linked to religious, not political institutions.

By way of example, in the writings of the Deuteronomistic historian in Kings we are given the formulaic words, "For [God] they are your very own people that you freed from Egypt from the midst of the iron furnace . . . For you . . . God have set them apart for yourself from all the peoples of the earth . . . as you promised through Moses your servant" (1 Kgs 8:51–53). When the Chronicler tells this tale, "he cannot accept that the people of Israel became the people of God through a single act at a particular point of history."[11] Israel became God's people over many years as they developed a relationship. David was a key character in forming the ongoing bonds with God. As Knoppers writes, Chronicles "neither stresses the Exodus and Conquest nor ties these events to the founding of Israel as a

---

9. Japhet, "The Relationship between Chronicles and Ezra-Nehemiah," in *From the Rivers of Babylon*, 169–82.

10. Myers, *1 Chronicles,* lxiv.

11 Japhet, *I and II Chronicles,* 600.

nation ... [Chronicles] does not associate the Exodus with the crystallization of Israel's corporate identity."[12]

There are clear connections between Chronicles and the books of Samuel and Kings, and yet "salient ideological concepts in *Chronicles* set it apart from the earlier books. The greater voice given to the popular voice in public life indicates the evolving belief that the king must answer to the people (1 Chr. 13.1). The concept of reward and punishment based solely on the deeds or misdeeds of each generation (in contrast to the *Book of Kings*, in which punishment is cumulative from one generation to the next) seems to reflect the teachings of the exilic prophet Ezekiel."[13] Ezekiel prophesies early in the sixth century as part of the exilic community. He stresses individual over inherited responsibility/guilt (Ezek 3:16–21; 18; 33:1–20).

Chronicles includes the names of several women (often of royal families) not mentioned in the Deuteronomic histories. It also abbreviates or ignores certain episodes involving women that did appear in Samuel-Kings,[14] such as the narratives of Saul and the witch of Endor (1 Sam 28), Abigail and David (1 Sam 25), Bathsheba and David (2 Sam 11–12), and Bathsheba and the succession controversy (1 Kgs 1–2).

The Title; Contents

The Hebrew title for Chronicles is *Divrei ha-yamim*. This can translate as "matters of the days," "records of the times," or euphemistically "the chronicles of events." *Divrei ha-yamim* as a phrase is found only once in Chronicles (1 Chr 27:24), although it appears also in the allied book of Nehemiah (Neh 12:23). The one use of that expression contrasts with the fact that it is used over thirty times in the book of Kings, describing the record of the kings of Judah and Israel.

Chronicles relates the narrative of the story of Israel the people, from its origins in antiquity—indeed from creation itself—over thousands of years to the time of the Persian Empire. Chronicles contains many genealogies. It begins with Adam, and takes matters through the patriarchs, mentioning specifically Abraham and Isaac, although the Chronicler rarely mentions Jacob by that name, using instead the term Israel (e.g., "These are the sons of Israel: Reuben, Simeon, Levi, Judah"; 1 Chr 2:1). First Chronicles 3 takes the line of David from his firstborn son down to the time of the Chronicler.

12 Knoppers, *1 Chronicles 1–9*, 81.

13. Glatt-Gilad, "Book of Chronicles," 160.

14. Laffey, "1 and 2 Chronicles," 114–15. "Chronicles ... overwrites, effaces, and erases women." Mitchell, "1 and 2 Chronicles," 186.

Chapters 4–8 return to the genealogical table of the twelve tribes, but it does not list them in their traditional birth order. Beginning with Judah and Simeon, it moves to the descendants of Reuben, Gad, and the half-tribe of Manasseh.[15] This is followed by lists of the Levites, the descendants of Issachar, Benjamin, Naphtali, Ephraim, and Asher. There are no lineage listings for Zebulon or Dan.

While chapter 9 turns to the names of those who returned to Judah after the Babylonian Exile, suddenly beginning in verse 35 there is a repetition from chapter 8, with slight variations in wording, listing the line of Saul. This Saul lineage makes some sense, however, because beginning in chapter 10 the Chronicler moves to a history of Israel from the time of Saul to that of David. The narrative devoted to David and his reign is the major focus of the rest of 1 Chronicles and covers nearly twenty chapters, from the midst of chapter 10 through chapter 29.

Second Chronicles follows naturally on the words of 1 Chronicles. The first nine chapters are devoted to the reign of King Solomon. Solomon is a revered figure for the Chronicler. He is almost as idealized as David. Solomon's claim to glory is that he built the temple in Jerusalem. Chapters 10–36 continue with the history of Israel in the post-Solomonic world, the time of the divided kingdom, in which separate is certainly not equal. "As little notice as possible is given to the northern kingdom, which was [in the mind of the Chronicler] irredeemably false to God . . . Instead, the Chronicler pictures Judah as a kingdom with holy space (the temple) and holy servants (the priests, prophets and temple singers) at its center, and kings who are supposed to rule under stringent obligations to God."[16] These kings, with notable exceptions such as Hezekiah and Josiah, are not God-fearing. National upheavals and disasters befall Judah, eventually resulting in the destruction of the Jerusalem temple, the final days of the Davidic kingdom, and the Babylonian Exile. The book, however, concludes on a note of hope. God is the God of history. Under God's benevolent direction, Cyrus of Persia not only allows the exiles to return, but facilitates the rebuilding of the temple. Chronicles ends with this optimistic word: "Thus says King Cyrus of Persia: the LORD, the God of heaven, has given me all the kingdoms of the earth, and he has charged me to build him a house at Jerusalem, which is in Judah. Whoever is among you of all his people, may the LORD his God be with him! Let him go up" (2 Chr 36:23).

---

15. Manasseh and Ephraim were the sons of Joseph, and became tribal heads. Technically, there is no landed tribe of Joseph or Levi (the Levites included the priests and the assistants to the priests).

16. NOAB, Introduction to 2 Chronicles, 538.

These words then link naturally into the narratives of the books of Ezra and Nehemiah. The chapters in this volume devoted to Ezra and Nehemiah provide the historical context for the period at the end of Chronicles and the century following.

Authorship; Dating Chronicles; Historicity

Chronicles was authored by either an individual or by members of a school of thought that flourished around 400 BCE. Some scholars assert that Ezra, Nehemiah, and Chronicles share the same author, or at least they come out of a similar context or school.[17]

There are, however, compelling reasons to doubt that these books share similar authorship. To note one important point, "Scholars are almost unanimous in their opinion that the hallmark of the Chronicler is the emphasis on David . . . [but] although David dominates Chronicles, he is relatively unimportant in Ezra-Nehemiah . . . therefore . . . indicating different authors." Further, David's son "Solomon, far from being idealized, as he is in Chronicles, appears in Ezra-Nehemiah as a paradigm of sin (Neh 13:26)."[18]

Dates for Chronicles vary, but there is some consensus among modern scholars that it fits either later in the Persian period or early in the Hellenistic era, c. 400–300 BCE.[19]

As to the historicity of these books, they are history, but as mentioned in the opening section of this chapter, it is history written with a specific purpose. The Davidic house and kingdom is important for the Chronicler, but the primary concern is Jerusalem and the Jewish community of the late fifth to early–mid fourth century, and what would once again make them a viable community. To the extent that the Davidic institutions—Jerusalem, the temple, the cultus—are important, he stresses them. The Chronicler understands that the Davidic political institution is not viable in his day, nor is it likely to reappear soon, if ever. His concern is the furtherance of the Jewish community.

---

17. For a discussion about the authorship of Chronicles and its possible connections to Ezra-Nehemiah, see Klein, "Book of 1–2 Chronicles."

18. Eskenazi, *In an Age of Prose*, 22.

19. Klein, *1 Chronicles*, 16; see also Japhet, *I and II Chronicles*, 27–28.

The Book of Chronicles

Divisions in the Book of Chronicles

Broadly speaking, Chronicles divides into three major sections:

1 Chronicles 1–9	Prologue
1 Chronicles 10— 2 Chronicles 9	David and Solomon
2 Chronicles 10–36	Primarily the history of the kingdom of Judah

1 Chronicles 1–9; Prologue

Chapter 1 begins with Adam, his son Seth, and then further descendants through Noah and his sons, Shem, Ham, and Japheth. The list then describes first Japheth's sons, then those of Ham, and finally the line of Shem. Verses 27–28 note that Abraham, formerly Abram, had two sons, Isaac and Ishmael.

For the Chronicler, authority *"rested upon family relationships and continuity, both of which were important to maintain the pure religious community in his day. To him these lists were not just dry family registers; they represented living persons in the great chain of Israel's religious history."*[20] These lists have the same general purpose as do the genealogy lists in the Christian Scriptures, in the Gospels of Matthew and Luke, which link Adam to David to Jesus as the Messiah.

Abraham's descendants through Ishmael are listed, and then are followed by his offspring by Keturah (Gen 25:1ff.). After noting that Isaac's sons are Esau and Israel,[21] the list then follows the Esau line for several more verses to close out the chapter. These are selective genealogies, in that not every line is followed.

Chapter 2 begins with the list of Israel's (Jacob's) twelve sons, but they are not in strict birth order.

Several verses follow the Judah line. Judah's descendants are of particular interest for several reasons. They are the ancestors of the country of Judah, which is where the Chronicler presumably lives. This genealogy includes David, and these are likely to be the ancestors of the Chronicler himself.

Next comes the list of names that specifically mentions David and his siblings, his sisters Zeruiah and Abigail, as well as his six brothers (vv. 13–16). Several verses follow the dynasty of Caleb. This is important to the

---

20. Myers, *1 Chronicles*, 6 (emphasis added).

21. The Chronicler consistently uses the term Israel for Jacob (Jacob's other name, cf. Gen 32:28; 35:10), with two exceptions: 1 Chr 16:13, 17.

Chronicler because it mentions Bezalel, who was instrumental in building the ark and other sacred furniture at the time of Moses (Exod 31:2ff.; 35:30ff. et al.) Several other lines are followed.

The Davidic dynasty from the time of David to the exile and beyond forms the content of chapter 3.[22] Here, as in earlier genealogies, some wives and daughters are listed, including Ahinoam, Abigail, Maacah, Abital, Eglah, Bath-shua, Tamar, and Shelomith (vv. 1, 2, 3, 5, 9, 19).

Chapter 4 contains the southern tribal lists, primarily those associated with Judah, but also the tribe of Simeon, which eventually became absorbed into the Judah line. While the emphasis is on male names, including that of Jabez (vv. 9–10), females are mentioned, including Hazzelelponi, Helah, Naarah, and Bithiah daughter of Pharaoh (vv. 3, 5, 17).

Chapter 5 features the Reubenite line, as well as descendants of Gad and the half-tribe of Manasseh.

The Levite dynasty list is the subject of chapter 6 (in the Hebrew Bible, Masoretic Text, the Levite line begins in 1 Chr 5:27). The opening verses begin with Levi himself and continue with his descendants, including the important names of Aaron, Moses, and Miriam; followed by the Aaronide priestly line through Jehozadak, who was sent into exile at the time of the temple's destruction. Specific mention is made of a priest Azariah, "who served as priest in the house that Solomon built in Jerusalem" (1 Chr 6:10 [5:36 H]). Several verses are devoted to other Levites who were not priests, followed by a group of Levitical singers (1 Chr 6:31–48 [6:16–33 H]). The rest of the chapter mentions both descendants of Aaron who are priests with special functions, and the territorial location of various Aaronide and other Levitical families. Chapter 6 is the longest chapter in Chronicles, whether in Jewish or Christian versions (66 or 81 verses respectively). The importance for the Chronicler of these Levitical names is evident.

Chapter 7 turns to the northern tribes of Issachar, Naphtali, Manasseh, Ephraim, and Asher, but it also includes the line of Benjamin.

Chapter 8 features the Benjamin line, including Saul and his sons. This list, as with others, contains the names of some wives, including Hushim, Baara, Hodesh, and Maacah (vv. 8, 9, 29).

Those who returned from Babylon are the major subject matter of chapter 9. The chapter begins with a verse that serves as a conclusion to the previous chapter. "So all Israel was enrolled by genealogies; and these are written in the Book of the Kings of Israel. And Judah was taken into exile in Babylon because of their unfaithfulness" (v. 1). Of note is the reference to the "Book of the Kings of Israel," by which the Chronicler means

---

22. For a schema of the Davidic line in 1 Chr 3, see Myers, *1 Chronicles*, 22.

both the northern and southern kingdoms. It clearly refers to material found in the books of Samuel and Kings, since the books of Samuel list Saul and David's monarchies.

Typical of the interest of the Chronicler, chapter 9 quickly mentions not only Israelites, who are laity, but priests, Levites, and temple servants (v. 2).

Verse 3 likewise contains important information. It reads, "And some of the people of Judah, Benjamin, Ephraim, and Manasseh lived in Jerusalem." Ephraim and Manasseh are a euphemism for the northern tribes. Back in the days of the divided kingdoms, these tribes lived separately as part of the northern kingdom. They are not associated with Jerusalem, but now, in the time of the Chronicler, they are part of Judah and Jerusalem.

Chapter 9 closes out the genealogies that begin with Adam and continue through the return of the exiles. Technically, the Chronicler returns to the line of Saul at the end of the chapter, because this serves as a bridge to what follows, which will be a history of the monarchy and some of the attendant institutions.

1 Chronicles 10—2 Chronicles 9; David and Solomon

The opening lines of chapter 10 return to the final days of the monarchy of Saul. The Philistines and Israel are at war again. The enemy presses its advantage, and Saul is wounded mortally. Rather than be abused by the Philistines, Saul commits suicide, falling on his sword (v. 4). When the Philistines find Saul's body, they desecrate it. There are some discrepancies between this account and that in 1 Samuel 31. The Chronicler then concludes this chapter with some unfavorable remarks about Saul (vv. 13–14). These criticisms reflect the theology and values of the Chronicler (see the Text Study at the close of this chapter, "Exit Saul; Enter David".) The closing words are important. "Therefore the LORD put [Saul] to death and turned the kingdom over to David son of Jesse" (v. 14).

Chapter 11 presents David's rise to power. The opening verses are a ringing endorsement of David and his monarchy. True to his purpose, the Chronicler simply ignores the years of conflict between David and Saul, and the seven years David rules at Hebron while Saul's living sons are the nominal successors to their father. David and the Davidic kingdom are the theological ideal for the Chronicler.

The Chronicler makes subtle but important changes in his recounting of past events. Second Samuel 5:6 says that David and "his men marched to Jerusalem against the Jebusites." In 1 Chronicles 11, the parallel passage reads, "David *and all Israel* marched to Jerusalem . . . where the Jebusites were" (v. 4; emphasis added). "By this slight twist he indicates that 'all Israel' had a share in the capture of the city which became the holy city and the place of the temple, the religious as well as political focus of the kingdom."[23]

Jerusalem becomes known as the City of David because David first captures it and then resides there. This section ends with the descriptive endorsement that "David became greater and greater, for the LORD of hosts was with him" (v. 9).

The rest of chapter 11 names David's mighty warriors.

Chapter 12 is a long and somewhat exaggerated list in terms of the numbers of fighting men who join with David, both at Hebron and earlier at Ziklag. The large numbers of fighting men, listed in the thousands, has a possible solution. It is likely that the Hebrew word for thousand, *elef*, may also be a term for a contingent or a unit.[24]

Chapter 13 considers the initial attempt by David to bring the ark of God to Jerusalem. As in the Samuel account, while the ark's transfer to Jerusalem is begun, it does not arrive in the holy city. Several interesting items appear in this chapter. In the parallel passage in Samuel, David gathers his military supporters, and they bring the ark towards Jerusalem (2 Sam 6:1-2). This is a political move. In Chronicles, David speaks "to the whole assembly of Israel" and suggests that they include "the priests and the Levites" in the enterprise. The text then explains that the "whole assembly agreed to do so" for this was pleasing for "all the people" (1 Chr 13:2, 4). The Chronicles version includes not only the leaders of the cultus, but "all the people," not just a select group of David's warriors.

David's early reign in Jerusalem and his additional wives and children form part of chapter 14. The information that King Hiram of Tyre sends cedar logs, masons, and carpenters to build a house of David precedes a list of the names of David's sons and daughters. The chapter likewise details various skirmishes that David has with the Philistine forces. On each occasion, David consults with God, seeking advice on whether or not to attack. In one instance, God not only offers consent but also suggests what proves to be a successful strategy. It follows naturally that as Chronicles relates, "The fame of David went out into all lands, and the LORD brought the fear of him on all nations" (1 Chr 14:17).

---

23. Ibid., 85.

24. Myers (ibid., 98) points to G. E. Mendelhall's article "The Census Lists of Numbers 1 and 26," which proposes elef/1000 not as a thousand, but as a word for "unit" or the like.

The same problem surrounds the issue of how many people left Egypt with Moses. The traditional number is 600,000 men, plus women, children, and animals. See the companion volume Zucker, *The Torah*, 77-78, and the sources listed there in the endnotes.

Chapter 15 details David's second attempt to bring the ark to his capital. From the first verse on, it is clear that David wants to bring the ark to Jerusalem. While he "built houses for himself in the city of David," he also prepares a place for the "ark of God" by pitching a tent for it (v. 1). Respectful of religious authority, "David commanded that no one but the Levites were to carry the ark of God, for the LORD had chosen them to carry the ark of the LORD" (v. 2). David assembles "all Israel in Jerusalem" to bring—or more accurately to accompany the bringing of—the ark. David gathers together not only the descendants of Aaron and the Levites but also the priests Zadok and Abiathar. Many of the specific names of these Levites are mentioned (vv. 3–12).

Mindful of pageantry, David commands the "chiefs of the Levites to appoint their kindred as the singers to play on musical instruments, on harps and lyres and cymbals, to raise loud sounds of joy" (v. 16). Verses 17–24 list about forty Levites engaged in this process.

Chapter 15 basically repeats information recorded in 2 Samuel 6:12–23, in the sense that this earlier passage also describes how the ark is brought to Jerusalem. There are, however, significant differences between the two versions (see the Text Study at the close of this chapter, "Bringing the Ark to Jerusalem: The Viewpoint from Chronicles").

The establishment of the ark in Jerusalem itself is the central focus of chapter 16. After settling the ark inside the tent that David has pitched for it, various sacrifices are offered. Levites are appointed to minister before the ark, and the text provides a list of names. Verses 8–36 contain a psalm of praise to God, led by Asaph and his kindred. The psalm is a composite taken from parts of Psalms 105, 96, and 106.[25]

There is mention of gatekeepers and people playing instruments and singing sacred songs. It is not clear that these functionaries are Levites, but they act in a Levite-like way. This interest with the cultus is typical of the concerns of the Chronicler.

Chapter 17 portrays David as desiring to build a structure for God's ark. David says to the prophet Nathan that while he, the king, is living in a permanent structure, "the ark of the covenant of the LORD is under a tent" (v. 1). Nathan tells David to do what he has in mind, for God is with the monarch. That night, however, God gives instructions to Nathan that David is not to build God's house. God has other plans for him. David is to establish a lasting dynasty. When eventually David dies, God will raise up David's offspring, and will establish his kingdom. "He shall build

---

25. In 1 Chr 16, Asaph's hymn is based on Pss 105:1–15 (vv. 8–22); 96:1–13 (vv. 23–33); 106:1, 47–48 (vv. 35–36).

a house for me, and I will establish his throne forever . . . I will not take my steadfast love from him . . . I will confirm him in my house and in my kingdom forever, and his throne shall be established forever" (vv. 12–14). The closing verses of this chapter essentially repeat 2 Samuel 7:18–29. David gives thanks for the privilege of being God's servant, and requests that God's promise be valid forever.

Chapters 18–20 relate various battles fought by David and his soldiers. These chapters parallel events in 2 Samuel 8 and 10, and selected verses from 2 Samuel 12 and 21. The grouping together of these battles and skirmishes, as well as the materials *omitted* from the parallel sections from Samuel, is quite purposeful on the part of the Chronicler.

In chapter 17 God informs David that he is not the one who will build the temple. God says explicitly that this is because David is a warrior-king, and not a peaceful ruler. There are indications that David's very successes as a military leader preclude his taking on the role of establishing a permanent structure for the ark of God. God's hints are contained in such phrases as "I took you . . . to be ruler over my people Israel . . . I have . . . cut off your all your enemies before you . . . I will subdue all your enemies" (vv. 7–8, 10). That chapters 18–20 then contain various military campaigns makes sense; they follow naturally in this context (see, however, 1 Chr 22, where David is the one who receives the instructions from God about building the temple).

What is even more significant is which materials from 2 Samuel are ignored or excised by the Chronicler. Second Samuel 9 contains a standalone narrative about David first enquiring about and then making arrangements for the welfare of King Saul's descendants. On its literal level, the Samuel account shows David as a caring ruler, reaching out to make sure that Saul's progeny are protected. Another way to read the text is that David wants to make sure that Saul's descendants will not be a threat to him. David wants to know where they are, and whom they are seeing.

The presentation of David, and David's family, is denser and darker in Samuel than it is in Chronicles. David is a powerful and resourceful leader; he captures Jerusalem and he establishes a dynasty that will rule for over four hundred years. David, as many great leaders, is flawed in his moral judgments. He often makes good decisions, but occasionally he makes very bad ones, notably the Bathsheba affair (see the Text Study "David and Bathsheba" in the chapter on Samuel in the companion volume *The Bible's PROPHETS*).

Not only does Chronicles ignore David's acts of assignation and assassination, but it likewise deletes a series of passages in 2 Samuel 13:1—21:17. Missing from the Chronicles text are several narratives that deal largely with the violent side of David and his family. The Chronicler chooses to ignore the sordid rape of David's daughter Tamar, sister of Absalom, by her half-brother Ammon; Absalom's revenge on Ammon, and the necessity of his going into exile (2 Sam 13); Joab, David's general, taking charge of the situation and cunningly arranging for Absalom's repatriation; and then Absalom's ungrateful attitude toward Joab (2 Sam 14). Other material not in Chronicles includes Absalom's conspiracy and rebellion against his father David, and David's being forced to flee (2 Sam 15); Absalom's temporary capture of Jerusalem (2 Sam 16); various skirmishes between Absalom and David, and then eventually Absalom's defeat and death (2 Sam 17–18). David's personal weakness in mourning Absalom, and how Joab needs to remind David of his need to serve as leader; David's regaining Jerusalem; and some further examples of revolts against David (2 Sam 19–20) are also left out by the Chronicler. Missing also are some details of David executing some of Saul's descendants (2 Sam 21).

First Chronicles 21 parallels 2 Samuel 24. Each chapter begins with a census, but with significant differences: in Chronicles, the instigator of David's serious breach of good judgment is not God, but Satan (see the Text Study at the close of this chapter, "Satan in Chronicles"). What is at issue is that David authorized a census. David's loyal general, Joab, strongly advises against such a numbering of the people (for a discussion of the popular sentiment against a census, see the "The Census" section in the companion volume, *The Torah*, 143–44). In terms of the census numbers, it is clear that the crucial term *elef* needs to mean "unit" or some synonym, not "thousand," for certainly there were not over a million men who could draw the sword (1 Chr 21:5; see comments on ch. 12 above).

That the Chronicles version substitutes Satan for God is not the only difference between the accounts. The Chronicles text lacks details found in Samuel, and adds other touches. The Samuel version is much more human centered; the Chronicles version features greater heavenly personnel.

In Samuel, Joab takes close to ten months to conduct the census, and the text lists a number of the areas visited. In Chronicles, Joab simply "went throughout all Israel, and came back to Jerusalem" (v. 4).

In 2 Samuel 24:10 David himself is remorseful and claims his own wrongdoing in conducing a census. In Chronicles, it is God who is displeased and therefore punishes Israel. Only then does David admit that he sinned (vv. 7–8).

In both versions, God communicates some possible punishments for David through David's seer (prophet) Gad. David chooses God's punishment upon the land for three days. In Samuel, God sends a severe pestilence, and many die. Then the text mentions that when "the angel stretched out his hand toward Jerusalem to destroy it, the LORD relented concerning the evil" and reined in this destructive figure (2 Sam 24:16). In Chronicles, God also sends the pestilence. Further, God specifically instructs the angel to destroy Jerusalem (1 Chr 21:15). God again stays the angel's hand, so that it does not destroy the city, but the Chronicles angel is a much more frightening figure. In both versions, David sees the angel and then claims that he, as king, is the one responsible for the wrongdoing, not the people of Israel.

In Samuel David merely sees the angel standing by a threshing floor owned by a local Jebusite (2 Sam 24:16–17).[26] In Chronicles, however, while David also sees the angel by the threshing floor, there are further details. "David looked up and saw the angel of the LORD standing between earth and heaven, and in his hand a drawn sword stretched out over Jerusalem." In Samuel, David appears alone. In Chronicles, "David and the elders, clothed in sackcloth, fell on their faces" (1 Chr 21:16).

In Samuel, David's seer Gad tells him to purchase that property and to erect an altar, which David does. In Chronicles, it is the angel of God who instructs Gad to tell David to do this. The negotiations for this property are considerably more elaborate in Chronicles. Then, when David does set up the altar, God "answered him with fire from heaven," and further, "the LORD commanded the angel, and he put his sword back into his sheath," a considerably more dramatic description than its counterpart in Samuel (1 Chr 21:26–27).

God's sending down fire from heaven to consume the burnt offering is reminiscent of the divine approval for Elijah's sacrifices in his contest with the prophets of Baal (1 Kgs 18:38).

First Chronicles 22:1 literally and thematically connects chapters 21 and 22; it states the all-important fact that David said, "Here shall be the house of the LORD God and here the altar of burnt offering for Israel," linking David and the place of the future temple.

Completely new material is featured starting with chapter 22. This previously unreported information continues to the close of 1 Chronicles. This narrative does not appear elsewhere in the Bible. As with Moses, David may bring Israel to the edge of the next stage (for Moses, the Promised Land, for David, the construction of the temple), but he is not personally to direct those events.

Chapter 22 pictures David as a wise parent making arrangements for his child Solomon, who will actually carry through the plans to build the

---

26. There are several discrepancies between the Samuel and the Chronicles accounts in terms of the owner of the threshing floor. In Samuel it is Araunah; in Chronicles his name is Ornan, and Ornan's four sons are mentioned as well. The two names are, however, very similar and may be explained by the Chronicler having a slightly different version of these events than the narrative that became the official canon.

temple. David labels Solomon as "young and inexperienced" and, if one reads between the lines, not qualified to build a house for God, which "must be exceedingly magnificent, famous and glorified throughout all lands" (v. 5). David explains to Solomon that God has said to the older monarch, you "have shed much blood and have waged great wars; you shall not build a house to my name, because you have shed so much blood in my sight on the earth. See, a son shall be born to you; he shall be a man of peace. I will give him peace from all his enemies on every side; for his name shall be Solomon" (vv. 8–9). In the Hebrew a pun is intended here, for the name Solomon and the word for "peace" share the same root letters *(sh-l-m, shin-lamed-mem: Shlomoh* vs. *shalom).*

Chapter 23 commences with David making Solomon king over Israel. There is none of the palace intrigue seen in 1 Kings 1–2. This chapter contains various Levitical lists. It makes clear that the duties of the Levites are to "assist the descendants of Aaron," that is, the priests (v. 28).

The following chapter, 24, contains another list of Levites.

Chapter 25 follows in a similar vein, although here the focus is on the names of the personnel who formed the musical guilds, those who would "prophesy with lyres, harps, and cymbals" (v. 1).

A list of gatekeepers and keepers of the treasury is at the center of chapter 26.

The military, as well as other kinds of civil authorities and their names, forms chapter 27. The closing chapters of 1 Chronicles, 28 and 29, are David's final addresses. These chapters flow more logically as a continuation of chapter 22, but the intervening material contains lists important in the view of the Chronicler.

In chapter 28 David, even though an old man, appears full of vigor. He explains to those "assembled in Jerusalem"—officials of Israel, officials of the tribes, officers of the army, stewards, palace officials, and various warriors—that while he planned to build God's house, the task will fall to Solomon. The speech is self-serving, and at the same time seeks to praise Solomon. Lest there be any doubt of who is in charge, however, the text makes it clear that "David gave his son Solomon the plan of the vestibule of the temple, and of its houses, its treasuries" and other details (v. 11ff.) David's plan goes on in some detail, and then ends with the words, "All this, in writing at the LORD's direction, he made clear to me [to David]—the plan of all the works" (v. 19). The message is clear: do it this way and do not deviate.

The Chronicler's casting David in a Moses-like image, mentioned above in the description of chapter 22, is underscored when David says to Solomon, "Be strong and of good courage, and act. Do not be afraid or dismayed; for the LORD God, my God, is with you. He will not fail you or forsake you" (v. 20). In like manner, Moses had said to Joshua, "Be strong and bold . . . It is the LORD who goes before you. He will be with you; he will not fail your or forsake you. Do not fear or be dismayed" (Deut 31:7-8).

Should the assembled not understand David's message, he repeats key sentiments in chapter 29. Solomon is young and inexperienced; David has provided for the house of God; much of the building cost is borne by David himself. David then asks, who among those present are also willing to offer assistance? Many come forward and make offerings, or perhaps pledges. Verses 10-19 are David's final confession of faith. Then the people anoint and appoint Solomon to take David's place on the throne. David's death is noted, and there is a summary report of the royal record of David's reign.

The second book of Chronicles begins with the reign of Solomon (chs. 1-9), and then the next twenty-eight chapters (10-36) record matters about the monarchies of Israel and Judah, to the time of the destruction of the Jerusalem temple, and the early years of the exile. Chronicles emphasizes the southern kingdom of Judah. For the Chronicler, the division into two kingdoms is a matter of great evil. "For him the Northern Kingdom was conceived in sin, born in iniquity, and nurtured in adultery. There was only one way to salvation for its rulers and people and that was to recognize their sins of defection, humble themselves, and submit to the appointed way of the Lord, which was through the Davidic dynasty and the temple of the Lord at Jerusalem."[27]

The time frame for 2 Chronicles is c. 961-22 BCE (Solomon), 922-586, and then an addendum c. 539/538. The sources for this book come primarily from the book of Kings.[28]

Chapter 1 begins with a statement lauding Solomon, for "God was with him and made him exceedingly great." A few verses later God appears to Solomon at night (but not in a dream, as in the version in 1 Kgs 3) and asks Solomon what should be given to him. Solomon asks for "wisdom and knowledge" so that he can rule well (v. 10). Since he does not ask for material wealth or honor, or for his enemies' lives, nor even for a long life, God grants Solomon his request. In addition, God promises possessions and honor (vv.

---

27. Myers, *1 Chronicles*, xxxiii.

28. For a detailed description of parallel sources for 2 Chronicles, see Myers, *2 Chronicles*, xxiv-xxxi.

As noted earlier, however, while for the Chronicler, "the most frequently used canonical source is the Samuel-Kings corpus from the Deuteronomistic History," the "Chronicler's use of Samuel-Kings is, of course, selective . . . passages about the northern kingdom were omitted unless interaction with the south required their inclusion (e.g., 2 Chr 18:2-34, the joint campaign of Ahab and Jehoshaphat). At times his selective citations ignored the original context." Klein, "Book of 1-2 Chronicles," 1:996.

11–12). The rest of the chapter, addressing the breadth of Solomon's stables, is taken from 1 Kings 10:26–29.

As noted earlier, the bloody battle for the succession of the throne of David, detailed in the early chapters of Kings, is missing from Chronicles. Missing likewise is the episode of Solomon's judgment of the two prostitutes (1 Kgs 3:16–28).

Chapter 2 commences with the statement that "Solomon decided to build a temple for the name of the LORD, and a royal palace for himself " (2:1 [1:18 H]). Solomon, appropriately, speaks of God's greatness, and of his own modesty ("Who am I build a house for him?"; v. 6). As in the parallel passage in Kings, Solomon sends a letter to the ruler of Tyre (here it is Huram; in Kings it is Hiram) and negotiates for cedar, cypress, and algum wood (v. 8 [v. 7 H]) to build the temple. Solomon speaks of building God's house. While David is mentioned in passing, there is no reference to the plans David gave to Solomon. Huram replies that he is sending a skilled artisan to oversee the project.

Chapter 3 describes the building of the "house of the LORD in Jerusalem on Mount Moriah, where the LORD had appeared to his father David, at the place that David had designated, on the threshing floor of Ornan the Jebusite" (v. 1). It differs significantly from the account in 1 Kings 6–7. The Chronicles version is considerably shorter. It uniquely mentions Moriah, the mountain associated with the binding of Isaac (Gen 22). Specific details, such as those pertaining to the cherubim, are more detailed in the Kings narrative.

The temple equipment (the altar, the molten sea set above twelve cast metal oxen, three each facing in the direction of the compass; basins, lampstands, and so on) is the subject of chapter 4. The details here differ somewhat from the parallel account in Kings. The Chronicler, who wants to understand the passage, adds that the purpose of the sea was a place for the priests to wash.[29] The twelve oxen seem to connect with the twelve tribes of Israel.

This was a very elaborate building, with enormous amounts of gold and bronze required for the structure and its furnishings.

Chapter 5 details the celebration surrounding the actual transportation of "the ark of the covenant of the LORD to its place, in the inner sanctuary of the house, in the most holy place, underneath the wings of the cherubim" (v. 7). It follows the description in 1 Kings 8, with the expected addition of a Levite list.

---

29. Kalimi, 83; Japhet, *I and II Chronicles*, 565.

Chapter 6 features Solomon's dedicatory address/prayer. It is taken almost verbatim from 1 Kings 8:12–52. The king first speaks to the people, reminding them that God chose both Jerusalem as the place of divine dwelling and David as the ruler of Israel. He then mentions that while David wanted to build the temple, God explained to David that this task would fall to his son. Lest there be any doubts, Solomon then proclaims, "I have succeeded my father David, and sit on the throne of Israel, as the LORD promised, and have built the house for the name of the LORD, the God of Israel. There I have set the ark, in which is the covenant of the LORD that he made with the people of Israel" (vv. 10–11).

Now Solomon, standing before the altar of God, spreads out his hands and offers a long prayer to God. Notable within this speech is the description of God's omnipresence. "But will God indeed reside with mortals on earth? Even heaven and the highest heaven cannot contain you, how much less this house that I have built!" (v. 18).

Seven petitions, mainly dealing with national affairs, comprise the rest of chapter 6:[30]

Verses 22–23	Community order
Verses 24–25	If Israel sins, is defeated by an enemy, but then repents
Verses 26–27	Drought
Verses 28–31	Famine, plague, pestilence, etc.
Verses 32–33	Foreigners who come should have prayers answered
Verses 34–35	Military success
Verses 36–39	Release from captivity after repentance

As is the case with David's dedication of the altar (see 1 Chr 21:26), chapter 7 indicates that God shows divine approval for Solomon's words by sending fire from heaven to consume the offering. This fiery divine display is not found in the version in 1 Kings 8. God's glory fills the temple. That the "priests could not enter the house of the LORD, because the glory of the LORD filled the LORD's house" (v. 2) is reminiscent of Exodus 40:34–35. The dedication ceremonies are set in the seventh month; they take a full seven days, followed by an eighth day of solemn assembly. Verse 8 refers to "the Festival," one of the titles for the holy period of *Succot*/Booths/Tabernacles. Verses 11–22 parallel 1 Kings 9. They reflect the Deuteronomistic viewpoint: obey God's laws and you will prosper; disobey and follow other gods, and you will be cast out of God's sight and be a byword among all peoples.

---

30. Myers, *2 Chronicles*, 37.

Chapter 8 lists various activities of Solomon. They parallel, with some discrepancies, part of 1 Kings 9. The Chronicler assumes Solomon's marriage to Pharaoh's daughter is known to the reader (cf. 1 Kgs 3:1; 7:8; 9:24). Solomon moves her away from the palace of David, because the latter place is holy. As a foreigner (cf. Ezek 44:9), and perhaps as a woman who might be ritually unclean (cf. Lev 15:19ff.), she must not be in proximity to the sacred temple.

Chapter 9 completes the narrative devoted to Solomon. It is largely taken from the materials that the Chronicler had in hand from 1 Kings 10, the visit of the queen of Sheba. It also details at some length Solomon's wealth. Wisdom and wealth are the hallmarks of Solomon's reign in the mind of the Chronicler. The Chronicler consciously excised 1 Kings 11:1-40, which lists in great detail the excesses of Solomon, in particular Solomon's legion of foreign wives and the fact that these "wives turned away his heart after other gods; and his heart was not true to the LORD his God, as was the heart of his father David" (1 Kgs 11:4). Solomon's wrongdoing and failings fill that chapter. The Chronicler ignores those acts, because he wants to portray Solomon as the heroic builder of the temple. Chapter 9 concludes with Solomon's death and burial, and a notice that his son Rehoboam succeeded him.

2 Chronicles 10-36; Primarily the History of the Kingdom of Judah

Chapters 10-36, as noted earlier, are devoted to the years following Solomon until the destruction of Jerusalem, and the early years of the exile.

Chapter 10 repeats information stated in 1 Kings 12. It details the division of the united monarchy into two separate sections: the ten northern tribes, which become the kingdom of Israel, and the two remaining southern tribes (Judah and Benjamin), which become the kingdom of Judah. It is about 922 BCE. At issue is the burden of taxes, felt to be unduly heavy by the northern tribes. Rehoboam, Solomon's son, seeks advice from the elders, but then rejects it in favor of counsel from his contemporaries. Led by Jeroboam son of Nebat, the northern tribes secede. "When all Israel saw that the king [Rehoboam] would not listen to them, the people answered the king, [with these words,] 'What share do we have in David? We have no inheritance in the son of Jesse. Each of you to your tents, O Israel! Look now to your own house, O David'" (v. 16). Reflecting the Chronicler's own bias, chapter 10 concludes, "so Israel has been in rebellion against the house of David to this day."

Chapter 11 begins with Rehoboam mustering troops to fight against Jeroboam and the northern tribes. Then the word of God comes to Shamaiah, the man of God, who counsels against this action, so it does not take place. Rehoboam, however, builds up a number of cities for defensive purposes. The chapter notes that various Levites from the north come to Jerusalem, either because they are displeased with the religious direction that Jeroboam is taking in the north, or because Jeroboam has excluded them. Rehoboam's various wives and concubines are listed in the final verses of the chapter.

As chapter 12 commences, the text explains that although initially Rehoboam ruled wisely, after several years, once he felt more established, then "he abandoned the law of the LORD." In the mind of the Chronicler, turning from God brings predictable results. King Shishak of Egypt mounts an attack on Judah, fortified by many cavalry. They come as far as Jerusalem. Shamaiah (here called a prophet; see 11:2ff.) explains that this threat stems from the fact that the king and his officers have abandoned God. They take his words seriously, repent, and God limits the punishment meted out by Shishak of Egypt. The text explains that Rehoboam "did evil, for he did not set his heart to seek the LORD" (v. 14). The chapter closes out with an announcement of the king's death and burial, succeeded by his son Abijah (named Abijam in 1 Kgs 14:31; c. 915 BCE).

Much of chapter 13 is without parallel in Kings. King Abijah of Judah leads an attack on the northern kingdom. He delivers a caustic address to Jeroboam and his followers, defining many of them as "worthless scoundrels." Abijah berates them for exiling the Levites, and explains that in the southern kingdom the priests lead true worship to God, morning and evening. He warns the northerners not to fight against the "LORD, the God of your ancestors; for you cannot succeed" (v. 12). Jeroboam, however, sends an ambush, intending to rout the southern warriors. This attack fails, and Abijah and his forces win a great victory, and claim back cities that had been part of Jeroboam's sphere of influence. The chapter closes with a note that God strikes down Jeroboam and he dies.

Chapters 14–16 are devoted to the rule of King Asa of Judah (ruled c. 913–873 BCE), a king favored by the Chronicler (at least for most of his life). Much of this material is not found in Kings.

Following a statement that there was peace in the land for a decade, chapter 14 records that Asa did "what was good and right in the sight of the LORD his God." What does this mean? Asa "took away the foreign altars and the high places, broke down the pillars, hewed down the sacred poles . . . and the incense altars" (vv. 2–3, 5 [vv. 1–2, 4 H]). There is no attempt by the Chronicler to address the question of why all these pagan shrines are still in existence. Are they part of the syncretistic legacy of Solomon and Rehoboam? Solomon died less than twenty years before Asa became king, even though Solomon was his great-grandfather. Was this the influence from the northern tribes? The text is silent on the matter.

The rest of chapter 14 details a failed attack by Zerah the Ethiopian. Zerah may be part of a buffer force left behind by Shishak the Egyptian, just a few years earlier. Asa and his armies repulse the assault. They pursue their enemies and bring back great amounts of plunder.

On their return homeward to Jerusalem (ch. 15), Azariah son of Oded meets the forces and tells them that as long as they—Judah and Benjamin—seek God, God will be with them. Conversely, if they turn from God, God will abandon them. When Asa hears the prophecy, he puts away (further?) "abominable idols from all the land of Judah and Benjamin and from the towns that he had taken in the hill country of Ephraim" (v. 8). The closing four verses of chapter 15 parallel the information given in 1 Kings 15:13–15: that Asa removes his mother, Maacah, from the status of queen mother, because she has made an abominable cult image. Asa destroys the image, crushes and burns it. Peace then reigns for many years.

Nonetheless, embedded in the text is a statement that, despite all these moves against syncretism, "the high places were not taken out of Israel" (v. 17). The high places are some kind of pagan shrines. They will continue to be a problem (cf. 2 Chr 20:33 and 1 Kgs 22:43 [22:44 H]).

The Chronicler largely ignores the rulers of the northern kingdom. This is a significant difference from the account one finds in Kings.

Now, however, as chapter 16 commences, the Chronicler needs to address that kingdom. King Baasha of Israel builds some barriers at Ramah to limit trade and religious connections between Israel and Judah (c. 880 BCE). Asa of Judah forms an alliance with King Ben-hadad of Aram (Syria). Essentially, Asa invites Ben-hadad to harass King Baasha of Israel, so that Baasha will no longer be a threat to Judah. Hanani the seer then comes forward and severely criticizes Asa's actions: how dare the king form a military alliance; he should have simply relied on God! Asa is unrepentant, and further he puts Hanani in stocks in prison. Asa also mistreats some other people (v. 10). The last years of Asa's life are marred by ill health. The Chronicler is disappointed with Asa; he states that the king puts his faith in physicians instead of God, despite the fact that his condition worsens. Asa dies and is buried.

Chapters 17–20 are devoted to King Jehoshaphat of Judah (reigned 873–49 BCE). Jehoshaphat, as his later successors Hezekiah and Josiah, is a particular favorite of the Chronicler. There is considerable more material in Chronicles regarding Jehoshaphat's monarchy than found in Kings. The Chronicler undoubtedly has additional sources of information beyond Samuel-Kings.

Chapter 17 commences with great praise for this king. He fortifies his country (vv. 1–2) and he rejects foreign worship. He walks with God, receives tribute from his people, and actively removes high places, thereby earning God's approval (vv. 3–6). Jehoshaphat is proactive in his promoting religiosity: he sends out officials accompanied by Levites and priests to the cities of Judah. They take with them "the book of the law of the LORD" (v. 9).

The rest of the chapter details tribute brought to Jehoshaphat from neighboring kingdoms, and a list of various soldiers and mighty warriors and some of their equipment.

Although the central focus of the Chronicler is the southern kingdom of Judah, as opposed in his mind to the apostate northern kingdom of Israel, he cannot completely ignore the north. Chapter 18 is close to a verbatim copy of 1 Kings 22. It contains the greatest amount of descriptive material devoted to the kingdom of Israel. It is difficult to know why this particular narrative is included. On one hand, it focuses on the activities of a prophet, in this case Micaiah son of Imlah.[31] On the other hand, the Chronicler ignores the stories surrounding the better-known prophets Elijah and Elisha. The only reference to Elijah is probably an invention of the Chronicler (see 2 Chr 21:12). It may be that the Elijah-Elisha narratives are excluded because they do not impinge on the history of Judah, while at least with Micaiah, he also addresses the Judean monarch.

The narrative describes an alliance between King Jehoshaphat and his contemporary, King Ahab of Israel. At question is whether they should attack Ramoth-gilead, an area east of the Jordan along the Israel-Aram (Syria) border. King Ahab is accompanied by four hundred prophets, led by Zedekiah son of Chenaanah. These four hundred (court?) prophets counsel a successful military venture.

King Jehoshaphat of Judah, nonetheless, is skeptical. He asks if there is not another prophet from whom the kings might seek direction. King Ahab of Israel mentions Micaiah son of Imlah. In the same sentence, he dismisses him, as Micaiah consistently prophesies unfavorably toward Ahab. In the event, Micaiah is summoned, and despite the fact that he eventually speaks against this expedition against Aram, the two kings commence the battle. The incursion is unsuccessful; Ahab is killed (for a more detailed description of this fascinating confrontation between competing prophets, see the discussion in the companion volume *The Bible's PROPHETS*, including the Text Study, "Micaiah and the Kings of Israel and Judah").

Chapter 19 finds King Jehoshaphat returning safely to his home in Judah, following the disastrous battle against Ramoth-gilead. Calculating by the death of King Ahab of Israel, this would be c. 850 BCE. Jehu son of Hanani the prophet goes out to meet Jehoshaphat. He criticizes the

---

31. See Zucker, "Cold Case," 8 n. 1; and *idem*, "Prophet Micaiah," 156–62.

monarch for his alliance with Ahab and Israel, "those who hate the LORD" (v. 2). Jehu tells Jehoshaphat that God is angry, but still credits him with having removed syncretistic materials from the land. This chapter praises Jehoshaphat's support for a judiciary based on Torah law (vv. 5–7). "The crucial portion of the section is vss. 8–11, which deal with the situation in Jerusalem where Levites, priests, and heads of families were appointed to handle cultic and civil cases. Of particular significance is the strong religious emphasis throughout."[32]

Chapter 20 details an invasion against Judah from her southern/southeastern neighbors, primarily the Moabites and Ammonites. They reach the oasis of En-gedi, near the Salt Sea. Jehoshaphat is shocked at this news. He proclaims a fast, goes to the temple, and offers a long and fervent prayer to God. None of this particular material appears in Kings. "The spirit of the LORD [*ruah YHWH*]" descends upon a Levite, Jahaziel son of Zechariah, who tells the assembled that this "battle is not yours but God's" (vv. 14–15). They shall go and be victorious, for God will be them. The next day, early in the morning, Jehoshaphat gives a similar "trust in God" speech. In Chronicles, according to Jahaziel's word, the result of the war is a complete rout of the enemy. In the confusion of the fog of war, the adversaries effectively defeat themselves. When the army of Jehoshaphat comes to the battlefield, all they find are corpses. A considerable result of this "victory" is that the "fear of God came on all the kingdoms of the countries when they heard that the LORD had fought against the enemies of Israel" (v. 29), and so for the remainder of his reign Jehoshaphat is at peace.

The closing words of chapter 20 recount the latter days of this king. He attempts to mount a maritime force, but it fails. In the parallel account in Kings, Jehoshaphat declines the invitation to further pursue this venture, a thought offered by his northern colleague, King Ahaziah, the son of Ahab of Israel (1 Kgs 22:48–49). In Chronicles, the two men form an alliance. It is this association with the wicked King Ahaziah that causes God to destroy Jehoshaphat's fleet. The two accounts do agree that despite Jehoshaphat walking in the ways of God, nonetheless certain pagan high places are not eradicated (1 Kgs 22:43 [22:44 H]; 2 Chr 20:33). The first verse of the next chapter records Jehoshaphat's death.

Chapter 21 is in stark contrast to the chapters devoted to Jehoshaphat. Jehoram succeeds his father. Once he establishes himself, he assassinates his brothers and others who threaten him. He rules for seven years (849–42 BCE). The Chronicler dismisses him with the observation that Jehoram "walked in the ways of the kings of Israel, as the house of Ahab had done; for the daughter

---

32. Myers, *2 Chronicles*, 108. See also Japhet, *I and II Chronicles*, 776–79.

of Ahab was his wife. He did what was evil in the sight of the LORD" (v. 6). The second part of the verse just reiterates the earlier sentiment.

Verses 12–15 set down the missive from Elijah the prophet, who berates Jehoram and prophesies his painful death. This letter likely is without historical basis. The rest of the chapter is an expanded version of information found in Kings, and confirms Jehoram's abdominal illness.

Chapters 22–23 detail the years following Jehoram's death. Since his other brothers are killed, the crown goes to Ahaziah, Jehoram's son by Athaliah, the daughter of King Ahab of Israel and his wife Jezebel. His mother and her advisors serve as his counselors. Following their direction, he does "what is evil in the sight of the LORD." He joins his uncle, Joram (Jehoram), king of Israel, Ahab's son, and they fight an unsuccessful battle against King Hazael of Aram.

The Arameans wound King Joram (Jehoram) during this attack. King Ahaziah goes to meet with him during his recuperation. It is a fatal mistake. Both Joram (Jehoram) and Ahaziah, as well as all of Ahaziah's cousins, are killed by Jehu son of Nimshi. Elisha the prophet commissions Jehu to assassinate Joram. Jehu achieves this task and more. The details of this bloodbath, not found in the Chronicles account, are described in 2 Kings 9.

Second Chronicles 22:10 explains that when Athaliah, the queen mother of the southern kingdom of Judah, learns about her son Ahaziah's death, she acts quickly to consolidate her own power. She starts her reign in 842 BCE and rules for about six years. Queen Athaliah begins her monarchy by intending to kill all of the royal family so that they will not be a threat to her. She almost succeeds. Unbeknownst to her, the late King Ahaziah's sister, Jehoshabeath (Jehosheba in 2 Kgs 11:2), who is married to the priest Jehoida, saves the life of one of Ahaziah's sons, a boy by the name of Joash (Jehoash in 2 Kgs 12:1). Joash hides out in the home of his aunt and her husband for six years. Joash is "hidden in the house of God, while Athaliah reigned over the land" (v. 12).

Chapter 23 relates the fall of Queen Athaliah and the rise of King Joash of Judah. It is clear that Athaliah institutes the worship of Baal. This is explicitly stated later in this chapter (v. 17). Athaliah's mother, the late Queen Jezebel, wife of King Ahab of Israel, is the daughter of the king of Sidon (Phoenicia). Jezebel introduced Baal worship in Israel, and Ahab endorsed this pagan practice (cf. 1 Kgs 16:29–33).

In the seventh year the (high?) priest Jehoida decides that it is time to act. He makes plans with various military commanders, who in turn reach out to people throughout Judah who sympathize with the idea of overthrowing Queen Athaliah. In the parallel account (2 Kgs 11:4–12), the coup is administered largely by military personnel. In Chronicles, there are additional details of the plot. As one would expect of the Chronicler, the primary instigators are Levites. The coup may have taken place on the Sabbath. The insurgents surround the new king with weapons drawn, and anoint Joash. They shout, "Long live the king!" (v. 11). A good part of the action, including the anointing of Joash, takes place adjacent to the temple.

The next part of the chapter recounts Athaliah's reaction. She enters the temple precincts and sees the new king surrounded by people rejoicing and blowing trumpets. She responds with the words, "Treason! Treason!" (v. 13). The priest Jehoida instructs the captains who are set over the army to bring her out of the building. "Do not put her to death in the house of the LORD." She is taken outside and executed.

The final verses of the chapter explain how the priest Jehoida seeks to reestablish the covenant between the people and God. He institutes certain religious reforms, and Joash is set on the royal throne.

Chapter 24 roughly parallels the account in 2 Kings 12:1-21. Yet, there are some significant differences. Both accounts note that the temple needs some repairs. In Kings these repairs are necessary due to priestly neglect (2 Kgs 12:6-7); in Chronicles the repairs are needed because the children of Queen Athaliah had broken into the house of God and desecrated it with Baal worship (v. 7). Both accounts agree that the Arameans under King Hazael invade Judah. In Kings, Joash takes money from the temple to bribe Hazael to retreat (2 Kgs 12:17-18); in Chronicles the invasion is God's punishment because of Joash's apostasy and evil ways (vv. 17-18, 22, 24). In Kings, Joash is pious all his life, then he is assassinated by his servants (2 Kgs 12:2, 20); in Chronicles Joash, following the death of his uncle, the priest Jehoiada, turns from God's ways and sets up pagan sacred poles (*Asherim*). Not only that, he has Zechariah the son of Jehoiada killed in the temple precincts when the latter criticizes the king. As in Kings, Joash is assassinated by his servants, but in the Chronicles account he also receives wounds in the war with King Hazael; his death is in revenge for Joash's ordering the death of the priest Zechariah (v. 25). Both accounts agree that his son Amaziah succeeds him.

In chapter 25, the Chronicler recounts the decades-long reign of King Amaziah (800-783 BCE). As soon as he feels that he has hold of the reins of power, he executes the killers of his father. He does not, however, wreak revenge on their children, because he follows the command from the "book of Moses, where the LORD commanded, 'The parents shall not be put to death for the children, or the children be put to death for the parents; but all shall be put to death for their own sins'" (v. 4; cf. Deut 24:16). King Amaziah then hires some mercenaries from Israel. A man of God counsels against this (vv. 7-8). He releases them, and then takes his own men and attacks the Edomites. Unfortunately, Amaziah, for some unknown reason, then takes the Edomite gods and sets them up as gods in Judah. A prophet sent by God asks Amaziah why he would do this, especially since it is clear that these pagan gods could not deliver their own people. Amaziah threatens the prophet with death if he does not stop speaking. The prophet complies, but then says that God has determined Amaziah's death because of his apostasy. Whether or not the prophet says this in the king's hearing is ambiguous.

In the middle of his reign, fresh from his victory over Edom, Amaziah tries to force an alliance with his northern neighbor, King Joash son of Jehoahaz of Israel. Joash forcibly rebuffs Amaziah's offer, but Amaziah refuses to be put off. He attempts to invade Israel, but the forces of Judah are thoroughly routed. King Joash of Israel captures King Amaziah, brings him to Jerusalem, destroys parts of the walls of Jerusalem, and takes back to Samaria "all the gold and silver, and all the vessels that were found in the house of God" (v. 24). King Amaziah lives several years after this defeat. Some unknown forces in Jerusalem plot against Amaziah. He flees to Lachish, about thirty miles southwest of Jerusalem, fifteen miles west of Hebron, in the Judean foothills. His foes pursue him and kill him there.

The reign of King Uzziah of Judah is recorded in chapter 26. (Note: in 2 Kings Uzziah is also called Azariah. Azariah may have been his personal name, Uzziah his throne name.) According to the text, he reigns for many decades, although he is ill in the latter part of his monarchy, and his son Jotham is coregent (c. 783–42 BCE).

For much of his reign "he did right in the sight of the LORD." He rebuilds Eloth (modern day Eilat, at the head of the Gulf of Aqaba). He takes instruction to be God-fearing, and as long as he follows in this path God favors him, explains the Chronicler (v. 5). Uzziah achieves many military successes.

Verses 6–15 are notable because they are another example demonstrating that the Chronicler has his own independent sources for information which do not parallel 2 Kings 15. These verses detail many of Uzziah's accomplishments. He fortifies Jerusalem, builds fortresses in the wilderness, and creates cisterns for herds in the foothills, the Shephelah and further westward in the plains. He favors both the raising of cattle and viniculture. In addition, he outfits his army with "shields, spears, helmets, coats of mail, bows, and stones for slinging" (v. 14). He also encourages the building of some kind of machines like catapults.

Success, according to the Chronicler, leads to arrogance, and thereby to Uzziah's destruction. At one point, in violation of what was by then accepted tradition, he goes into the temple to make an offering of incense on the altar. (At an earlier time, both David and Solomon brought offerings, the former in 1 Chr 21:26-27; the latter in 2 Chr 6:12; 7:1, 4.) The chief priest, Azariah, accompanied by eighty priests, challenges the king. He tells Uzziah that only priests who are consecrated can make offerings. At first Uzziah is angry, but then he suddenly seems to be struck by some kind of severe skin irritation. The Chronicler interprets this as a sign of divine disfavor. King Uzziah remains ill for the rest of his life; he is quarantined, and his son Jotham serves as coregent until Uzziah dies. Verse 22 mentions that Uzziah is known to "the prophet Isaiah son of Amoz"—the prophet we know as First Isaiah, or Isaiah of Jerusalem. This is about the time of the prophet Amos, although he is not mentioned by name (see the companion volume *The Bible's PROPHETS*).

Chapter 27 explains that Jotham, Uzziah's son, succeeds his father (742-35 BCE). Jotham, unlike his father, does not invade the temple, and "he did what was right in the sight of the LORD" although "the people still followed corrupt practices" (v. 2). Like his father, Jotham builds up the fortifications of Jerusalem. He also builds cities in the hill country of Judah, and towers (probably some kind of forts) in the wooded hills. He fights successfully against the Ammonites, who pay him tribute. His son Amaz follows him on the throne. Although none of the classical prophets are cited by name in this chapter, this is about the time of Isaiah of Jerusalem and Micah of Moresheth.

These are years of great changes geopolitically in the wider region. Assyria, located in what is now northern Iraq, around the upper region of the Tigris River, is coming into its own in terms of political might and armed strength.[33] During this time, the (Neo-)Assyrian Empire expands westward. It aims to challenge and, hopefully, to conquer the other major political power of that time, Egypt. The route to Egypt runs right through ancient Israel. The ongoing tensions and conflicts between Assyria and Egypt threaten both the northern kingdom of Israel and the southern kingdom of Judah.

About 735 BCE, Israel (which is also termed Ephraim),[34] forms a military alliance with her neighboring country, Aram (Syria). They intend to oppose Assyria. Since the addition of another partner to this coalition would lend added strength, Aram and Israel invite Judah to join with them. King Ahaz of Judah refuses this invitation. Consequently, Aram (Syria) and Israel (Ephraim) lay siege to Jerusalem (2 Kgs 16:5), but this fact is not mentioned in the Chronicles account. This is the Syro-Ephraimitic War, c. 735-32 BCE.

33. Machinist, "Empire of Assyria," 77.
34. Israel often is called Ephraim in the book of Isaiah. Ephraim was one of the traditional tribes that made up Israel. That Ephraim appears as a synonym for Israel reflects the importance of that particular tribe's holdings and influence.

During the siege of Jerusalem, the prophet Isaiah publicly meets with King Ahaz. Isaiah explains that this attack on Jerusalem will fail (Isa 7). Isaiah urges King Ahaz to stay calm. He advises the monarch against joining in the rebellion against Assyria. Isaiah likewise counsels against an alliance with Assyria. Simply trust in God (see the Text Study sections "Judah under Siege" and "The 'Immanuel' Passage" in the chapter on Isaiah in the companion volume *The Bible's PROPHETS*). King Ahaz ignores Isaiah's advice of absolute neutrality. Instead Ahaz opts to become a vassal of Assyria (2 Kgs 15:37—16:9; Isa 7:1–9). The Assyrian ruler, Tiglath Pileser III (745–27 BCE), attacks and subjugates both Aram and Israel.

During Ahaz's rule in Judah, the northern kingdom of Israel ends. Details of this final defeat in 722 BCE are recounted in 2 Kings 17. For three years the Assyrian forces, under the leadership of King Sargon II, besiege the capital of the northern kingdom, Samaria. Then they destroy the kingdom. They carry away the survivors to Assyria. This is the end of the nation formed by the ten tribes over two hundred years earlier.

King Ahaz's monarchy (735–15 BCE) forms chapter 28. Ahaz ranks among the most reviled kings of Judah. The Chronicler adds to the decidedly drastic account of this reign depicted in 2 Kings 16. A catalog of Ahaz's apostasy includes making cast images of Baals; child sacrifices, including his own sons; sacrificing on the high places and under every green tree (vv. 2–4); sacrificing to the gods of Damascus; building high places in Jerusalem; as well as making offerings to other gods (vv. 23, 25).

This is a very interesting chapter for what it records, and for what it does not record. As noted above, Aram and the northern kingdom of Israel lay siege to Jerusalem. Although this tactic fails, the combined Aram-Israel forces take many of the Judean population as captives. The Arameans take some captives to Damascus. Other captives are taken north to Samaria. When the army brings these prisoners to Samaria, an otherwise unknown prophet named Oded comes out to meet them. He explains that Israel defeated Judah because God is angry with the Judeans. To take the Judeans captive, however, will make God angry at the northern kingdom. Several leaders from the tribe of Ephraim join in with Oded and say, do not add to the sins of the northern kingdom, we are in enough trouble with God as it is. Their counsel prevails. These same leaders take the captives and repatriate them to Jericho.

Although reference is made to Oded, for some inexplicable reason there is no mention of the powerful figure of Isaiah, who is the most prominent prophet in Judah at this time.

Meantime, King Ahaz decides to ignore the advice of Isaiah to trust in God, and not to engage in treaties with an earthly ruler. Ahaz forms an alliance with the Assyrian ruler, Tiglath Pilneser (vv. 16, 20). The Assyrian ruler attacks Jerusalem and demands tribute, which Ahaz has to pay (vv. 20-21).[35] Taking advantage of Judah's weakness, the Philistines and the Edomites regain some land they lost in previous years.

Ahaz then turns even further from God. He sacrifices to the gods of Damascus, rationalizing that since they had aided Aram, perhaps these gods will help him. Ahaz also shuts the doors of the temple (v. 24); further he builds high places (pagan shrines) in Jerusalem and other cities in Judah. Foreign cult centers at this point fill the land of Judah; it is a religious low point. The chapter closes with Ahaz's death and notes that his successor, his son Hezekiah, takes the throne.

Chapter 29 marks the beginning of a change of fortune for Judah. Hezekiah is regarded as a good king. He reigns for nearly three decades (c. 715-687 BCE). "He did what was right in the sight of the LORD, just as his ancestor David had done" (v. 2). The Chronicler offers no higher praise. Chapters 29-32 relate the story of Hezekiah. The first three of these four chapters catalog the religious reforms and changes King Hezekiah institutes. Only beginning with chapter 32 does the narration turn to the political life of Judah. This is in stark contrast to the Hezekiah chapters in 2 Kings 18-20. Those chapters in Kings describe in detail the geopolitical conflicts of Hezekiah, and barely touch on his religious reforms (cf. 2 Kgs 18:3-6).

Chapter 29 explains that Hezekiah reopens the temple (his father had closed it); further, he brings priests and Levites to the temple square and addresses them at length, pledging his loyalty to God (vv. 5-11).

Characteristic of the ways of the Chronicler, the next three verses list the names of these Levites. They clear up the rubble in the temple; there is a division of labor; priests go to the inner sanctum; and the Levites assist them outside of these precincts. It takes them over two weeks to accomplish their tasks.

An elaborate dedication ceremony follows. Hezekiah commands the priests, the descendants of Aaron, to offer appropriate sacrifices on the altar. It is a celebration, with many musical instruments: cymbals, harps, lyres, trumpets, and singers singing praises of gladness.

---

35. Ahaz formed the alliance with the Assyrian ruler because he wanted relief from the pressure of Aram-Israel (Syro-Ephraim). The Assyrian ruler, called Tiglath Pilesner in v. 20, is Tiglath Pileser III. Tiglath Pileser attacks Aram and Israel and defeats them, but then also exacts tribute from Ahaz. See Matthews and Benjamin, *Old Testament Parallels*, 182-84.

The Chronicler's eye for detail, or perhaps his preference for his own group, the Levites, as opposed to the priests, is evident. He notes that the "priests were too few" and could not do all their necessary ritual work. Consequently, the Levites "helped them until the work was finished—for the Levites were more conscientious than the priests" (v. 34).

Chapter 30 describes in some detail the reinstitution of Passover as a major festival. The text indicates that it is many years since Passover was celebrated. Because the priests and the people are unprepared, the celebration is postponed a month from when it is supposed to be held (vv. 2–3, 13). The people are so enthusiastic that they follow the Passover traditions for an additional week (v. 23). "That some sort of religious celebration, apart from the rededication of the temple, took place soon after the accession of Hezekiah is extremely likely, especially in view of the character and ambitions of the king (cf. II Kings xviii 4–6)."[36]

Hezekiah's religious reforms continue to be highlighted in chapter 31. Hezekiah himself provides an example for the people by generously supporting the cult; the people emulate him (vv. 3–7). Many of the Levites are named, and there is an active enrollment of various priestly and Levitical families. Hezekiah follows in the positive aspects of the precedents of Solomon. "The space which the Chronicler has devoted to Hezekiah's story is one way of expressing that Hezekiah is the greatest Jewish monarch after David and Solomon."[37]

The reader of Chronicles is well served to remember that while this is a history of Israel, it is history with a purpose. The Chronicler sets down these narratives c. 400 BCE. It is the time of Ezra-Nehemiah. The Chronicler wants to inspire the people in his day. He wishes to encourage them to return to the ways of God, including the cultus, the religion/religious rites of Judaism of that day. There is a sermonic aspect to some of the writing of the Chronicler.

Hezekiah's reforms take place during the time of the prophecies of Micah of Moresheth and Isaiah of Jerusalem (see the chapters on Micah and Isaiah in the companion volume *The Bible's PROPHETS*). Undoubtedly, these prophets influence the king. Although there is no

> direct information, Hezekiah's reform undoubtedly had social aspects as well. A return to strict Yahwism would of necessity

---

36. Myers, *2 Chronicles*, 176.
37. Japhet, *I and II Chronicles*, 912.

have involved an attempt to remove the economic abuses that had existed, and against which Isaiah and Micah had thundered. We know (Jer 26:16-19; cf. Mic 3:12) that the preaching of Micah, who primarily attacked just such abuses, influenced Hezekiah in his efforts; and the fact that the equally stern Isaiah stood close to Hezekiah at least argues that that king was not guilty of condoning outrageous injustice. What measures Hezekiah may have taken we do not know.[38]

Chapter 32 turns to the political world of the eight century BCE: the Assyrian invasion of Judah. This one chapter condenses much of the information recorded in 2 Kings 18-20. Yet it provides greater details about the remarkable engineering feat where, at Hezekiah's orders, his people cut through solid rock in order to divert the spring waters outside of Jerusalem, so that they will only be accessible within the city—the Siloam project (cf. 2 Kgs 20:20; 2 Chr 32:3-4, 30) (see the Text Study at the close of this chapter, "Portraying Hezekiah: Chronicles versus Kings").

The Chronicles account excises much of the detailed description where the Assyrian forces come to the gates of Jerusalem and actively taunt Hezekiah—the Rabshakeh dialogue (2 Kgs 18:17-36). As here in Chronicles, in the Kings account of this incursion against Judah by the Assyrian king, Sennacherib, the text specifically mentions the presence of the prophet Isaiah son of Amoz. The Kings version is considerably more detailed than the Isaiah account (cf. 2 Kgs 19:5-7; 2 Chr 32:20-21; Isa 36-37). According to the biblical text, God intervenes on behalf of Judah, and the Assyrians return to their land where Sennacherib is assassinated.

Second Chronicles 32:24-32 detail the final days of King Hezekiah. He suffers an illness and almost dies. God first sends healing, but Hezekiah, in his pride, refuses to acknowledge divine intervention. When God brings additional suffering for Hezekiah and his people, the king relents, and humbles himself. Then God brings blessings once again. The final verses praise Hezekiah for his accomplishments, mentioning that there is additional material about Hezekiah in the words of Isaiah and in the "Book of the Kings of Judah and Israel" (v. 32). His son Manasseh follows him on the throne.

Chapter 33 covers the reigns of the next two kings of Judah, Manasseh (687-42 BCE) and Amon (642-40 BCE). The second verse says it clearly: Manasseh "did what was evil in the sight of the LORD, according to the abominable practices of the nations whom the LORD drove out before the people of Israel." Manasseh builds up the high places (pagan shrines) his father Hezekiah destroyed. He erects altars to the Baals, makes sacred poles,

---

38. Bright, *History of Israel*, 283.

and worships various celestial deities. He also builds pagan altars in the temple. The catalog of Manasseh's apostasy continues. "He made his son pass through fire in the valley of Hinnom, practiced soothsaying and augury and sorcery, and dealt with mediums and with wizards" (v. 6). Manasseh is condemned for his evil acts. He "misled Judah and the inhabitants of Jerusalem, so that they did more evil than the nations whom the LORD had destroyed before the people of Israel" (v. 9). Although God speaks to Manasseh and his people, they choose not to listen.

What motivates Manasseh to turn from the righteous ways of his father?

> As Ahaz before him, Manasseh was doubtlessly caught in the stream of world politics and had perforce to become subservient to Assyria. That meant, in part, the adoption of Assyrian religion which in turn compelled the nullification of the achievements of his father and earned for the king the enmity and violent opposition of prophets and religious officials, many of whom worked underground. Manasseh was, in all probability, not an unwilling tool—though certainly not the first—in the hands of the Assyrian kings. Prophecy was not altogether quiescent, as can be inferred from vs. 10 (cf. II Kings xxi 10), but its message availed little and was even met with violence (II Kings xxi 16).[39]

To punish Manasseh for his apostasy, God brings the forces of Assyria, who capture this king and bring him in manacles and fetters to Babylon (v. 11). In captivity Manasseh decides to repent. In the words of the Chronicler, when Manasseh "was in distress he entreated the favor of the LORD his God and humbled himself greatly before the God of his ancestors. He prayed to him, and God received his entreaty, heard his plea, and restored him again to Jerusalem and to his kingdom. Then Manasseh knew that the LORD indeed was God" (vv. 12–13). According to the text, not only does Manasseh return to Jerusalem, he builds up the defenses of the capital city, and fortifies much of Judah. In addition, he has a complete change of heart and puts away all the pagan shrines. A cryptic line explains that the people still sacrifice at the high places, but only to God (v. 17).

The parallel passages in 2 Kings 21 details many of the same offenses (cf. Jer 15:4). However, they do not record his captivity in Babylon, his acts of return to God, or the good deeds with which Chronicles credit him.

Verses 21–25 detail the short reign of Manasseh's son Amon (642–40 BCE), who in his two-year monarchy reverts back to the evil excesses of his father. Amon's servants assassinate him. Then the very last verses in the chapter explain that "the people of the land" (presumably "the free landowners of Judah who always acted decisively in times of crises to see that the

---

39. Myers, *2 Chronicles*, 198.

Davidic dynasty was perpetuated")[40] rebel against the anti-Amon forces and install Amon's son Josiah in his place.

Chapters 34–35 recount the glorious reign of King Josiah (640–609 BCE). In contrast to the negative report about Manasseh, here the Chronicler is quick to add, "He did what was right in the sight of the LORD, and walked in the ways of his ancestor David; he did not turn aside to the right or to the left" (v. 2). Although a youngster when he becomes king, he soon purges Jerusalem and Judah of foreign practices and religious rites (vv. 3–7).

How is it that Josiah could achieve these reforms? The first answer is that they do not come about immediately. Josiah is a child of eight when he becomes ruler; these changes begin when he is older. By that point he may have begun to make a shift in national policy.

> It seems that in Josiah's twelfth year (629/8) the opportunity came. By that point [the king of Assyria] Asshurbanapal was old and his son Sin-shar-ishkun had come to the throne as his coregent; Assyria, whose effective control of the west had already begun to loosen, was no longer in a position to interfere. It is reasonable to suppose that at this time (cf. II Chron. 3b-7) Josiah... launched a sweeping reform... [Those reforms] by far the most thoroughgoing in Judah's history, is described in detail in II Kings 22:3 to 23:25 and in II Chron. 34:1 to 35:19.[41]

Josiah turns his mind to the needed repairs of the temple. He organizes laity, priests, and Levites in this endeavor. Many of their names are listed. It is c. 622 BCE.

In the course of their work repairing the temple, the high priest, Hilkiah, finds "the book of the law of the LORD given through Moses" (v. 14). Hilkiah gives the book to Shaphan, the scribe who then reads from it aloud to the king (v. 18). The king is devastated by the words that he hears. It is clear to him that the country is failing to keep God's word. He tears his clothes as a sign of mourning (vv. 19, 21). It is likely that the "book" refers to Deuteronomy, or some version of it (see the Text Study section "The Discovery of the 'Book of the Law'" in the chapter on Kings in the companion volume *The Bible's PROPHETS*).

Josiah then seeks to know what is to be done. He sends a delegation to meet with the female prophet, Huldah the wife of Shallum, who is an official of the court (see the Text Study section at the end of this chapter, "Huldah the Prophet"). Huldah offers a prophecy (vv. 23–28) that difficult days are coming to "this place and upon its inhabitants." Since this people forsakes

---

40. Ibid., 200. Myers suggests that these landowners ousted the anti-Amon forces because they were fearful of a negative reaction from Assyria.

41. Bright, *History of Israel*, 317.

God and makes offerings to other gods, divine "wrath will be poured out on this place and will not be quenched" (v. 25). Yet the king, because his heart is penitent, will go to his grave in peace, and he shall not see the disaster that God will bring in future time (vv. 27–28).

Huldah's prophecy concerning the fate of Judah, and more specifically the future of Josiah, is not entirely accurate. "The prophecy concerning the peaceful end of Josiah was not fulfilled ([Chr] xxxv 23f.). Yet the Chronicler did not revise the prophecy. There were, however, two aspects to it, and one was realized: that he would not see the destruction of the city and nation. It is rather remarkable that the prophecies were faithfully preserved intact regardless of conformity in detail to what was known to have happened."[42]

Josiah's reaction is to send word to the elders of Judah and Jerusalem. He goes to the temple and reads in their hearing "all the words of the book of the covenant that had been found in the house of the LORD" (v. 30). The king makes a public covenant with God to follow these statutes. He asks the people of Judah and Benjamin to do likewise, and they assent to this. Josiah then puts away (further?) abominations from the territory that belongs to the people of Israel. It is likely that Josiah's initial reforms are in the more limited areas of Judah and Benjamin, but that he then reaches out further to the traditional territorial lands of what was the northern kingdom, and effects religious reforms there.

Chapter 35 describes Josiah's great Passover celebration in Jerusalem. He also appoints priests to their offices and encourages the Levites in their duties. The Passover ritual is described in great detail. The text explains that "No passover like it had been kept in Israel since the days of the prophet Samuel; none of the kings of Israel had kept such a passover as was kept by Josiah, by the priests and the Levites, by all Judah and Israel who were present, and by the inhabitants of Jerusalem" (v. 18).

The "discovery" of the book of the law and this great celebration takes place in Josiah's eighteenth regnal year, c. 622/621 BCE.

As the seventh century BCE draws down, great changes are taking place in the ancient Near East. Assyria is in serious decline. It was the "superpower" of its day for about three hundred years. That era is ending. The Babylonians and the Medes bring Assyria to the ground in 612 BCE with the fall of Nineveh. Even as the prophet

> Nahum rejoiced over the tyrant's fall, rival powers were gathering like vultures to divide the corpse. Whichever would win, it

---

42. Myers, 2 *Chronicles*, 207.

was certain that Judah would lose, for the day of the independent petty state in western Asia was long over. Lose she did—first her independence, then her life . . .

Since the Medes contented themselves for the moment with consolidating their holdings east and north of the mountains, control of the western part of Assyria's defunct empire lay between Babylon and the Egyptians, who, hoping among other things to gain a free hand in Palestine and Syria, had been allies of Assyria. Between the two Judah was brought to disaster.

The blow fell (II Kings 23:29f.; II Chron 35:20–24) in 609 [BCE]. In that year [the Egyptian ruler, Pharaoh] Neco II . . . marched with a large force to Carchemish on the Euphrates to assist Asshur-uballit [the Assyrian ruler] in a last effort to retake Haran from the Babylonians. Near Megiddo, probably where the coastal road now passes through the Carmel range, Josiah tried to stop him. Whether Josiah was formally an ally of the Babylonians, as Hezekiah once had been, or whether he acted independently, we do not know. But he certainly could not have wished an Egypto-Assyrian victory the result of which would have been to place him at the mercy of Egypt's ambitions. The outcome, in any event was tragic. Josiah was killed in battle, and brought dead in his chariot to Jerusalem amid great lamentation. His son Jehoahaz was made king in his place.[43]

The rest of chapter 35 concentrates on the final days of Josiah. It provides material not found in 2 Kings 23:29–30, which simply lays out the bare information about Josiah's death. In Chronicles, Neco, the king of Egypt, warns off Josiah, telling him not to get involved in the conflict between Egypt-Assyria and Babylon. Neco tells Josiah that God is on Neco's side. "Cease opposing God, who is with me, so that he will not destroy you" (v. 21). But Josiah persists in engaging the Egyptian forces at Megiddo, and he is killed. He is brought back to Jerusalem and buried amongst widespread grief. The text explains that the prophet Jeremiah specifically wrote a lament for Josiah (v. 25), although we no longer have a copy of it. For some reason Jeremiah is not mentioned in the parallel Kings account.

Chapter 36, the final chapter of Chronicles, catalogs the final days of the nation of Judah. "The people of the land" take Josiah's son Jehoahaz and make him king in place of Josiah. He reigns but three months and is deposed by Neco, the king of Egypt. Neco takes Jehoahaz to Egypt. He then replaces him on the throne with another of Josiah's sons, Eliakim.

43. Bright, *History of Israel*, 324–25.

The Egyptian ruler changes Eliakim's name to Jehoiakim, and then exacts an enormous tribute from Judah.

Jehoiakim (609-598 BCE) remains an Egyptian vassal for several years. In the eyes of the Chronicler he is an evil king (cf. Jer 22:13-19). Although the Chronicles text does not explains this, Jehoiakim then becomes subservient to Babylon when the (Neo-)Babylonians defeat the Egyptians in 605 BCE at Carchemish. A fuller account of these years is presented in 2 Kings 23:36—24:7 (cf. Jer 46:2.)

At Jehoiakim's death, his son Jehoiachin[44] succeeds him (598 BCE), but reigns for only a few months. Then King Nebuchadnezzar of Babylon replaces Jehoiachin with an uncle Zedekiah (mistakenly labeled Jehoiachin's brother in 2 Chr 36:10).[45] Zedekiah is a son of the late revered King Josiah. Zedekiah will be the last king of Judah.

The Chronicles account is much briefer than the parallel record in 2 Kings 24.

At this point, King Nebuchadnezzar deports a large number of people to Babylon. These include King Jehoiachin, the king's mother, a large number of officials, warriors, and artisans, along with a sizeable amount of the temple treasury. These events take place 598/597 BCE. They are more clearly described in the Kings account.

In terms of the welfare of Judah, Zedekiah is a disastrous choice. "He did not humble himself before the prophet Jeremiah who spoke from the mouth of the LORD. He also rebelled against King Nebuchadnezzar" (vv. 12-13).

Although God sent messengers to the king, the priests, and the leading officials, all turned from the ways of God; the words of these prophets are rebuffed.[46]

The fall of Jerusalem begins with verse 17. The Babylonians (called here the Chaldeans) show no mercy on the young, the aged, or the feeble; all fall into captivity. The vessels of the house of God are taken, as is the temple treasury and the king's treasury. Large numbers of people are deported to Babylon. The temple is destroyed, and the walls of Jerusalem are broken down.

---

44. Jehoiachin is known by various names. He is also called Jeconiah (1 Chr 3:16-17; Est 2:6; Jer 24:1; 27:20; 28:4; 29:2) and Coniah (Jer 22:24, 28; 37:1).

45. These events are much more clearly set out in the Kings account (2 Kgs 24). 2 Kings 24:17 states, "The king of Babylon made Mattaniah, Jehoiachin's uncle, king in his place, and changed his name to Zedekiah." See Matthews and Benjamin, *Old Testament Parallels*, 195-97.

46. "The Chronicler does not condemn the Levites and musicians." "The Chronicler is fond of the theme of the unheeded prophet (compare 12.5-8; 15.1-8; 19.1-3; 21.12-15; 25.7-9, 15-17; Jer 26.20-24; 29.16-20; 25:14-15)." *NOAB*, 579, notes to vv. 14, 15-16.

The book closes with a series of statements that clearly were written after the facts of that time.

The second half of verse 20 explains that the captives in Babylonia remained there "until the establishment of the kingdom of Persia." Verses 22-23 take place fifty years after the beginning of the exilic period. It is the first year of King Cyrus of Persia. Cyrus explains that "The LORD, the God of heaven . . . has charged me to build him a house in Jerusalem . . . Whoever is among you of all his people, may the LORD his God be with him! Let him go up" (v. 23).

This note of hope is a paraphrase of the opening verses of the book of Ezra. In the Christian Bible, Chronicles precedes Ezra, so there is a natural flow of ideas. "1 and 2 Chronicles portrayed the downfall, and Ezra/Nehemiah the restoration, of God's people."[47]

Chronicles in the Christian Scriptures

In Luke's genealogy of Jesus, he mentions a number of names that are also found in the genealogy at the beginning of Chronicles, including Adam, Seth, and Noah. There are some variant spellings in Luke, for example, Cainan for Canaan, Arphaxad for Arpachshad, and Enos for Enosh (Luke 3:36-38). Luke links Jesus with Adam, highlighting the connections with all humankind, in contrast to Matthew's specific connections to Jesus' Jewish heritage (Matt 1:1ff.)[48]

Luke's rendition of the Davidic connection (Luke 3:31-33) reflects some of the names in 1 Chronicles 2:1-15 (cf. Matt 1:3-12).

The words in Acts 26:17, "I will rescue you from your people and from the Gentiles—to whom I am sending you," echoes the praises of Asaph in 1 Chronicles "Save us, O God of our salvation, and gather and rescue us from among the nations, that we may give thanks to your holy name, and glory in your praise" (1 Chr 16:35).

David's desire to build a house for God is remembered in Acts (Acts 7:45-46; 1 Chr 17:1-14).

Hebrews 1:5-13 is made up of seven quotations from the Hebrew Scriptures. Verse 5 says in part, "I will be his Father, and he will be my Son." This reflects a verse in Chronicles, "I will be a father to him, and he shall be

---

47. *NOAB*, comment on 2 Chr 3:22-23.

48. "Matthew . . . follows the listing in Chronicles where possible . . . [yet] he makes a few theologically significant adjustments to Chronicles . . . by subtle midrashic allusions he connects Jesus to priestly and prophetic threads in Israel's history." Keener, *Commentary on the Gospel of Matthew*, 76-77.

a son to me" although in the Chronicles text the reference is to Solomon (1 Chr 17:13; cf. 2 Sam 7:14).

In the final book of the Christian Scriptures, Revelation, the author reports that he hears angels singing, "Worthy is the Lamb that was slaughtered to receive power and wealth and wisdom and might and honor and glory and blessing" (Rev 5:12). This phrasing shows familiarity with David's words in Chronicles, "Yours, O LORD, are the greatness, the power, the glory, the victory, and the majesty . . . yours is the kingdom" (1 Chr 29:11).

David's desire to build the temple and Solomon's actual construction of the house of God are mentioned in Acts (Acts 7:46–47; 2 Chr 3:1; 5:1; 6:2, 7–8, 10).

The Queen of Sheba's desire to meet with Solomon to search out his wisdom is used as an example in Matthew and Luke (Matt 12:42; Luke 11:31; 2 Chr 9:1ff.).

Azariah son of Oded addresses King Asa in Chronicles. As part of his foreboding message, Azariah says, "They were broken in pieces, nation against nation and city against city, for God troubled them with every sort of distress" (2 Chr 15:6). The writers of the Synoptic Gospels all take up this image describing the times of trouble that will precede the coming of the Messiah (Matt 24:7; Mark 13:8; Luke 21:10).

The prophet Micaiah's image of chaos, the people scattered "like sheep without a shepherd," is utilized in Matthew and Mark (2 Chr 18:16; Matt 9:36; Mark 6:34).

In his address to Kings Jehoshaphat and Ahab, Micaiah describes God sitting on a throne, surrounded by the host of heaven. The concept of God's throne appealed to the writer of the book of Revelation, who repeated the throne image many times (2 Chr 18:18; Rev 4:2, 9–10; 5:1, 7, 13 et al.).

God's impartiality in justice (2 Chr 19:7) is a theme mentioned in Acts and several of the Epistles (Acts 10:34; Rom 2:11; Eph 6:9; Col 3:25; 1 Pet 1:17).

Chronicles in Rabbinic Literature

Children, rabbis, and learning. In Asaph's prayer he explains that God has rebuked rulers with the words, "Do not touch my anointed ones; do my prophets no harm" (1 Chr 16:22). The anointed are schoolchildren; the latter are the rabbis, explains a midrash. Stressing the value of learning, this midrash continues, "Resh Lakish in the name of Rabbi Judah Nesiah says: Let not the children be kept back from school, even to help in the building of the Temple" (*Babylonian Talmud Shabbat* 119b).

Israel praises God as one; God praises Israel as one. Just as Israel proclaims God's unity in the *Sh'ma*, "Hear, O Israel: The LORD is our God, the Lord alone [or 'is one']" (Deut 6:4), so God proclaims Israel's unity, "Who is like your people Israel, one nation on the earth" (1 Chr 17:21) (*Mekilta de Rabbi Ishmael, Shirata*, 3.13–16).

Prayer, repentance, charity. Rabbi Yudan says in the name of Rabbi Elazar: Three things annul the evil decree: prayer, repentance, and charity. All three are contained in one verse, "If my people who are called by my name humble themselves, pray, seek my face, and turn from their wicked ways, then I will hear from heaven, and I will forgive their sin" (2 Chr 7:14), for to seek my face is charity, as it says, "I shall behold your face in righteousness [*tzedeq*, which has the same root letters as *tzedaqah*, 'charity'—*tz-d-q, tzadeh-dalet-quf*]" (Ps 17:15) (*Pesikta de-Rab Kahana, Piska* 28.3).

God accepts the penitent. If someone were to say that God does not receive the penitent, King Manasseh would come and give witness. There was never anyone as wicked as Manasseh, and yet in the hour of his repentance, God accepted him. When Manasseh "was in distress he entreated the favor of the LORD his God and humbled himself greatly before the God of his ancestors. He prayed to him, and God received his entreaty, heard his plea, and restored him again to Jerusalem and to his kingdom. Then Manasseh knew that the LORD indeed was God" (2 Chr 33:12–13) (*Midrash Numbers Rabbah* 14.1).

True wickedness precludes someone from attaining the World to Come. The rabbis are divided over the destiny of evil King Manasseh. On one hand, there is the line that "God received his entreaty, heard his plea, and restored him again to Jerusalem and to his kingdom. Then Manasseh knew that the LORD was indeed God" (2 Chr 33:13). Yet Rabbi Judah says, God returned him to his kingdom; God did not give him life in the World to Come (*Mishnah Sanhedrin* 10.2; *Babylonian Talmud Sanhedrin* 90a).

Israel is one people. Jacob takes twelve stones of the stones of the altar where his father Isaac was nearly sacrificed, and he sets them for his pillow in that place to indicate that twelve tribes are to arise from him. And they all fuse into one stone, to indicate to him that all (the tribes) are destined to become one people on earth, as it is says, "Who is like your people Israel, one nation on the earth" (1 Chr 17:21) (*Pirke de Rabbi Eliezer*, ch. 35[49]). This midrash bases itself on the fact that according to the Genesis text, Jacob takes literally from the "stones" (plural) of that place for his

---

49. See this title in the bibliography.

pillow, and the next morning he takes a "stone" (singular) and anoints it (cf. *Midrash Genesis Rabbah* 68.11).

His fame shall be his name. Six were called by their name before they were born, and these are Isaac, Ishmael, Moses, Solomon, Josiah, and Messiah ... How do we know this concerning Solomon? Because it is said, "See, a son shall be born to you ... for his name shall be Solomon [*Shlomoh*] and I will give peace [*shalom*] and quiet to Israel in his days" (1 Chr 22:9) (*Pirke de Rabbi Eliezer*, ch. 32 beginning). (*Midrash Genesis Rabbah* 45.8 lists but three names, Isaac, Solomon, and Josiah.)

The physical direction of prayer. In Judaism, the physical direction of prayer is toward Jerusalem. "Those who are outside of the land must face toward the Land of Israel when they pray, as it is said, They are to 'pray to you toward their land, which you gave to their ancestors, the city that you have chosen, and the house that I have built for your name' (1 Kgs 8:48). Those who are in the Land of Israel must face toward Jerusalem when they pray, as it is said, 'and they pray to you toward this city that you have chosen' (2 Chr 6:34). Those who are in Jerusalem must face toward the Temple when they pray, as it said, 'and pray toward this house' (2 Chr 6:32). Those who are within the Temple must direct their hearts toward the Holy of Holies when they pray, as it is said, 'they pray toward this place' (2 Chr 6:26). Thus those who are in the north must face the south, and those in the south must face the north, those who are in the east must face the west, and those in the west must face toward the east; thus all Israel will pray toward the same place" (*Sifre Deuteronomy, Piska* 29).

Huldah was one of seven female prophets. There are seven female prophets listed in the Bible: Sarah, Miriam, Deborah, Hannah, Abigail, Huldah, and Esther (*Babylonian Talmud Megillah* 14a).

Precious are chastisements: they bring one to God. King Manasseh's father, Hezekiah, is a righteous ruler. He teaches proverbs to Israel. "These are other proverbs of Solomon that the officials of King Hezekiah of Judah copied" (Prov 25:1). Do you think that Hezekiah did not instruct his son? Yet his son was wicked. Only chastisements availed him. When Manasseh "was in distress he entreated the favor of the LORD his God and humbled himself greatly before the God of his ancestors. He prayed to him" (2 Chr 33:12–13) (*Sifre Deuteronomy, Piska* 32).

Ecclesiastes is correct. The sages discourse on the words of Ecclesiastes, "The same fate comes to all, to the righteous and the wicked, to the good and the evil ... to those who sacrifice and those who do not sacrifice" (Eccl 9:2).

They note that both Ahab, who was regarded as a wicked king, and Josiah, who was a virtuous king, offered sacrifices (although they question Ahab's sincerity). In either case, both were killed by arrows (Ahab in 2 Chr 18:33; Josiah in 2 Chr 35:23) (*Pesikta de-Rab Kahana, Piska* 26.1).

The descendants of Jethro [Moses' father in law] seek God and are rewarded. "When the Holy One, blessed be He, reveals his Shekinah [divine presence], He will richly reward Jethro and his descendants." Now how did the descendants of Jethro make their living? By pottery work, for it is said, "The families also of the scribes that lived at Jabez . . . the Kenites" (1 Chr 2:55) and it says, "These were the potters" (1 Chr 4:23). They had been people of importance, householders and owners of fields and vineyards, but for the sake of service of the King of kings, the Holy One, blessed be He, they gave up everything and went off. Where did they go? To Jabez, to study Torah; and (thus) they became God's people. At that time Jabez—the good and worthy man, the man of truth and saint—was sitting and expounding the Torah, as it is said, "Jabez called upon the God of Israel . . . and God granted what he asked" (1 Chr 4:10) (*Avot de Rabbi Natan*, ch. 35).

Punishing the arrogant. Rabbi Simeon ben Eleazar . . . used to say, Upon the arrogant of spirit plagues come. For thus we find concerning Uzziah "But when he had become strong he grew proud, to his destruction . . . King Uzziah was leprous to the day of his death" (2 Chr 26:16, 21) (*Avot de Rabbi Natan*, ch. 9).

Chronicles is not to be taken literally. Rabbi Simon says in the name of Rabbi Joshua ben Levi, and Rabbi Hama, the father of Rabbi Hosea, in the name of Rabbi [Judah], The book of Chronicles was given only for the sake of [midrashic, i.e., sermonic] interpretation *Lo natnu divrei hayamim eleh lidrosh.* (*Midrash Ruth Rabbah* 2.1 beginning; *Midrash Leviticus Rabbah* 1.3 beginning). Oftentimes the rabbis took names, especially from the genealogical lists, and then, using midrashic (homiletic/sermonic) interpretation, conflated names, i.e., said that this person was the same as that person. (Examples of this are found in *Midrash Exodus Rabbah* 1.17 and *Babylonian Talmud Sotah* 12a.)

Chronicles in the liturgy. Some of the praises associated with David, the song of Asaph, form part of the traditional morning service in Judaism. These verses are taken from 1 Chronicles 16:8–36.

Text Study

1 Chronicles 10; Exit Saul; Enter David

The main focus of Chronicles is the Davidic line, and even more so institutions connected with the Davidic line such as Jerusalem, the temple, and the cultus. As noted earlier, the term "cult," or "cultus," in this context in Chronicles is used as a synonym for the religion/religious rites of Judaism of that day.

The first nine chapters of Chronicles bring Israelite history from creation to the time of David, catalog David's descendants, and then provide a list of some of the people who return to Jerusalem following the Babylonian Exile.

These nine chapters serve as a prelude to his major theme, but the Chronicler wants at least to acknowledge, although in limited manner, the monarchy of Saul.

Chapter 10 allows the Chronicler to close out the past, and explain why Saul was not chosen to father the royal Judean dynasty. The final two verses provide a summary of Saul's failings. "So Saul died for his unfaithfulness; he was unfaithful to the LORD in that he did not keep the command of the LORD; moreover, he had consulted a medium, seeking guidance, and did not seek guidance from the LORD. Therefore the LORD put him to death and turned the kingdom over to David son of Jesse" (1 Chr 10:13–14).

The Chronicler expects that the reader will know the details behind these acts of wrongdoing. In 1 Samuel 13, Saul has not waited for the arrival of the prophet/priest Samuel, but offers sacrifices on his own authority. Then, when Saul defeats the Amalekites, he does not follow Samuel's command when he tells Saul that God demands the utter annihilation of this tribe and all its property (1 Sam 15:2–3). Saul spares the Amalekite king and takes booty.

In his final days, Saul tries to seek God's advice, but fails to do so. "When Saul inquired of the LORD, the LORD did not answer him, not by dreams, or by Urim, or by prophets" (1 Sam 28:6). In desperation, Saul seeks out the advice of the medium at Endor. This is a last step, the actions of a man distressed and distraught, utterly lacking hope. The medium conjures up the spirit of the recently deceased Samuel, who confirms for Saul the monarch's own worst fears. The final criticism, that Saul "did not seek guidance from the LORD," is a gratuitous denigration. Saul does try to seek God's word, but as just noted, "the LORD did not answer him."[50]

With Saul dead, chapter 11 begins with the words, "Then all Israel gathered together to David at Hebron," and they invite David to rule over

---

50. The Chronicler suggests that God is angry with Saul because he consulted ghosts, a great sin in the Chronicler's mind. Kalimi, *Reshaping of Ancient Israelite History*, 328.

them. This conveniently ignores the report in 2 Samuel 1–4 that there is an interim monarchy led by Saul's sons, and that David skirmishes with them for some time.

1 Chronicles 15; Bringing the Ark to Jerusalem: The Viewpoint from Chronicles

This chapter describes how David brings the "ark of the LORD" to Jerusalem. The narrative has scant relation to the account of the same event found in 2 Samuel 6. There are two major sections: transporting the ark itself, and then how David's wife Michal reacts to David's dancing before the ark.

Transporting the Ark

The book of Samuel dedicates less than three verses (2 Sam 6:12–14) to the moving the ark to Jerusalem. Part of verse 12 explains, "David went and brought up the ark of God from the house of Obed-edom to the city of David with rejoicing." Verse 13 simply notes that there are people "who bore the ark of the LORD," but it does not identify them. In verse 14, David is girded with a linen ephod, and he dances with all his might.

The Chronicles account is considerably more elaborate in its description. The text explains that David commands that no one but Levites are to carry the ark, because they are God's designees for this task; the "LORD had chosen them to carry the ark of the LORD and to minister to him forever" (v. 2). Then David "assembled all Israel in Jerusalem" to achieve this goal. David specifically "gathered together the descendants of Aaron and the Levites" (vv. 3–4). Verses 5–12 are filled with the names of these Levites and priests.

Beginning with verse 16 comes a list of singers, who play on musical instruments, harps, lyres, and cymbals, raising loud shouts of joy. Verses 17–24 list out their names, as well as additional personnel who are blowing trumpets. Between the two lists, about forty people are named. Like the Levites, David is clothed with a robe of fine linen, and he also wears a linen ephod.

Michal's Reaction to David's Dancing

David's dancing with all his might, or dancing and leaping, differs little in the accounts of Samuel and Chronicles. They both agree that Michal, Saul's daughter and David's wife, is horrified and despises David in her heart. The Samuel version of this episode, however, adds some colorful additions (2 Sam 6:20–23) that are absent in Chronicles.

When David finishes offering the burnt offerings, and distributes food to the assembled, he eventually goes home. His intent is to bless his household. Instead, Michal greets him with a scathing critique of his behavior. "How the king of Israel honored himself today, uncovering himself today before the eyes of his servants' maids, as any vulgar fellow might shamelessly uncover himself!" (2 Sam 6:20). David angrily replies that he was dancing before God, and further, that God has chosen him to be king (a veiled reference to the fact that the crown had passed from Saul to David). He then says that he will continue to do what he wants, and that he will be honored by the maids of whom she speaks. That chapter in 2 Samuel closes with the statement that Michal remains childless to the day of her death, hinting that either this was her punishment or that David did not visit her.

1 Chronicles 21; Satan in Chronicles

The Chronicler faces a difficult dilemma. The narrative of David's conducting a census, clearly against the advice of his loyal general, Joab, is too well known simply to ignore. There was then (as there is today) a certain sentiment against taking a national census: if the government knows too much about us, it will find ways to exploit us, often to tax us. In David's day this might include being forced into some kind of national service at the will of the ruler—a corvée. In the Davidic narrative, in addition, there is the tradition that a plague accompanies this census, which is interpreted by the prophet Gad as further punishment for the census.

In the account in 2 Samuel, for some unspecified reason God is angry at Israel. "Again the anger of the LORD was kindled against Israel, and he incited David against them, saying 'Go, count the people of Israel and Judah'" (2 Sam 24:1).

The Chronicler chooses not to attribute such an unpopular act to God. "For the writer, the incitement of Satan accounts for the persistence of David despite the violent objection of Joab, though it is to be noted that Satan does not have the power to thwart the purposes of God."[51] God ultimately allows David a way to atone for his wrongdoing.

"There are three occasions" in the Hebrew Scriptures where the term Satan

> is used for a supernatural being. In Job (1:6, 2:2) and Zech. (3:1f.) the word is used with the definite article, and is clearly not a proper name but a common noun, i.e. "the (supernatural)

---

51. Myers, *1 Chronicles*, 147.

adversary." ... Here the word is used without the article and is probably to be rendered as a proper name. Yet even here he is not presented as the devil of ... Christian teaching ... His function is little more than to test David; will he trust wholly in God, or will [David], like other kings, put his confidence in military strength? Furthermore, the Chronicler and his readers would be clearly aware that the term was replacing and therefore in some sense interpreting the phrase in Sam., "the anger of the Lord." ... David's action ... is the sin of self-assertion and mistrust.[52]

2 Chronicles 28–32 / 2 Kings 18–20; Portraying Hezekiah: Chronicles versus Kings

The portrayal of King Hezekiah in Chronicles is radically different from that presented in Kings. The differences in approach between these two passages highlight well the concerns of the Deuteronomist (the author of Kings, writing some time after 622 BCE) and the Chronicler, living two centuries later (some time around 400 BCE).

> The Hezekiah material must be evaluated in the light of the Chronicler's theology, since he departs rather widely from the presentation in II Kings ... Kings [the work of the Deuteronomist] was written under the spell of the Deuteronomic reform set in motion by Josiah, and the writer was charmed by his early achievements. The Chronicler, on the other hand, was under no historical illusions about the Davidic kings ... His aim is predominately to present the religious situation with a view toward the orientation of the nation in his own day. Hence he severely limits the historicopolitical details and stresses the points appropriate to his purpose.[53]

Taking a look at the two passages, 2 Kings 18–20 and 2 Chronicles 28–32, one sees that while technically they cover the same time, the emphases are quite different. As Japhet notes, the attention given to Hezekiah is extraordinary in Chronicles; it covers about seventy more percent than the parallel passages in Kings.[54] The Chronicler devotes two chapters to Hezekiah's religious reforms. "The Deuteronomist dismissed the reformation with only four verses (II Kings xviii 3–6). But the Chronicler did not deal

---

52. Herbert, "I and II Chronicles," 362.
53. Myers, *2 Chronicles*, 169.
54. Japhet, *I and II Chronicles*, 912.

as curtly with the political events as his predecessor had with Hezekiah's reformation. However, the political involvements of the period as presented by the writer are so telescoped that they cannot be understood without the records of Kings, the references in Isaiah, and the Assyrian inscriptions."[55]

2 Chronicles 34:22–28; Huldah the Prophet

The figure of Huldah is somewhat of a mystery. What is known about her from the Bible is limited to 2 Chronicles 34:22–28 and its parallel passage in 2 Kings 22:14–20. These are the basic facts: When King Josiah learns of the "discovery" of the "Book of the law of the LORD given through Moses" (most likely a form of the book of Deuteronomy), he is very distressed. His first response is a command to Hilkiah, the high priest, "Go, inquire of the LORD for me . . . concerning the words of the book that has been found" (2 Chr 34:21). Hilkiah does not seem to hesitate. He does not ponder from whom to seek this advice. The next verse states that Hilkiah "went to the prophet Huldah." Huldah is the wife of Shallum who is an official, the keeper of the king's wardrobe. She resides in Jerusalem.

Hilkiah speaks to her, and presumably shows her the book. Huldah then offers her prophecy. At some length, she explains that God will bring destruction and devastation upon the people for their faithlessness. More specifically, she speaks of God bringing "disaster upon this place and upon its inhabitants, all the curses that are written in the book that was read before the king of Judah" (2 Chr 34:24). She also says that the king will go to his grave in peace.

There is no indication that Huldah took the book and read it. Did she know its contents beforehand? Was she part of the group that either produced the book, or was aware of it?

Many other questions abound. Undoubtedly, in terms of collected addresses and prophecies, Jeremiah was the premier prophet of the day. When, about a dozen years later, Josiah is killed in battle, it is Jeremiah who utters a lament for the king (2 Chr 35:25). Zephaniah also prophesied at that time.

In addition to Huldah, why were Jeremiah and Zephaniah not consulted?

In the absence of the Bible giving information on Huldah's life, the sages of the rabbinic period provide some answers. They explain that Josiah makes a conscious decision to go to Huldah and not to Jeremiah. They suggest that Huldah and Jeremiah work in tandem, addressing different constituencies. The rabbis also offer an explanation of how Huldah becomes a prophet. Huldah's more nurturing qualities as a woman persuade Josiah

55. Myers, *2 Chronicles*, 188.

that she would be more open and empathetic to his request to plead his case, and the case of the people, before God (*Babylonian Talmud Megillah* 14b). Perhaps, listening to Jeremiah's preaching, which at times could be quite harsh, Josiah feels that this latter prophet will be too judgmental.

According to the rabbis, Huldah is a near relative of Jeremiah, and hence he does not object to the king going to her. Without saying so directly, this indicates Jeremiah's endorsement of Huldah's capabilities.

Another sage, Rabbi Johanan, suggests that in the event, Jeremiah is out of the city on a mission to bring the ten tribes back to Judah (*Babylonian Talmud Megillah* 14b). The three prophets of that day, Jeremiah, Zephaniah, and Huldah, each speak to different groups, explains a midrash. Jeremiah speaks publicly in city squares, Zephaniah in the temple and in synagogues, and Huldah addresses the women (*Pesikta Rabbati, Piska* 26.1/2).

A midrash suggests that Huldah becomes a prophet because of her husband Shallum. He is one of the most important men of his generation. He gives to charity daily. His custom is to fill up a bottle of water and to go to the entrance of the city. There he offers refreshments to visitors. Because of Shallum's generous behavior the Holy Spirit rests on Huldah, for just as he pours out water for the thirsty, so does the spirit pour out on Huldah (*Pirke de Rabbi Eliezer*, ch. 33).

Another source suggests that Huldah the prophet teaches at a Torah academy in Jerusalem, and that is where Josiah's representative speaks with her (Targum* to 2 Kgs 22:14; Rashi, Rabbi Shlomoh Itzhaki, eleventh-century CE commentator, to 2 Chr 24:22).

Rally 'Round the Temple, Not Rally 'Round the Ruler[56]

The viability and the necessity for the Davidic dynasty come into question in the later biblical (exilic and post-exilic) period. The repatriation of the exiles to Judea and the rebuilding of the temple, with the reestablishment of its cultus, become the community's paramount goals. This reflects a shrewd calculation by the biblical leadership of the realpolitik of the Persian and later Hellenistic eras.

A major role of the monarchy as depicted in Chronicles is to see that the cult flourishes, and for that to happen there has to be a functioning temple. God, so to say, rules from the temple. Without that structure, God still rules in heaven, but God's rule over earth—and more specifically over the Jewish people—is limited. Many of God's commands to the Jewish people

---

56. Adapted from Roddy L. Braun's title, *The Message of Chronicles: Rally Round the Temple*.

depend on them living on the land and bringing sacrifices to the temple. The theocracy depends upon God, not God's human agent, the ruler. God's temple is more important than any flesh-and-blood person.

An independent political Davidic monarchy was incompatible with the realpolitik of the times. By the time of Chronicles the process has become "Rally 'round the temple" and not "Rally 'round the ruler."

Glossary

BCE, CE — Before the Common Era, Common Era. The same periods as the religiously exclusive terms Before Christ (BC) and Anno Domini (AD)

Bible — The Hebrew Scriptures; the Jewish Scriptures; the Hebrew Bible; the Jewish Bible; the *TANAKH*; the holy scriptures of Judaism; are comprised of three sections: *Torah*/Teaching, *Neviim*/Prophets, and *Ketuvim*/Writings. The newest standard Jewish translation is *Tanakh: The Holy Scriptures* (Philadelphia: Jewish Publication Society, 1985) (see NJPS/NJPS *TANAKH* below).

Note: Christians will refer to the Bible as comprised of two sacred documents, the Old Testament and the New Testament. While Jews recognize that the Christian Scriptures are sacred to Christians, only those books Christians term the Old Testament are sacred for Jews.

Christian Scriptures — The holy scriptures of Christianity; those books produced by the early Christian church; the New Testament.

Epistles — Part of the Christian Scriptures; the letters written to the early Christian communities (Romans, Corinthians, Galatians, etc.)

Exilic — Referring to the time of the Babylonian Exile, c. 586–538 BCE.

Gospels — The first four books of the Christian Scriptures: Matthew, Mark, Luke, John.

Haftarah	The addition scriptural reading on a Shabbat or Holy Day taken from the Prophets.
Halakhah	Lit. "the Way"; the normative traditional Jewish law/teaching.
Hebrew	Ancient (and modern) Semitic language; the language of the Jewish Bible.
Hebrew Bible, Hebrew Scriptures	The holy scriptures of Judaism (see Bible above).
Jewish Bible, Jewish Scriptures	See Hebrew Bible, Hebrew Scriptures above.
Judaism	The religion and culture of the Jewish people.
Ketuvim	The Writings, the third section of the *TANAKH*, the Hebrew Bible; comprising Psalms, Proverbs, Job, Song of Songs, Ruth, Lamentations, Ecclesiastes, Esther, Daniel, Ezra, Nehemiah, and 1 and 2 Chronicles.
Lectionary	The tradition of reading set biblical selections at the regular worship service.
Masoretic Text, MT	The traditional exact wording of the Hebrew Bible in Hebrew.
Midrash	A collection of rabbinic sermons and interpretations that supplements the Bible, compiled c. 400–1550 CE, involving many genres: tales and allegories, ethical reflections, epigrams and legends.
Midrashim	Plural of midrash.
Mishnah	Initial section of the Talmud, six volumes, compiled 200 CE.
NAB	New American Bible (a Roman Catholic Bible).
NEB	New English Bible.
Neviim	The Prophets, the second section of the *TANAKH*, the Hebrew Bible; comprising Joshua, Judges, 1 and 2 Samuel, 1 and 2 Kings, and the fifteen literary prophets: Isaiah, Jeremiah, Ezekiel, Hosea, Joel,

	Amos, Obadiah, Jonah, Micah, Nahum, Habakkuk, Zephaniah, Haggai, Zechariah, and Malachi.
New Testament	See Christian Scriptures above.
NIV	New International Version.
NJPS/NJPS *TANAKH*	The newest translation of the Hebrew Scriptures, *Tanakh: The Holy Scriptures* (Philadelphia: Jewish Publication Society, 1985.)
NRSV	New Revised Standard Version.
NOAB	*The New Oxford Annotated Bible with the Apocryphal/Deuterocanonical Books* (New York: Oxford University Press, 1991); the specific edition used in this volume.
Old Testament	See Bible and Hebrew Scriptures above.
Pentateuch	The first five books of the Bible, the Torah: Genesis, Exodus, Leviticus, Numbers, and Deuteronomy.
Post-exilic	The period following the Babylonian Exile (c. 586–538 BCE.
Pre-exilic	The period prior to the Babylonian Exile (c. 586–538 BCE).
Prophets	See Neviim above.
Reed Sea/ Sea of Reeds	The "sea" the Israelites passed through (see Exod 14), mistakenly called the Red Sea.
RSV	Revised Standard Version.
Septuagint	The Greek translation of the Torah, completed c. 250 BCE.
Sheol	The underground place where the dead go for a short period of time before they cease to exist.
Sh'ma	"Hear"; first word of the Bible's statement, "Hear, Israel, the LORD is your God, the LORD alone" (Deut 6:4).
Synoptic Gospels	The Gospels of Matthew, Mark, and Luke.

Talmud	The vast compendium of Jewish thought developed in the post-biblical world c. 200 BCE to 500 CE. There are two Talmuds: the Babylonian Talmud, which is more authoritative, and the Jerusalem Talmud.
TANAKH, TANAK	An acronym for the titles of the three divisions of the Hebrew Scriptures: **Torah**/Teaching, **Neviim**/Prophets, and **Ketuvim**/Writings.
Targum	The translation of the Bible into Aramaic.
Torah	Teaching, the first section of the *TANAKH*, the Hebrew Bible; comprising Genesis, Exodus, Leviticus, Numbers, Deuteronomy. Can also mean "a Jewish teaching," or by extension Jewish learning in general.
Vulgate	The Latin translation of the Greek Bible by Jerome in the fourth century CE.
Writings	See Ketuvim above.

Bibliography

Ackroyd, Peter R. "The Book of Nehemiah." In *Harper's Bible Dictionary*, edited by Paul J. Achtemeier. San Francisco: Harper & Row, 1985.
———. *Israel under Babylon and Persia*. Oxford: Oxford University Press, 1970.
Adler, Rachel. *Engendering Judaism: An Inclusive Theology and Ethics*. Philadelphia: Jewish Publication Society, 1998.
Allen, Leslie C., and Timothy S. Laniak. *Ezra, Nehemiah, and Esther*. New International Bible Commentary. Peabody, MA: Hendrickson, 2003.
Aschkenasy, Naomi. "Language as Female Empowerment in Ruth." In *Reading Ruth: Contemporary Women Reclaim a Sacred Story*, edited by Judith A. Kates and Gail Twersky Reimer. New York: Ballantine, 1994.
Avot de Rabbi Natan (The Fathers According to Rabbi Nathan). Translated by Judah Goldin. New York: Schocken, 1974.
The Babylonian Talmud. Edited by Rabbi Dr. I. Epstein. 18 vols. London: Soncino, 1938.
Berlin, Adele. *Esther: The Traditional Hebrew Text with the New JPS Translation*. JPS Commentary. Philadelphia: Jewish Publication Society, 2001.
Bickerman, Elias. *From Ezra to the Last of the Maccabees: Foundations of Postbiblical Judaism*. New York: Schocken, 1962.
Boadt, Lawrence. *Reading the Old Testament: An Introduction*. Revised and updated by Richard Clifford and Daniel Harrington. 2nd ed. New York: Paulist, 2012.
Braun, Roddy L. "The Message of Chronicles: Rally 'Round the Temple." *Concordia Theological Monthly* 42 (1971) 502–14.
Brenner, Athalya. "On Feminist Criticism of the Song of Songs." In *A Feminist Companion to the Song of Songs*, edited by Athalya Brenner. Sheffield: Sheffield Academic, 1993.
———. "Ruth as Foreign Worker and the Politics of Exogamy." In *Ruth and Esther*, edited by Athalya Brenner, 158–62. The Feminist Companion to the Bible, 2nd ser., 3. Sheffield: Sheffield Academic, 1999.
———. *The Song of Songs*. Sheffield: JSOT, 1989.
Bright, John. *A History of Israel*. 4th ed. Louisville: Westminster John Knox, 2000.
Bronner, Leila Leah. "Esther Revisited: An Aggadic Approach." In *A Feminist Companion to Esther, Judith and Susanna*, edited by Athalya Brenner. The Feminist Companion to the Bible 7. Sheffield: Sheffield Academic, 1995.

———. "The Regime of Modesty: Ruth and the Rabbinic Construction of the Feminist Ideal," 61–86, *From Eve to Esther: Rabbinic Reconstructions of Biblical Women*, Louisville, KY: Westminster John Knox, 1994.

Brueggemann, Walter. *An Introduction to the Old Testament: The Canon and Christian Imagination*. Louisville: Westminster John Knox, 2003.

Carruthers, Jo. *Esther Through the Centuries*. Malden, MA: Blackwell, 2008.

Childs, Brevard S. *Introduction to the Old Testament as Scripture*. Philadelphia: Fortress, 1979.

Clines, David J. A. *Ezra, Nehemiah, Esther*. New Century Bible Commentary. Grand Rapids: Eerdmans, 1984.

———. *Job 1–20*. Word Biblical Commentary 17. Waco, TX: Word, 1989.

Cohen, A. *Everyman's Talmud*. New York: Dutton, 1949.

Cohen, Shaye J. D. *The Beginnings of Jewishness: Boundaries, Varieties, Uncertainties*. Berkeley: University of California Press, 1999.

Collins, John J. "The Book of Daniel." In *Harper's Bible Dictionary*, edited by Paul J. Achtemeier. San Francisco: Harper & Row, 1985.

———. "Book of Daniel." In *The Anchor Bible Dictionary*, edited by David Noel Freedman, vol. 2. New York: Doubleday, 1992.

Cottrill, Amy C. "The Articulate Body: The Language of Suffering in the Laments of the Individual." In *Lamentations in Ancient and Contemporary Cultural Contexts*, edited by Nancy C. Lee and Carleen Mandolfo, 103–12. Atlanta: Society of Biblical Literature, 2008.

Craven, Toni. "Daniel and Its Additions." In *The Women's Bible Commentary*, edited by Carol A. Newsom and Sharon H. Ringe. Louisville: Westminster John Knox, 1992.

Crawford, Sidney White. "Esther." In *Women's Bible Commentary*, edited by Carol A. Newsom, Sharon H. Ringe, and Jacqueline E. Lapsley. 3rd ed. Louisville: Westminster John Knox, 2012.

Crenshaw, James L. "Book of Ecclesiastes." In *The Anchor Bible Dictionary*, edited by David Noel Freedman, vol. 2. New York: Doubleday, 1992.

———. "Book of Job." In *The Anchor Bible Dictionary*, edited by David Noel Freedman, vol. 3. New York: Doubleday, 1992.

———. "Book of Proverbs." In *The Anchor Bible Dictionary*, edited by David Noel Freedman, vol. 5. New York: Doubleday, 1992.

Davies, Gordon, F. *Ezra and Nehemiah*. Berit Olam. Collegeville, MN: Liturgical, 1999.

Davies, Philip R. *Daniel*. Old Testament Guides 4. Sheffield: Sheffield Academic, 1985.

Davis, Ellen F. *Proverbs, Ecclesiastes, and the Song of Songs*. Westminster Bible Companion. Louisville: Westminster John Knox, 2000.

Day, Linda M. *Esther*. Abingdon Old Testament Commentaries. Nashville: Abingdon, 2005.

DeClaissé-Walford, Nancy L. "Psalms." In *Women's Bible Commentary*, edited by Carol A. Newsom, Sharon H. Ringe, and Jacqueline E. Lapsley. 3rd ed. Louisville: Westminster John Knox, 2012.

Dobbs-Allsopp, F. W. *Lamentations*. Interpretation. Louisville: John Knox, 2002.

Eaton, John. *The Psalms: A Historical and Spiritual Commentary with an Introduction and New Translation*. New York: Continuum, 2003.

Ehrlich, Bernard. "The Book of Job as a Book of Morality." *Jewish Bible Quarterly* 34/1 (January–March, 2006) 30–38.

Eskenazi, Tamara Cohn. "Ezra-Nehemiah." In *Women's Bible Commentary*, edited by Carol A. Newsom, Sharon H. Ringe, and Jacqueline E. Lapsley. 3rd ed. Louisville: Westminster John Knox, 2012.

———. *In an Age of Prose: A Literary Approach to Ezra-Nehemiah*. Society of Biblical Literature, Monograph Series 36. Atlanta: Scholars, 1988.

———. "The Structure of Ezra-Nehemiah and the Integrity of the Book." *Journal of Biblical Literature* 107/4 (1988) 641–56.

Eskenazi, Tamara Cohn, and Tikva Frymer-Kensky. *Ruth: The Traditional Hebrew Text with the New JPS Translation*. JPS Bible Commentary. Philadelphia: Jewish Publication Society, 2011.

Exum, J. Cheryl. "Song of Songs." In *Women's Bible Commentary*, edited by Carol A. Newsom, Sharon H. Ringe, and Jacqueline E. Lapsley. 3rd ed. Louisville: Westminster John Knox, 2012.

Falk, Marcia. *The Song of Songs: A New Translation and Interpretation*. San Francisco: HarperSanFrancisco, 1990.

Farmer, Kathleen A. "Psalms." In *The Women's Bible Commentary*, edited by Carol A. Newsom and Sharon H. Ringe. Louisville: Westminster John Knox, 1992.

Fishbane, Michael. *Biblical Interpretation in Ancient Israel*. Oxford: Clarendon, 1985.

Fisch, Harold. "Ruth and the Structure of Covenant History." *Vetus Testamentum* 32/4 (October 1982) 425–37.

Flesher, LeAnn Snow. "Lamentations." In *The IVP Women's Bible Commentary*, edited by Catherine Clark Kroeger and Mary J. Evans. Downer's Grove, IL: InterVarsity, 2002.

Fontaine, Carole R. "Ecclesiastes." In *The Women's Bible Commentary*, edited by Carol A. Newsom and Sharon H. Ringe. Louisville: Westminster John Knox, 1992.

———. "Proverbs." In *The Women's Bible Commentary*, edited by Carol A. Newsom and Sharon H. Ringe. Louisville: Westminster John Knox, 1992.

Fox, Michael V. *Character and Ideology in the Book of Esther*. 2nd ed. Grand Rapids: Eerdmans, 2001.

———. *Ecclesiastes: The Traditional Hebrew Text with the New JPS Translation*. JPS Bible Commentary. Philadelphia: Jewish Publication Society, 2004.

———. *Proverbs 1–9*. Anchor Bible 18A. New York: Doubleday, 2000.

Fuchs, Esther. "Feminist Hebrew Literary Criticism: The Political Unconsciousness." *Hebrew Studies* 48 (2007) 195–216.

———. "Who Is Hiding the Truth? Deceptive Women and Biblical Androcentrism." In *Feminist Perspectives on Biblical Scholarship*, edited by Adela Yarbro Collins. Chico, CA: Scholars, 1985.

Garrett, Duane. *Song of Songs*. Word Biblical Commentary 23b. Nashville: T. Nelson, 2004.

Ginsberg, H. L. "Book of Daniel." In *Encyclopedia Judaica*. 16 vols. New York: Macmillan; Jerusalem: Keter, 1972.

———. "The Book of Job." In *Encyclopedia Judaica*. 16 vols. New York: Macmillan; Jerusalem: Keter, 1972.

Gladson, Jerry A. *The Five Exotic Scrolls of the Hebrew Bible: The Prominence, Literary Structure, and Liturgical Significance of the Megilloth*. Lewiston, NY: E. Mellon, 2009.

Glatt-Gilad, David A. "Book of Chronicles." In *The Oxford Dictionary of the Jewish Religion*, edited by R. J. Werblowsky and Geoffrey Wigoder. New York: Oxford University Press, 1997.

Goldingay, John E. *Daniel*. Word Biblical Commentary. Dallas: Word, 1989.

———. *Psalms*. Vol. 1, *Psalms 1–41*. Baker Commentary on the Old Testament Wisdom and Psalms. Grand Rapids: Baker Academic, 2006.

Gordis, Robert. *Koheleth: The Man and His World*. New York: Schocken, 1968.

Gottwald, Norman K. *A Light to the Nations: An Introduction to the Old Testament*. New York: Harper & Row, 1959.

Greenspahn, Frederick E., editor. *Scripture in the Jewish and Christian Traditions: Authority, Interpretation, Relevance*. Nashville: Abingdon, 1982.

Grossman, Jonathan. *Esther: The Outer Narrative and the Hidden Reading*. Siphrut 6. Winona Lake, IN: Eisenbrauns, 2011.

Hamilton, Victor. "Marriage." In *The Anchor Yale Bible Dictionary*, edited by David N. Freedman, 4:564–65. New York: Doubleday, 1992.

Hancock, Maxine. "The Wise Woman, the Foolish Woman & the Righteous Woman." In *The IVP Women's Bible Commentary*, edited by Catherine Clark Kroeger and Mary J. Evans. Downer's Grove, IL: InterVarsity, 2002.

Hartley, John E. *The Book of Job*. New International Commentary on the Old Testament. Grand Rapids: Eerdmans, 1988.

Hartman, Louis F., and Alexander A. Di Lella. *The Book of Daniel*. Anchor Bible 23. Garden City, NY: Doubleday, 1978.

Herbert, A. S. "I and II Chronicles." In *Peake's Commentary on the Bible*, edited by Matthew Black. New York: Nelson, 1962.

———. "Lamentations." In *Peake's Commentary on the Bible*, edited by Matthew Black. New York: Nelson, 1962.

Herr, Moses David. "Lamentations Rabbah." In *Encyclopedia Judaica*. 16 vols. New York: Macmillan; Jerusalem: Keter, 1972.

Hess, Richard S. *Song of Songs*. Baker Commentary on the Old Testament Wisdom and Psalms. Grand Rapids: Baker Academic, 2005.

Hillers, Delbert R. "Book of Lamentations." In *The Anchor Bible Dictionary*, edited by David Noel Freedman, vol. 4. New York: Doubleday, 1992.

Huwiler, Elizabeth, *Biblical Women: Mirrors, Models, and Metaphors*. Cleveland: United Church Press, 1993.

Japhet, Sara. *I and II Chronicles: A Commentary*. Old Testament Library. Louisville: Westminster John Knox, 1993.

———. *From the Rivers of Babylon to the Highlands of Judah: Collected Studies on the Restoration Period*. Winona Lake, IN: Eisenbrauns, 2006.

———. "Periodization between History and Ideology II: Chronology and Ideology in Ezra–Nehemiah." In *Judah and the Judeans in the Persian Period*, edited by Oded Lipschitz and Manfred Oeming. Winona Lake, IN: Eisenbrauns, 2006.

Jeansonne, Sharon Pace. *The Women of Genesis: From Sarah to Potiphar's Wife*. Minneapolis: Fortress, 1990.

The Jerusalem Bible, Garden City: Doubleday, 1966.

The Jewish Annotated New Testament—New Revised Standard Version. Edited by Amy-Jill Levine and Marc Zvi Brettler. New York: Oxford University Press, 2011.

Josephus, Flavius. *The Antiquities*. Translated by William Whiston. In *The Complete Works of Josephus*. Boston: Walker, 1823.

Kalimi, Isaac. *The Reshaping of Ancient Israelite History in Chronicles*. Winowa Lake, IN: Eisenbrauns, 2005.

Kates, Judith A., and Gail Twersky Reimer, editors. *Reading Ruth: Contemporary Women Reclaim a Sacred Story*. New York: Ballantine, 1994.

Keener, Craig S., *A Commentary on the Gospel of Matthew*. Grand Rapids: Eerdmans, 1999.

Klagsbrun, Francine. "Ruth and Naomi, Rachel and Leah: Sisters Under the Skin." In *Reading Ruth: Contemporary Women Reclaim a Sacred Story*, edited by Judith A. Kates and Gail Twersky Reimer. New York: Ballantine, 1994.

Klein, Lillian R. *From Deborah to Esther: Sexual Politics in the Hebrew Bible*. Minneapolis: Fortress, 2003.

———. "Honor and Shame in Esther." In *A Feminist Companion to Esther, Judith and Susanna*, edited by Athalya Brenner. Sheffield: Sheffield Academic, 1995.

Klein, Ralph W. *1 Chronicles: A Commentary*. Hermeneia. Minneapolis: Fortress, 2006.

———. "Book of 1–2 Chronicles." In *The Anchor Bible Dictionary*, edited by David Noel Freedman, vol. 1. New York: Doubleday, 1992.

"Books of Ezra-Nehemiah." In *The Anchor Bible Dictionary*, edited by David Noel Freedman, vol. 2. New York: Doubleday, 1992.

Knoppers, Gary. *1 Chronicles 1–9: A New Translation with Introduction and Commentary*. Anchor Bible 12. New York: Doubleday, 2003.

———. *1 Chronicles 10–29: A New Translation with Introduction and Commentary*. Anchor Bible 12A. New York: Doubleday, 2004.

Kraemer, David. *Responses to Suffering in Classical Rabbinic Literature*. New York: Oxford University Press, 1995.

Kroeger, Catherine Clark, and Mary J. Evans, editors. *The IVP Women's Bible Commentary*. Downer's Grove, IL: InterVarsity, 2002.

Kugel, James L. "The Psalms." In *Harper's Bible Dictionary*, edited by Paul J. Achtemeier. San Francisco: Harper & Row, 1985.

Lacocque, André. *Ruth: A Continental Commentary*. Translated by K. C. Hanson. Minneapolis: Fortress, 2004.

Laffey, Alice L. "1 and 2 Chronicles." In *The Women's Bible Commentary*, edited by Carol A. Newsom and Sharon H. Ringe. Louisville: Westminster John Knox, 1992.

Lee, Eunny P. "Ruth," In *Women's Bible Commentary*, edited by Carol A. Newsom, Sharon H. Ringe, and Jacqueline E. Lapsley. 3rd ed. Louisville: Westminster John Knox, 2012.

Lee, Nancy C. *Lyrics of Lament: From Tragedy to Transformation*. Minneapolis: Fortress, 2010.

Levenson, Jon D. *Esther*, Old Testament Library. Louisville: Westminster John Knox, 1997.

Levine, Amy-Jill. "Ruth." In *The Women's Bible Commentary*, edited by Carol A. Newsom and Sharon H. Ringe. Louisville: Westminster John Knox, 1992.

———. "Settling at Beer-lahai-roi." In *Daughters of Abraham: Feminist Thought in Judaism, Christianity and Islam*, edited by Yvonne Yazbeck Haddad and John L. Esposito. Gainesville: University of Florida Press, 2001.

Limburg, James. "Book of Psalms." In *The Anchor Bible Dictionary*, edited by David Noel Freedman, vol. 5. New York: Doubleday, 1992.

Linafelt, Tod. *Surviving Lamentations: Catastrophe, Lament, and Protest in the Afterlife of a Biblical Book*. Chicago: University of Chicago Press, 2000.

Lohfink, Norbert. *Qoheleth: A Continental Commentary*. Translated by Sean McEvenue. Minneapolis: Fortress, 2003.

Longman, Tremper, III. *Jeremiah, Lamentations*. New International Biblical Commentary, Old Testament Series 14. Peabody, MA: Hendrickson, 2008.

Lucas, Ernest. *Daniel*. Apollos Old Testament Commentary. Downers Grove, IL: InterVarsity, 2002.

Machinist, Peter B. "Empire of Assyria." In *Harper's Bible Dictionary*, edited by Paul J. Achtemeier. San Francisco: Harper & Row, 1985.

Maggay, Melba Padilla. "The Power and Potential of Women." In *The IVP Women's Bible Commentary*, edited by Catherine Clark Kroeger and Mary J. Evans. Downer's Grove, IL: InterVarsity, 2002.

Matthews, Victor H. *Judges and Ruth*. New Cambridge Bible Commentary. New York: Cambridge University Press, 2004.

Matthews, Victor H., and Don C. Benjamin. *Old Testament Parallels: Laws and Stories from the Ancient Near East*. 3rd ed. New York: Paulist, 2006.

Meadowcroft, Tim. *Haggai*. Readings. Sheffield: Sheffield Phoenix, 2006.

Mekilta de Rabbi Ishmael. Translated by Jacob Z. Lauterbach. Philadelphia: Jewish Publication Society, 1949.

Mendelhall, G. E. "The Census Lists of Numbers 1 and 26." *Journal of Biblical Literature* 77 (1958) 52–66.

Meyers, Carol L. *Discovering Eve: Ancient Israelite Women in Context*. New York: Oxford University Press, 1988.

———. "Every Day Life: Women in the Period of the Hebrew Bible." In *The Women's Bible Commentary*, edited by Carol A. Newsom and Sharon H. Ringe. Louisville: Westminster John Knox, 1998.

Meyers, Carol L., and Eric M. Meyers. *Haggai, Zechariah 1–8*. Anchor Bible 25B. Garden City, NY: Doubleday, 1987.

The Midrash on Proverbs. Translated by Burton L. Visotzky. New Haven, CT: Yale University Press, 1992.

The Midrash on Psalms. Translated by William G. Braude. 2 vols. New Haven, CT: Yale University Press, 1959

Midrash Rabbah (The Midrash). Edited by H. Freedman and Maurice Simon. 10 vols. London: Soncino, 1939.

Midrash Tanhuma. Vol. 1, *Genesis*. Buber recension. Translated by John T. Townsend. Hoboken, NJ: Ktav, 1989.

Midrash Tanhuma. Vol. 3, *Numbers and Deuteronomy*. Buber recension. Translated by John T. Townsend. Jersey City, NJ: Ktav, 2003.

The Mishnah. Edited by Philip Blackman. 6 vols. New York: Judaica, 1965.

Mitchell, Christine. "1 and 2 Chronicles." In *Women's Bible Commentary*, edited by Carol A. Newsom, Sharon H. Ringe, and Jacqueline E. Lapsley. 3rd ed. Louisville: Westminster John Knox, 2012.

Moore, Carey A. "Book of Esther." In *The Anchor Bible Dictionary*, edited by David Noel Freedman, vol. 2. New York: Doubleday, 1992.

———. *Esther*. Anchor Bible 7B. Garden City, NY: Doubleday, 1971.

Moore, George Foot. *Judaism in the First Centuries of the Christian Era*. Vol. 1. New York: Schocken, 1971.

Murphy, Roland E. *Proverbs*. Word Biblical Commentary 22. Nashville: T. Nelson, 1998.

Myers, Jacob M. *1 Chronicles, 2 Chronicles*. Anchor Bible 12, 13. Garden City, NY: Doubleday, 1965.

———. *Ezra–Nehemiah*. Anchor Bible 14. Garden City, NY: Doubleday, 1965.

———. "Ezra." In *Encyclopedia Judaica*. 16 vols. New York: Macmillan; Jerusalem: Keter, 1972.

———. "Ezra and Nehemiah, Book of." In *Encyclopedia Judaica*. 16 vols. New York: Macmillan; Jerusalem: Keter, 1972.

New American Bible, (NAB) Cleveland, OH: Collins World, 1970.

The New English Bible with the Apocrypha (NEB), Oxford, Cambridge: Oxford University Press, Cambridge University Press, 1970.

New International Version (NIV), [The Holy Bible: New International Version], Grand Rapids: Biblia/Zondervan, 2011.

New Jewish Publication Society (NJPS)—See *TANAKH: The Holy Scriptures*.

New Oxford Annotated Bible with the Apocryphal/Deuterocanonical Books. Edited by Bruce M. Metzger and Roland E. Murphy. New York: Oxford University Press, 1991.

New Revised Standard Version (NRSV)—See *New Oxford Annotated Bible with the Apocryphal/Deuterocanonical Books*.

Newsom, Carol A. *The Book of Job: A Contest of Moral Imaginations*. New York: Oxford University Press, 2003.

———. "Daniel." In *Women's Bible Commentary*, edited by Carol A. Newsom, Sharon H. Ringe, and Jacqueline E. Lapsley. 3rd ed. Louisville: Westminster John Knox, 2012.

———. "Job." In *Women's Bible Commentary*, edited by Carol A. Newsom, Sharon H. Ringe, and Jacqueline E. Lapsley. 3rd ed. Louisville: Westminster John Knox, 2012.

Newsom, Carol A., and Sharon H. Ringe, editors. *The Women's Bible Commentary*. Louisville: Westminster John Knox, 1998.

Newsom, Carol A., Sharon H. Ringe, and Jacqueline E. Lapsley, editors. *Women's Bible Commentary*. 3rd ed. Louisville: Westminster John Knox, 2012.

Nielsen, Kirsten, *Ruth: A Commentary*. Old Testament Library. Louisville: Westminster John Knox, 1997.

O'Connor, Kathleen M. "Lamentations." In *Women's Bible Commentary*, edited by Carol A. Newsom, Sharon H. Ringe, and Jacqueline E. Lapsley. 3rd ed. Louisville: Westminster John Knox, 2012.

Oesterley, W. O. E. *The Psalms*. London: SPCK, 1962.

Pardes, Ilana. *Countertraditions in the Bible: A Feminist Approach*. Cambridge, MA: Harvard University Press, 1992.

Perkins, Pheme. *Reading the New Testament: An Introduction*. Rev. ed. New York: Paulist, 1988.

Pesikta de-Rab Kahana: Rabbi Kahana's Compilation of Discourses for Sabbaths and Festal Days. Translated by William G. Braude and Israel J. Kapstein. Philadelphia: Jewish Publication Society, 1975.

Pesikta Rabbati: Discourses for Feasts, Fasts, and Special Sabbaths. Translated by William G. Braude. New Haven, CT: Yale University Press, 1968.

Pirke de Rabbi Eliezer. Translated by Gerald Friedlander. New York: Sepher-Hermon, 1981.

Pritchard, James B., editor. *Ancient Near Eastern Texts Relating to the Old Testament*. Princeton, NJ: Princeton University Press, 1958.

Rabinowitz, Louis Isaac. "Book of Psalms." In *Encyclopedia Judaica*. 16 vols. New York: Macmillan; Jerusalem: Keter, 1972.

Reis, Pamela Tamarkin. *Reading the Lines: A Fresh Look at the Hebrew Bible*. Peabody, MA: Hendrickson, 2002.

———."Uncovering Jael and Sisera. A New Reading." *Scandinavian Journal of the Old Testament* 19/1 (2005) 24–47.

Reiss, Moshe, and David J. Zucker, (2013) "Chronicles as Revisionist Religious History," *The Asbury Journal*: Vol. 68: No. 2, p. 120–33.

Rosenblatt, Naomi Harris, *After the Apple: Women in the Bible*, New York: Miramax/Hyperion, 2005.

Rowell, Gillian M. "Ruth." In *The IVP Women's Bible Commentary*, edited by Catherine Clark Kroeger and Mary J. Evans. Downer's Grove, IL: InterVarsity, 2002.

Sarna, Nahum M. *Songs of the Heart: An Introduction to the Book of Psalms*. New York: Schocken, 1993.

Schaefer, Konrad, *Psalms*. Berit Olam. Collegeville, MN: Liturgical, 2001.

Schonfield, Jeremy, "Esther: Beyond Murder." *European Judaism* 99/1 (1999) 11–25.

Schwartz, Baruch J. "Ecclesiastes." *The Oxford Dictionary of the Jewish Religion*. Edited by R. J. Werblowsky and Geoffrey Wigoder. New York: Oxford University Press, 1997.

Schwartz, Seth. *Imperialism and Jewish Society, 200 B.C.E. to 640 C.E.* Princeton, NJ: Princeton University Press, 2001.

Scott, Robert B. Y. "Book of Proverbs." In *Encyclopedia Judaica*. 16 vols. New York: Macmillan; Jerusalem: Keter, 1972.

———. *Proverbs, Ecclesiastes*. Anchor Bible 18. Garden City, NY: Doubleday, 1965.

Sifre: A Tannaitic Commentary on the Book of Deuteronomy. Translated by Reuven Hammer. Yale Judaica Series 24. New Haven, CT: Yale University Press, 1986.

Signer, Michael A. "Searching the Scriptures: Jews, Christians, and the Book." In *Christianity in Jewish Terms*, edited by Tikva Frymer-Kensky and David Novak, et al. Boulder, CO: Westview, 2000.

Simon, Maurice. "Introduction." In *Midrash Rabbah*, edited by Freedman and Maurice Simon, vol. 9, *Esther, Song of Songs*. London: Soncino, 1939.

Smith, Daniel L. *The Religion of the Landless: The Social Context of the Babylonian Exile*. Bloomington, IN: Meyer-Stone, 1989.

Smith-Christopher, Daniel L. "The Mixed Marriage Crisis in Ezra 9–10 and Nehemiah 13: A Study of the Sociology of the Post Exilic Judaean Community." In *Second Temple Studies*, vol. 2, *Temple and Community in the Persian Period*, edited by Tamara Cohn Eskenazi and Kent H. Richard. JSOT 175. Sheffield: Sheffield Academic, 1994.

Suter, David W. "The Rest of the Book of Esther." In *Harper's Bible Dictionary*, edited by Paul J. Achtemeier. San Francisco: Harper & Row, 1985.

TANAKH: The Holy Scriptures. Philadelphia: Jewish Publication Society, 1985.

Tanna Debe Eliyyahu: The Lore of the School of Elijah. Translated by William G. Braude and Israel J. Kapstein. Philadelphia: Jewish Publication Society, 1981.

Tigay, Jeffrey H. "Lamentations, Book of." In *Encyclopedia Judaica*. 16 vols. New York: Macmillan; Jerusalem: Keter, 1972.

Trible, Phyllis. *Texts of Terror: Literary-Feminist Readings of Biblical Narratives*. Philadelphia: Fortress, 1984.

Walfish, Barry D. "Kosher Adultery: The Mordecai-Esther-Ahasuerus Triangle in Talmudic, Medieval, and Sixteenth Century Exegesis." In *The Book of Esther in Modern Research*, edited by Sidnie White Crawford and Leonard J. Greenspoon. Journal for the Study of the Old Testament, Supplement Series 380. New York: Continuum, 2003.

Walsh, Carey Ellen. *Exquisite Desire: Religion, the Erotic, and the Song of Songs*. Minneapolis: Fortress, 2000.

Waltke, Bruce K. *The Book of Proverbs*. Vol. 1, *Chapters 1–15*. New International Commentary on the Old Testament. Grand Rapids: Eerdmans, 2004.

Weems, Renita J. "Song of Songs." In *The Women's Bible Commentary*, edited by Carol A. Newsom and Sharon H. Ringe, eds. Louisville: Westminster John Knox, 1992.

Werblowsky, R. J., and Geoffrey Wigoder, editors. *The Oxford Dictionary of the Jewish Religion*. New York: Oxford University Press, 1997.

West, James King. *Introduction to the Old Testament*. 2nd ed. New York: Macmillan, 1981.

Westermann, Claus. *Lamentations: Issues and Interpretations*. Translated by Charles Muenchow. Minneapolis: Fortress, 1994.

Whiteley, Raewynne J. "Song of Solomon." In *The IVP Women's Bible Commentary*, edited by Catherine Clark Kroeger and Mary J. Evans. Downer's Grove, IL: InterVarsity, 2002.

Williamson, H. G. M. *Ezra, Nehemiah*. Word Biblical Commentary 16. Waco, TX: Word, 1985.

Wilson, Gerald H. *Job*. New International Biblical Commentary, Old Testament Series 10. Peabody, MA: Hendrickson, 2007.

Wolde, E. J., van. *Mr and Mrs Job*. Translated by John Bowden. London: SCM, 1997.

Wright, N. T. *Jesus and the Victory of God: Christian Origins and the Question of God*, Vol. 2. Minneapolis: Fortress, 1996.

Yoder, Christine Roy. "Proverbs." In *Women's Bible Commentary*, edited by Carol A. Newsom, Sharon H. Ringe, and Jacqueline E. Lapsley. 3rd ed. Louisville: Westminster John Knox, 2012.

Zucker, David J., *The Bible's PROPHETS: An Introduction for Christians and Jews*, (Wipf and Stock, 2013).

———. "Cold Case: The Micaiah Mysteries." *CCAR Journal/Reform Jewish Quarterly* 58/4 (Fall 2011) 3–9.

———. "The Importance of Being Esther: Rabbis, Canonicity, Problems, and Possibilities." *European Judaism*, forthcoming, 2014.

———. "The Prophet Micaiah in Kings and Chronicles." *Jewish Bible Quarterly* 41/3 (2013) 156–62.

———. "The Riddle of Psalm 49." *Jewish Bible Quarterly* 33/3 (2005) 143–52.

———. "Throwaway Women: Ruth as Response." *CCAR Journal/Reform Jewish Quarterly*, 60/4 (Fall 2013) 185–96.

———. *The Torah: An Introduction for Christians and Jews*. New York: Paulist, 2005.

www.ingramcontent.com/pod-product-compliance
Lightning Source LLC
Chambersburg PA
CBHW052102230426
43662CB00036B/1757